FLORENCE

INSIGHT *City* GUIDES

Edited by Christopher Catling
Principal photography by Albano Guatti and Patrizia Giancotti
Editorial Director: Brian Bell

A P A
PUBLICATIONS

FLORENCE

First Edition (2nd Reprint)
© **1992 APA PUBLICATIONS (HK) LTD**
All Rights Reserved
Printed in Singapore by Höfer Press Pte. Ltd

ABOUT THIS BOOK

Florence is not the easiest of cities to get to know. All the contributors to this guide have experienced the feeling of being overwhelmed by it all. Tourists in Henry James's day hired themselves a *cicerone*, a personal guide to make sense of the maze and show them all that Florence has to offer. We have done our best to write *Cityguide Guide: Florence* in the same spirit.

We cannot accompany you round the streets in person, of course, but we have tried to get beneath the skin of the city and show you— like a guide at your side—aspects of Florence that you will not find in any other guidebook, insights that only come with familiarity and repeated visits.

Our unique approach concentrates as much on modern Florence as it does on the obvious tourist attractions; it is a blinkered traveller who ignores the late 20th-century city, in all its vitality, and looks only for the relics of the Renaissance.

Enjoyable, not Indigestible

The hardest task facing each contributor was to keep our enthusiasm for Florence within bounds. We could have written volumes (several of us have) on the art and architecture, but instead chose the harder path of distilling out the essence of Florence, to produce a guide that is enjoyable without being indigestible. Even so, it would take even an energetic visitor at least two weeks, perhaps a month, to cover all the sights we have packed into these pages.

The book's project editor, **Christopher Catling**, first fell in love with Florence as a student archaeologist excavating Roman villas in the Tuscan countryside. The discovery that buildings as old as recorded time are still inhabited sent him wandering every corner of Florence, seeking out churches that were built by the first Christians and streets that would still be recognisable today to Dante or Botticelli.

He describes his contribution to the book as a painless guide to what really matters amongst all the competing demands on the visitor's time. The only thing he dislikes about Florence is bookish art historians, since he believes that much of the city's best art is deliberately erotic and meant to be enjoyed by the senses.

Lisa Gerard-Sharp agrees. Resident in Florence for many years and presenter of TV programmes in both Rome and Florence, Gerard-Sharp interviewed some of the city's top designers for this book. Love of the beautiful figure—*bella figura*—is, she says, in the genes of all Florentines. She has also taken up the challenge of describing the lifestyles and beliefs of contemporary Florentines, and loves the city because it is, at heart, one big village.

Timothy Harper, an American lawyer and journalist, first visited Florence with his wife, Nancy Bobrowitz, and their infant daughter Elizabeth. They were amazed that, in such a cosmopolitan, tourist-weary city, the baby drew such interest wherever they went. Harper's interest in antique maps led him to the bowels of the National Library, where he made many friends among the restorers working to reverse the damage of the 1966 flood. He has given us an insider's view of that never-ending task, and of the issues confronting the city as it approaches the 21st century.

Catling

Gerard-Sharp

Harper

Paul Holberton, as an art historian specialising in Renaissance poetry, art and architecture, is equally at home amongst the archives and art galleries. He is also to be found lecturing in the city, from time to time, and leading art lecture tours. All of Holberton's boundless knowledge has been compressed into an admirable introduction to the city's rich art.

David Clement-Davies, actor, writer and film producer, says his first memory of Florence was of arriving in a heat wave and diving for the nearest air-conditioned café. He now knows most of the city's restaurants and has given us an account of the local food and wine. He warns that the hearty meals beloved of Florentines will prostrate the strongest constitutions and says there are few pleasures to beat picnicking in the Boboli Gardens.

Susie Boulton, who compiled the Travel Tips section, finds any excuse to revisit Florence, and once sold ice cream to tourists to pay for her accommodation. That was in student days. Subsequently she spent many years working for the consumer magazine *Holiday Which?* and has applied its high standards to provide a guide to the best of the city's hotels and shopping.

People, we are told, buy Apa Guides because the stunning photography brings memories of many an enjoyable holiday back into sharp focus. Florence, in all its variety, leaps from these pages thanks principally to two of Italy's top photographers.

Albano Guatti, born in Udine, studied film in Florence and now divides his time between Italy and the United States. He is well known for his strongly graphic shots and his eye for ironic juxtapositions. He does not exclude the traffic, the advertising hoardings, the messy, garish and trashy because they are just as much a part of Florence as the pristine palace façades.

Patrizia Giancotti, who comes from Turin, is well-known for her work in many leading Italian magazines, especially her photo reports from South America. She has a way of photographing people that captures the expressive gesture, the typical scenes that sum up Florence and tell an intriguing story; we can just about tell what the people in her pictures were thinking at the moment the shutter clicked.

Supervising the book's progress from conception into print was Apa's London-based editorial director **Brian Bell**. Vital cogs in the production machine were typists **Janet Langley** and **Valerie Holder**, proofreader and indexer **Rosemary Jackson Hunter** and computer tamers **Audrey Simon** and **Karen Goh**.

Holberton   *Clement-Davies*   *Boulton*   *Guatti*

FLORENCE IN HISTORY

23 Inexhaustible City
—by Timothy Harper

24 Decisive Dates
—by Christopher Catling

27 Etruscan Genius
—by David Clement-Davies

33 City and Countryside
—by Timothy Harper

34 Public Planning
—by Timothy Harper

37 Dynasties and Vendettas
—by David Clement-Davies

43 Milestones of the Renaissance
—by Paul Holberton

53 Rulers of Florence
—by Christopher Catling

57 Florentine Firsts
—by Timothy Harper

59 The Grand Tour
—by Lisa Gerard-Sharp

FLORENCE TODAY

67 After the Flood
—by Timothy Harper

71 Grandeur and Reality
—by Timothy Harper

72 The Political Maze
—by Lisa Gerard-Sharp

79 Class and Society
—by Lisa Gerard-Sharp

85 Pucci, Gucci and Ferragamo
—by Lisa Gerard-Sharp

93 Contemporary Art
—by Lisa Gerard-Sharp

98 Festivals
—by Lisa Gerard-Sharp

103 Wine and Food
—by David Clement-Davies

104 A Night Out
—by Lisa Gerard-Sharp

109 Street Markets
—by David Clement-Davies

PLACES
—by Christopher Catling

117 Introduction

121 The Religious Centre

129 The Political Centre

139 Art and Nature

150 Bargello and Santa Croce

163 Central Florence

173   **Florence of the Medici**

183   **The University Quarter**

193   **Santa Maria Novella**

203   **Arno and Oltrarno**

219   **The Florentine Countryside**

227   **Fiesole**

235   **Suburbs and Excursions**

MAPS

  34 Historic Florence
118 Street Plan
152 Bargello and Santa Croce
163 Central Florence
174 Northern Florence
183 San Marco District
193 Western Florence
204 Arno and Oltrarno
219 Southern Florence
228 Fiesole

TRAVEL TIPS

GETTING THERE
242 By Air
242 By Rail
242 By Bus
242 By Car

TRAVEL ESSENTIALS
243 Visas & Passports
243 Health Tips
243 Money Matters
243 Customs Formalities
243 What to Wear

GETTING ACQUAINTED
244 Time Zones
244 Climate
244 Culture & Customs
245 Language
245 Business Hours
245 Electricity
245 Holidays
245 Festivals
246 Religious Services

COMMUNICATIONS
246 Media
246 Telephone
247 Postal Services
247 Telegrams & Telexes

EMERGENCIES
247 Security & Crime
247 Medical Services
248 Loss of Belongings
248 Left Luggage

GETTING AROUND
248 From the Airport
248 Orientation
249 Recommended Maps
249 Buses
249 Taxis
249 Walking & Cycling
249 By Car
250 Getting out of Florence
250 Hitchhiking

WHERE TO STAY
250 Hotels
252 Camping
252 Youth Hostels
252 Villas

FOOD DIGEST
253 What to Eat
254 Where to Eat
256 Drinking Notes

THINGS TO DO
256 Lectures
257 Libraries
257 City Tours

CULTURE PLUS
257 Museums & Art Galleries
257 Key Sights
258 Music, Opera & Ballet
258 Theatre
258 Cinema

NIGHTLIFE
259 Night Spots

SHOPPING
259 Shopping Hours
259 What to Buy
260 Markets
260 Export Procedures

SPORTS

SPECIAL INFORMATION
261 Children
261 Disabled
261 Students
262 Parks & Gardens

FURTHER READING

USEFUL ADDRESSES
263 Consulates
263 Airlines
263 Tourist Information

FLORENCE, INEXHAUSTIBLE CITY

Getting acquainted with Florence is a little like taking up chess; the more you know about it, the more you realise there is to learn. Consequently, to many visitors Florence can be one of the most intimidating cities in the world.

Trying to see all the highlights only reveals more highlights to be seen, and the impossible task is especially frustrating because of the physical compactness of this city of fewer than half a million people. Everything is so near—just down the street or around the corner is yet another "must see" gallery or museum or chapel. Visitors frequently drive themselves to distraction or exhaustion or both in their desire to see everything the city has to offer.

Florentine hospitals actually document about a dozen cases a year of what is commonly known as "Stendhal Syndrome." First described by the French writer, who suffered from it in 1817, the syndrome is a reaction to the overwhelming beauty of Florence. Symptoms range from mere dizzy spells to complete collapse requiring bed rest. "Sensory overload" is how modern travellers describe their feelings of too much art, too much culture, too much history, and just plain too much Florence.

A glass of wine, a Florentine steak and an hour or two of reading a trashy novel or watching the students play out their coquetry in the city's squares and cafes; these are usually adequate therapy to renew the spirits and revive one's interest in seeing some more of Florence's almost numberless treasures.

All this is to say that visitors to Florence shouldn't try to do too much too fast. The people who seem to enjoy and appreciate the city most are those who leave parts of the city unseen, reserving something for their next visit—for Florence is a city to which nearly every visitor vows to return.

Florentines describe themselves as an inhospitable people, wary of foreigners. Many visitors know this not to be true. Reticence is reserved for those who see Florence only as a museum city, its people only as servants to the tourist industry.

For them, the pleasures of carrying out life's routines amid such splendour are matched by the frustrations; narrow streets pose the daily problems of how to get to work or where to park whilst momentous issues, such as the proposal to build a new satellite city, provoke passionate debate.

These complex undertows highlight the real marvel of Florence: the fact that it has survived at all, despite floods, warfare and the threat from development; the fact that it is very much part of the modern world as well as a monument to past achievements, with one foot in the 21st century and the other in the Renaissance.

Preceding pages: dappled light on a renaissance fresco; under restoration: Loggia Dei Lanzi; the cathedral from Giotti's belltower; bicycles for rent: the cathedral; reproductions, San Lorenzo market; city reflections; Henry Moore exhibition at the Belvedere Fort. Following pages: Vasari's vision of the foundation of Florence; the siege of Florence: fresco in Palazzo Vecchio.

DECISIVE DATES

8th century B.C. First settlements on the site of Florence.

4th century B.C. Fiesole well-established as a powerful Etruscan city with walls and temples.

351 B.C. Etruria conquered by the Romans.

59 B.C. Foundation of the Roman colony of Florentia which grows rapidly at the expense of Fiesole.

3rd century A.D. Christianity brought to Florence by eastern merchants. Martyrdom of St Miniato.

5th century: Florence repeatedly sacked by Goths and Byzantines.

570: Lombards occupy Tuscany, ruling Florence from Lucca. Two centuries of peace, during which the Baptistry was built.

774: Charlemagne becomes king of the Lombards and appoints a marquis to rule Tuscany, still based in Lucca.

1001: Death of Marquis Ugo, who made Florence the new capital of Tuscany. Florence now a prosperous trading town.

11th century: Most of the city's churches rebuilt.

1115: Death of Countess Matilda, last of the marquis, leaving her title to the pope. Florence becomes a self-governing commune and begins a campaign to conquer the surrounding countryside, forcing robber barons to abandon their castles and live in the city.

1125: Florence conquers and destroys Fiesole.

1215: Beginning of civil strife between rival supporters of the pope and of the Holy Roman Emperor over issues of temporal power and politics fuelled by class warfare and family vendettas. The papal party is uppermost in Florence and the city is at war with Pisa, Pistoia and Siena, old trade rivals and supporters of the emperor.

1248: New town walls erected that define the limits of Florence until 1865. Despite continuing strife, Florence is now one of Europe's richest banking and mercantile cities and the florin is the established currency of European trade.

1260: Florentines suffer disastrous defeat by the Sienese at Montaperti. Sienese plan to raze the

city but are persuaded to desist by Florentine supporters of the emperor.

1293: Strife between Guelf (papal) and Ghibelline (imperial) parties now an outright class war. The merchant Guelfs pass an ordinance excluding aristocratic Ghibellines from holding public office.

1294: Construction of the cathedral begins.

1299: Palazzo Vecchio begun.

1302: Dante exiled in a mass purge of Ghibellines.

1322: Palazzo Vecchio completed.

1338: Florence at the height of its prosperity, despite continuing instability. Population now 90,000.

1339: Edward III of England defaults on massive debts incurred fighting the 100 Years War. The two most powerful banking families, the Bardi and Peruzzi, go bankrupt and the Florentine economy is in crisis.

1348: The Black Death sweeps through Tuscany and, over the next 50 years, kills three-fifths of the population of Florence.

1378: Revolt of the *ciompi*, the lowest paid wool industry workers, demanding guild representation and a voice in government. Nominally their demands are met but in reality the merchant families reinforce their oligarchy.

1400-01: Competition to design new doors for the Baptistry announced. Taken by art historians as the beginning of the Renaissance and the rise of Florence to intellectual and artistic pre-eminence in Europe.

1406: Florence defeats old rival Pisa and gains a sea port.

1433: Cosimo de' Medici sent into 10 years exile, his growing popularity in Florence a threat to the merchant oligarchy.

1434: Cosimo de' Medici returns to Florence, to popular acclaim, and becomes "godfather" figure, presiding over 30 years of stability and artistic achievement, adroitly reconciling the interests of rival factions.

1464: Death of Cosimo, hailed as Pater Patriae—Father of his Country. Beginning of brief reign of his sickly son, Piero the Gouty.

1469: Lorenzo, later called the Magnificent, grandson of Cosimo takes charge of the city at the age of 20 and proves an able leader.

1478: Pazzi conspiracy seeks to destroy the Medici dynasty but only reinforces the popularity of Lorenzo.

1492: Death of Lorenzo, aged 44. His son, Piero, takes over.

1494: Charles VIII of France invades Italy and Piero surrenders Florence to him. In disgust, citizens expel Piero and, under the influence of Savonarola, declare Florence a republic with Christ as its only ruler.

1498: Alexander VI, the Borgia pope, orders the trial of Savonarola for heresy and fomenting civil strife. He is burned at the stake, but the republic survives.

1512: Florence defeated by an invading Spanish army. The Medici take advantage of the city's weakness to re-establish control, led by Giovanni, son of Lorenzo the Magnificent and now Pope Leo X, and his cousin, Giulo (later Pope Clement VII).

1527: Clement VII tries to rule Florence from Rome but, when Rome is attacked by imperial troops, Florentines expel the Medici again and return to a republican constitution.

1530: Pope Clement signs a peace treaty with Emperor Charles V and together they hold Florence to siege. Florentines resist bravely, with Michelangelo taking a leading role.

1531: Florence falls. Alessandro de' Medici, Charles V's son-in-law is made Duke of Florence.

1537: Alessandro assassinated by his cousin, Lorenzaccio. Cosimo I, from a lateral branch of the Medici family, is made Duke, defeats an army of republican opponents and begins a 37-year reign. Many artists, including Michelangelo, leave Florence, which goes into decline as a centre of artistic excellence.

1555: Beginning of Cosimo I's campaign to reunite Tuscany by force.

1564: Cosimo I unexpectedly resigns and his son, Francesco, is appointed Regent.

1570: Cosimo I created Grand Duke of Tuscany by Pope Pius VI in belated recognition of his absolute control over the region.

1574: Cosimo I dies of cerebral haemorrhage, aged 54.

1610: Galileo made court mathematician to Cosimo II. Florence pre-eminent in the sciences.

1631: Galileo tried by the Inquisition and excommunicated, spending the rest of his life virtually under house arrest.

1737: Gian Gastone, last of the Medici Dukes, dies without a male heir. The title passes, by treaty, to the Austrian imperial House of Lorraine.

1743: Anna Maria Lodovica, last of the Medici line, dies bequeathing her property to the people of Florence.

1799: The French defeat Austria and Florence is first ruled by Louis of Bourbon, then by Napoleon's sister.

1815: After the defeat of Napoleon, Florence is once again ruled by the House of Lorraine, but clandestine organisations, dedicated to securing independence from foreign control, are gaining popular support.

1848: First Italian War of Independence; Tuscany is the vanguard of the uprising.

1860: Tuscany votes to become part of the emerging United Kingdom of Italy.

1865: Florence declared the new capital of the kingdom.

1871: Rome becomes the capital.

1887-1912: Tuscany remains economically buoyant, helped by textile production, and Florence becomes a haven for foreign poets and novelists.

1919: Mussolini founds the Fascist Party.

1940: Italy enters World War II.

1944: Despite the best efforts of the wartime German consul, Gerhard Wolf, retreating Nazis destroy three of the bridges of Florence, leaving only the Ponte Vecchio.

1946: Marshall Plan aid helps rebuild the Tuscan economy and Florence establishes itself as a centre of fashion.

1957-65: The period of the "long boom". Florence transforms from an agricultural to a service and culture based economy.

1966: Florence devastated by floods. Many works of art destroyed.

1988: Florentines vote for measures to control traffic and pollution. Plans to build a satellite city are approved in principle and the city prepares to host the 1990 World Cup.

All Florentine work of the finest kind… is absolutely pure Etruscan, merely changing its subjects and representing the Virgin instead of Athena, and Christ instead of Jupiter.

— Ruskin, *Mornings in Florence*

Florence was originally a Roman settlement and the classical flowering of the Renaissance owes much to Rome's rich civilisation. But the vitality of that 15th-century Florentine art is indebted at least as much to a culture that pre-dated Rome by several centuries, that of Etruria.

Rising above Florence to Fiesole, where the sunset steeps the city in colour, you come upon the remains of an ancient Etruscan town. The massive stone walls were laid in the late 7th century B.C., long before Latins ever settled the Arno's banks. Today Fiesole is just a satellite of the city and for the traveller the Renaissance obscures an earlier dawn. But throughout Tuscany hilltop villages founded by the Etruscans, harbours, tombs and statuary testify to a remarkable and often overlooked civilisation.

Craftsmen and traders: The Etruscans (*Tusci* to the Romans, *Rasenna* as they called themselves) first flourished around 800 B.C. in the coastal regions of Tuscany and Lazio. Building their cities on high plateaus for defence, but with access to the sea, they quickly rivalled the Greeks and Phoenicians as traders. Their wealth was founded on the rich metal deposits of the mainland and the island of Elba. With a genius for craftsmanship these metals were worked and exchanged for luxury goods and trading links soon extended as far as Mesopotamia, Syria, Cyprus and Egypt.

The Etruscans thrived as powerful traders for 300 years. At their peak their cities covered Italy from Campania to the Po valley. By forging links with the Greeks in the 8th century they established an outpost in La-

Left, the flute player: Etruscan tomb painting in Tarquinia.

tium. This primitive encampment was destined to become the city of Rome, and Rome would one day eclipse Etruria.

Unlike Rome the Etruscans never established anything resembling a centralised empire. Their settlements retained considerable independence from one another and though the 12 main cities of Etruria were grouped in a loose confederation, this was primarily for religious purposes.

That religion was primitive and magical. Vases and tombs are haunted by their gods and demons; the Lasa or winged women, symbolic of death, Tulchulcha a demon of the underworld. Temples and votive statues abound, while the Etruscans' special preserve was augury, interpreting the will of the gods in the entrails of wild animals, forks of lightning and the flight of birds.

The Romans later absorbed these beliefs and, as late as the Emperor Julian, every legion of the army contained an Etruscan soothsayer. But who knows if Etruscan soothsayers ever predicted the fate of their own people, for the Etruscans, powerful in the 5th century, had, by the 4th, completely succumbed to Roman rule.

The great enigma: Why this civilisation should have proved so fragile is just one of the tantalising enigmas that surround the Etruscans. Though their alphabet has been deciphered as Greek Chaldean, much of their language remains incomprehensible to modern scholars and a recent controversial theory even roots their language in Indian Sanskrit.

Similarly their origins elude us. Herodotus believed they came from Lydia in Asia Minor, led by Tyrrhenos, son of Athis, to settle on the shores of the sea that still bears his name. Dionysius of Halicarnasus, on the other hand, says that the Etruscans themselves claimed to be indigenous to Italy and the lack of any evidence of warfare at early archaeological sites might support this.

These lingering mysteries have captured the imaginations of writers from the Emperor Claudius, who wrote a 20-volume history on the Etruscans, to Virgil, Livy and D.H. Lawrence. All were, above all, fascinated by the art that these people produced: marble statues, colourful frescoes, powerful bronzes, pottery of great delicacy, potent, erotic and above all humane.

Tarquinia: The search for the spirit of Etruscan art, which many have seen as remarkably akin to that of the Florentine Renaissance, begins not in Florence itself, nor in Fiesole, but on the parched hillsides of Lazio, in the underground necropoli or citadels of the dead that cluster round the hilltop city of Tarquinia. Most remnants of Etruscan civilisation come from tombs such as these; their myriad funerary urns, painted sarcophagi and many household objects which accompanied the wealthy into the afterlife.

Though empty now, the tombs of Tarquinia, buried safe from the dust that blows hard across the region's wild landscape are covered in remarkable frescoes, vivid paintings that light the magic lantern of the past. Scenes of hunting, fishing, wrestling and feasting evoke a lively and luxurious people, fond of music and dancing, while erotic figures capture a sensuality and naturalism rare in any art.

A central element in these paintings is the wildlife; animals that inhabit this twilight world. Dolphins, bulls and seahorses leap to life from the walls. In Tarquinia's terracotta horses and the famous bronze she-wolf, later to become the symbol of ancient Rome, the Etruscans displayed an extraordinary empathy with their natural environment and a supreme ability to record life in movement.

Tarquinia's frescoes are the most complete. Elsewhere we only have tantalising scraps, "fragments of people at banquets, limbs that dance without dancers, birds that fly into nowhere" as D.H. Lawrence put it.

Illicit trade: How many new tombs remain to be discovered, even in the vicinity of Florence, no-one really knows. Tomb robbers are more active than the archaeologists, and neither, with good reason, is prepared to disclose their discoveries to the public.

Yet it is not unusual, amongst trusted friends at intimate aristocratic dinner parties in the villas of the Florentine countryside, for some pristine Etruscan bronze figurine,

mirror or brooch to be offered for admiration or sale. By law all objects discovered underground automatically become the property of the Italian state but an ordinance of 1934 permits Italians to keep the antiquities they owned before that date. The difficulty of proving exactly when an object was acquired clearly works in favour of the tomb-robbers, and so the regrettable business continues.

Florentines justify their illicit trade by pointing to the inactivity of archaeologists, by asserting that art should be enjoyed, not left forgotten underground and, above all, by claiming that, "it is our heritage; we are

Etruscans."

There is some truth in this statement even if there is not in the arguments it is used to support. Cosimo I justified his conquests of Pisa and Siena as an attempt to re-unify the ancient kingdom of Etruria, and the citizens of Florence certainly warmed to this appeal even if their victims were less convinced. Renaissance artists saw themselves as inheritors of the Etruscan talent for sculpture and bronze casting, and many of the objects in the Archaeological Museum in Florence were once owned by the likes of Michelangelo and his contemporaries.

Images of death: This compact museum, tucked away in the Via della Colonna, exists in a peaceful vacuum, off the beaten track, untouched by the hectic traffic of visitors to the city. In the Room of Urns, you often find yourself alone amongst sculptures of the dead and intricate marble friezes that rival the best Greece and Rome produced.

The museum's prizes, however, are two bronzes, the *Arringatore* and the *Chimera*. The *Arringatore*, (or orator), dates from the third century B.C., by which time Etruria had already been conquered by Rome. It portrays a member of the Metelli family, once powerful Etruscan aristocrats who had adopted a

bursts with a desperate energy as it struggles in mortal combat. Discovered near Arezzo in 1554, the *Chimera* caused a sensation among contemporary artists. It was entrusted to the care of Cellini who restored the two left legs, marvelling at the skill of the original makers.

The Etruscan demise: Thus, in Florence and all over Tuscany, one stumbles across remains which bring the Etruscans vividly back to life. A candelabra in Cortona, an arch in Volterra, Tarquinia's frescoes, Florence's *Chimera*. They tell the story of a natural people, of a magical religion and of a once primitive culture that attained a high degree of civilisation.

new name and achieved new status by winning Roman citizenship. At once dignified and disturbing, it captures the tension between new energies and a sense of melancholy for a culture destined to lose its own identity. It is a wonderful example of Etruscan realism and their mastery of bronze.

The wounded *Chimera* is one of the most celebrated masterpieces of high Etruscan art. The straining beast, part goat, lion and snake,

Left, the Chimera, Florence Archaeological Museum. Above, dancing youths: Etruscan tomb painting in Tarquinia.

But Etruscan glories were fleeting. By the fifth century B.C. they were threatened by Gauls in the north and by local Italic tribes. The Romans, taking advantage of their vulnerability rapidly overcame the whole of Etruria. The Etruscans survived for two centuries as Roman subjects but their culture became diluted, their leaders decadent and eventually they were completely absorbed into the fabric of a new society. Yet there is a unique vitality in the best of Etruscan art and a genius for colour and movement which has survived and which many believe was reborn in Florence 2,000 years later.

One of the best-known European cities, Florence is not only one of the smallest but also one of the youngest. The Etruscans first settled the area in the fifth or sixth century B.C., but their city was Fiesole, situated in the hills overlooking modern Florence.

The Etruscans, however, did have a regular market at the ancient ford across the Arno, near the Ponte Vecchio. A dispute in the Etruscan community apparently led some of Fiesole's residents to establish a separate community near the ford, but around 300 B.C. the Romans engulfed it when they established a camp on the site.

The actual date of the founding of Florence is generally agreed to be 59 B.C., when it was established as a *colonia* for retired Roman soldiers, distinguished veterans of Caesar's campaigns.

City of flowers: The source of the Roman name, *Florentia*, remains open to question. Perhaps the new city was named after the many wild flowers that grow in the Arno plain and on the surrounding hillsides, perhaps after Fiorinus, one of Caesar's generals, or from the word *fluentia* because the Arno "flows" through the city.

The retired Roman soldiers built the first city walls almost in a perfect square, with sides of about 1300 ft (400 metres) in length. The southwestern corner, not far from Ponte S. Trinita, was the closest point the walls came to the Arno. The fact that the river embankment was not, itself, defended suggests that the Arno played little part in the economy of the Roman city, initially at least.

Instead, the Roman settlers lived chiefly by farming the perimeter of the city. Out of this developed what was to become one of the principal industries, both in Roman times and in the centuries to follow—wool dyeing.

Even in those earliest days, the city was setting itself apart in style and attitude. The Romans who settled Florence were dedicated to the Horatian/Virgilian ideal of *rus in*

Preceding pages: Florence at dusk. Left, Florence viewed from Fiesole.

urbe—the countryside in the town. It is an ideal that has characterised Florence through the ages for even now, whereas many Italians aspire to a chic city apartment, Florentines all desire a country villa with its own vineyard and olive grove.

The wealth and splendour of Florence from the 13th century on owed much to this same marriage of town and country, of nature and necessity. As the city became prosperous, she grew to resent the parasitical habits of country landowners who would descend from their hilltop fortresses to rob any mule trains that passed through their domain. Armies were formed to counter the threat and defeated landowners were forced to live in Florence to learn to read and write.

Bandits tamed: Forced to be civilised, they nevertheless built in the style of the countryside. Travellers over the centuries have commented on how much the 12th and 13th-century Romanesque churches of Florence, with their wide arcades and shallow aisles, their decorative motifs of leaves, flowers, sea shells and sun rays, have a chapel-in-the-woods atmosphere.

Palaces, *palazzi*, the grandiose term that Florentines give to any townhouse of pretension, were built with massive fortress-like walls and towers, gaunt reminders of their rural prototypes. Yet, in both public and private construction, the emphasis was on sunlight and warmth, bringing the glorious golden outdoors of Tuscany inside, past the columns and through the spacious arches and open windows. Courtyards were filled with greenery, potted plants and flowers, in part because of the *rus in urbe* heritage but also to deflect the intense midsummer heat—another example of Florence's traditional mix of the pragmatic and the ideal.

Early suburbs: Through the 14th century, there was little building outside the city walls but as the robbers and murderers, the highwaymen and renegade soldiers were tamed, the hills around Florence once again became dotted with villas built by the Medici and other wealthy families. These villas were the

PUBLIC PLANNING

Unlike many cities in Europe which evolved piecemeal, only to have rationality imposed upon them in the 19th century, or the inter-war years, Florence was a planned city from the start. Much of its appeal stems from the grid system of its streets, oriented on the cardinal points of the compass, that one moment creates a grand vista, the next opens into an intimate *piazza*, and frequently provides intriguing glimpses of the cathedral or one of the city's other domed churches.

Public buildings too, like the cathedral, the Palazzo Vecchio and successive town walls, were planned and built by a combination of property

could be more than 95 feet (29 metres) high, and the families began scaling them down to conform with the horizontal, close-to-the-ground building style that has characterised Florence ever since. Students of the history of town planning view this limit on tower height as one of the earliest attempts to define the modern relationship between public and private space in urban areas.

Other planning measures included an unsuccessful ban on *sporti*, the projecting upper stones corbelled out to gain more living space, that are a characteristic of Florentine buildings, and the compulsory provision of *muriccioli*, stone benches for public use running round the bases of palace walls.

By the last quarter of the 13th century, Florence was one of the five most populous cities

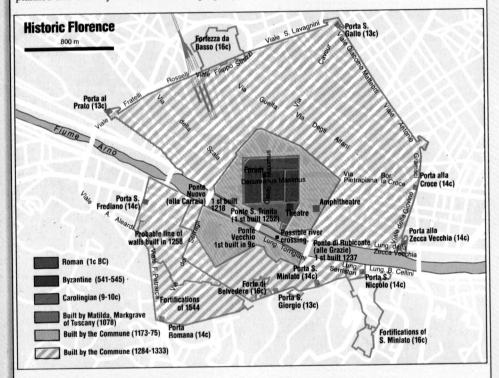

Historic Florence

800 m

- Roman (1c BC)
- Byzantine (541-545)
- Carolingian (9-10c)
- Built by Matilda, Markgrave of Tuscany (1078)
- Built by the Commune (1173-75)
- Built by the Commune (1284-1333)

Fortezza da Basso (16c)
Viale S. Lavagnini
Porta S. Gallo (13c)
Rosselli
Viale Filippo Strozzi
Cavour
Viale Giacomo Matteotti
Via
Porta al Prato (13c)
Fratelli
Via
Guelfa
Via
Viale Antonio
Via
della
Degli
Alfani
Scala
Gramsci
Flume Arno
Forum
Decumanus Maximus
Cardo Maximus
Via Pietrapiana
Bor. la Croce
Porta alla Croce (14c)
Viale
Ponte Nuovo (alla Carraia)
1st built 1218
Ponte S. Trinita (1st built 1252)
Amphitheatre
Porta S. Frediano (14c)
A. Aleardi
Theatre
Via della Giovine
Porta alla Zecca Vecchia (14c)
Probable line of walls built in 1258
Ponte Vecchio 1st built in 9c
Possible river crossing
Ponte di Rubiconte (alle Grazie) 1st built 1237
Lung. della Zecca Vecchia
Lung. Torrigiani
Lung. Serristori
Lung. B. Cellini
Porta S. Miniato (14c)
Porta S. Nicolo (14c)
Forte di Belvedere (16c)
Fortifications of 1544
Porta S. Giorgio (13c)
Porta Romana (14c)
Fortifications of S. Miniato (16c)

tax and the patronage of the guilds, striving to outdo each other in the splendour of the buildings they funded. The first fruits of this communal endeavour was the new set of walls, built by the Comune from 1173 to 1175 to protect the enlarged city that had grown beyond the limits of the Roman and later fortifications.

In 1250, the Comune's patrician leaders agreed to do something about the more than 100 towers, some of them 215 feet (65 metres) high, that the wealthy families had built to crown and protect their urban palaces. It was decided that no tower

in Europe, her walls scarcely able to contain an estimated 100,000 inhabitants. New walls, commenced in 1284, were intended to relieve the congestion and cater for future growth. The ambitious project, completed in 1334, encompassed 40 sq. miles (100 sq. km) but proved unnecessary! Plague, in the following decades, decimated the population and areas of the new city—around Santa Maria Novella—were still greenfield sites when expansion began again in the 19th century, when Florence was briefly capital of the United Kingdom of Italy.

start of the modern suburbs, though the people who built them as a refuge from the summer heat of the city also saw them as a vital ingredient of the humanistic philosophy that regarded a man as incomplete who did not study the natural world and find time for relaxing, reading, thinking and pursuing hobbies or sports.

The conscious link with nature is seen in many of Florence's most famous landmarks. The Medici, who themselves came from farming stock to become the city's dominant banking family, retained a rustic love of gardens and an affinity for the forces of nature throughout their generations of rule. Cosimo I ordered the construction of the Uffizi as a practical and architectural symbol linking the city centre with the Arno.

The river's symbolic importance cannot be over-estimated; in spring it revives the city with a torrent that flows fresh with meltwater from the Apennines and every autumn the rains bring the annual threat of catastrophic floods, capable of devastating the city and its treasures as it has so many times in the past, most recently in 1966.

Profit sharing: But to the successful bankers and merchants of Florence, the surrounding Tuscan hills were more than a reminder of their rustic ancestors or a convenient place to avoid the noise and congestion of town. The land was a good investment, both in terms of preserving hard-earned capital and of developing the feudal *mezzadria* agricultural system under which landowners split profits with the peasants in return for their labour.

Consequently, land has always been more of a financial focal point in Florence than, say, shares or other "paper" investments. And the 50-50 profit-sharing system, with less emphasis on subservience and class division than many other feudal arrangements, is regarded as one of the reasons for the pride and "nobility" of the Florentine peasant, which many believe extends to the city's working classes even today.

Designer olive oil: In recent years there has been yet another revival in the old *rus in urbe* ideal. The shops of Florence are no longer

filled with homogenous, mass-produced produce. Rich, cloudy green olive oils and a profusion of new wines compete for attention with their designer labels, the result of the aristocracy's renewed interest in making money to revive flagging family fortunes from the land.

If designers can sell fashions on the strength of a name why not brand the products of the countryside too. That is why, today, the animated café conversations of sophisticated Florentines is as likely to be about the progress of the harvest or the price of oil as it will be about politics or the arts.

Even in politics, there is a legacy of the

rural past. Private individuals see it as a right and a duty to be involved in public issues; politics, they say, is too important to leave to politicians. Everyone has their say, through referenda and the newspaper letters columns. Like all village politics the search for consensus is often slow and inconclusive.

In the golden Tuscan light of tradition, it makes sense that this compact city, settled in a bowl of hills alongside a usually sleepy but occasionally wild river, somehow remains so special, so urbane on the one hand and yet so in tune with both the laws of nature and the dreams of humankind.

Above, villas and vineyards of Tuscany.

DYNASTIES AND VENDETTAS

During the *quattrocento* Florence was virtually unrivalled as a cultural and commercial centre. Unique in its artistic contribution, it also enjoyed a singular political position, clinging doggedly to republicanism long after rival towns had succumbed to despotic rule, tolerating Cosimo de Medici's leadership so long as it remained unofficial and benign. In this the city had some justification in styling itself the "new Rome".

How Florence reached this state of commercial superiority and political independence is a story of self-awareness and creativity, emerging from centuries of continuous and often violent conflict.

The wool trade: As early as the 11th century, Florentine merchants began importing wool from Northern Europe and rare dye-stuffs from the Mediterranean and the east. They quickly developed specialised weaving and dyeing techniques that made the wool trade the city's biggest source of income, an industry that employed approximately one third of her inhabitants by 1250.

Soaring profits fuelled that other Florentine mainstay, banking. Financiers exploited the established trade routes, creating a network of lending houses. In 1250 a tiny gold coin was minted in the city that became the recognised unit of international currency, the Florin.

Emergent capitalism and the rapid expansion of the city served to fuel the long standing conflict between the Guelfs and the Ghibellines. It was a struggle that embroiled the whole Italian peninsula, but the prize—and therefore the vehemence of the feud—was all the greater in Florence.

In broad terms, the Guelfs supported the Pope and the Ghibellines the Holy Roman Emperor in a battle for territory and temporal power. In Florence, the parties fought in the streets, attacking their enemies and retreating to their defended palaces.

In the ups and downs of the conflict, there were no decisive victories and new alliances were created every time an old one was defeated or its supporters sent into exile. In general, though, the new men were in the ascendant. The Florentine banking system reached its zenith in the late 13th century when the Parte Guelfa secured a monopoly over papal tax collection and in 1293 the Ordinances of Justice barred the nobility from state office, concentrating power in the hands of the trade guilds.

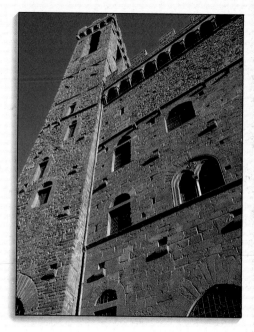

Black versus white: But just as the *magnati*, the aristocrats, survived as a powerful element in the city, so the Guelfs themselves began to split, as powerful families jostled for prominence, and the plague of the medieval city, the family vendetta, grew apace.

The origins of the new conflict—between the Blacks, the *Neri*, and the Whites, the *Bianchi*—lay outside Florence, in a feud between two branches of the Concellieri family in Pistoia. It was just the excuse that the rival Florentine Cerchi and Donati families were looking for. They took up opposite sides in a quarrel that gained momentum and

Left, Cellini's *Perseus*, Loggia Dei Lanzi. Above, the Bargello: typical 13th-century stronghold.

led, in 1302, to the exile of Dante, amongst others, who were all expelled from the city in a mass purge of the Whites.

Dante achieved his revenge by populating Hell and Purgatory with his enemies, inventing appropriate eternal punishments so that out of the conflict was born a great work of art, one that helped establish the Florentine dialect as the progenitor of the modern Italian language. Equally remarkable is the fact that Florence still prospered even though it was, in the poet's own words, like a fevered woman tossing and turning in bed in search of rest and relief.

The enigma of Florence: In the 14th century, hereditary dynasties, Florence for a long time (and despite the in-fighting) did not succumb. Instead, it evolved its own style of broadly based government.

The city was never democratic in any modern sense, for the huge artisan community had little real power. However the government did encompass a variety of interest groups, with a council whose members were elected from the city's 21 guilds and executive officers chosen from the seven major guilds, appointed to posts for a finite period so that no individual could dominate.

Capitalism in crisis: New-found stability was continually put to the test and yet sur-

Florence was the richest city in Europe; the cathedral, Palazzo Vecchio and Santa Croce were all begun, industry boomed and Florentine artisans were renowned for their skills in metalcasting and terracotta, as well as the weaving and dyeing of cloth. Pope Boniface summed up the enigma of the city when he described the world as composed of five elements; earth, air, fire and water...and the Florentines.

Moreover, whereas factionalism in other Italian city states favoured the rise of *signori*, despots who exploited instability to impose their own personal authority and establish

vived. In 1340, Edward III of England reneged on Florentine debts, precipitating a banking crisis, and, three years later, the first terrifying symptoms of the Black Death appeared in the city. It re-emerged seven times during the century, carrying off more than half the population.

Internal revolts, such as the 1378 rebellion of the *ciompi*, the lowest paid of the city's wool workers, demanding the right to form a guild and be represented on the council, often resulted in the powerful merchant families closing ranks against "popular" elements. But each time this happened the leaders were sent into exile: first the Alberti, then the Strozzi and finally the Medici.

Wars with foreign powers and neighbouring states tended, also, to unite factional leaders in a common cause: that of defence and then the expansion of the Florentine republic. Between 1384 and 1406, Florence won victories over Arezzo, Lucca, Montepulciano, and Pisa—the great prize that gave the city direct access to the sea.

Style wars: Her success helped to confirm that aggressive independence and sense of Florentine identity that played a shaping role in the cultural awakening of the *quattrocento*. By the beginning of the 1400s, the guilds, as well as individual patrons, had begun to find new ways of expressing the rivalry that was previously the cause of so much bloodshed, and one that was to benefit, rather than threaten, the city. Patronage of the arts became the new source of prestige, a means of demonstrating wealth and power. The oldest of the guilds, the wool-importers, the Arte di Calimala, set the precedent by its lavish expenditure on the Baptistry and its competition to choose the best artist to design the great bronze doors.

Florence's many religious foundations also began to compete in the sponsorship of artists, as well as private patrons. All could justify their patronage on grounds of piety—initially Renaissance art was religious, and only later secular and classical—or as an expression of community responsibility and civic pride. At root, though, it was the same old desire to excel, dressed in a new guise.

Nouveau riche artists: Patronage made many a Florentine artisan wealthy. Ghiberti, trained as a goldsmith and only 25 years old when he was awarded the commission for the Baptistry doors, founded a workshop and foundry that employed countless craftsmen, many of whom became famous and courted in their own right. Filippino Lippi's sexual peccadilloes were tolerated—he was even allowed to relinquish his monastic vows and marry the nun he seduced, so long as he continued to produce brilliant art.

Left, symbols of mercantile success: San Lorenzo Market. Above, Road to exile, fate of Date and the Medici.

Florentine humanism: In this changing environment, it was also possible for intellectuals and artists to play a role in political life. Humanist scolars emerged from their absorbtion in classical texts to make new claims for Florence as the true inheritor of Roman virtues. In 1375, Collucio Salutati, the greatest classical scholar of his day, became Florentine Chancellor, bringing to everyday politics all his immense learning, and swaying opinion by the power of his Ciceronian rhetoric. Other scholars followed his example: Leonardo Bruni, Poggio Braccilioni and Cosimo de Medici.

Cosimo proved too persuasive, too popu-

lar for the comfort of his political opponents. Heir to the banking network established by his father, Giovanni, he supported the guilds against government attempts to expropriate their funds to support its military operation. He suffered the fate of all who threatened to wrest or win power in Florence and was banished from the city in 1433.

Exile lasted only a year for, with the backing of Pope Eugenius IV, he returned in 1434, and acted as unofficial leader for the next 30 years. Thus began a period of unparalleled peace and stability, and the founding of what was to become the Medici dynasty.

MILESTONES OF THE RENAISSANCE

In his celebrated *Lives of the Most Excellent Painters, Sculptors and Architects,* published in 1550, Giorgio Vasari recounted the story of art up to his own time in terms of three great phases, which he called the first, second and third manners. Florentines were largely responsible for all three.

The first manner was created by Cimabue and Giotto in painting and by Nicola and Giovanni Pisano in sculpture. From the first manner evolved the second, in which Brunelleschi in architecture, Masaccio in painting and Donatello in sculpture finally achieved "beautiful" and "good" work, though it was still not yet, in Vasari's opinion, "perfect". Perfection, and consequently the fear that art in the future was more likely to decline than to progress, came with Leonardo, Raphael and Michelangelo, artists of the third manner.

The first manner was developing during the 14th century or the *trecento,* the 1300s, as art historians, following Italian practice, often call it. The second manner corresponds to the 15th century, the *quattreocento,* or what is now called the Early Renaissance. The third manner was achieved in the 16th century, the High Renaissance. It was followed by the style called Mannerism which, coming after the High Renaissance, is often regarded as something of a decline.

Although visitors to Florence can still follow Vasari's sequence in full by studying the paintings in the Uffizi, most of the greatest treasures of the rest of the city clearly belong to the second manner.

The highest points of the High Renaissance were reached elsewhere: in the Sistine Chapel, for instance, in Rome. Neither, with the exception of the damaged frescoes in Santa Croce, does Florence possess the best of the pre-Renaissance art. But for masterpieces of the Early Renaissance—in painting, fresco, sculpture and architecture—

Preceding pages: the Ponte Vecchio. Left, Michelangelo's *David*. Above, gothic sculpture in the Bargello.

nowhere in Italy or the world can rival the city of Florence.

Cathedral sculpture: The three fine arts of architecture, painting and sculpture developed in close association in this small city, although not all at the same time. Sculpture was the first to come to the fore at the beginning of the 15th century. The cathedral begun in 1294, was still unfinished a century later, but Florentines were keen to press ahead with its decoration and, from the end

of the 14th century, they began to commission a series of works of sculpture for its adornment.

Those responsible for the commissions were not the Archbishop or the clergy but members of the city's leading trade guilds, to which different parts of the cathedral were allocated. Rivalry between the guilds does much to explain the constant flow of commissions and the impetus that spurred the artists on to produce ever better work. In the winter of 1400-01, the Calimala, the guild of cloth importers, undertook a project which, if not the first of its kind, was certainly the most costly and prestigious to date: a new set of bronze doors with scenes from the Old Testament, to adorn the Baptistry.

The Baptistry already had a set of 14th-century bronze doors, but the guild wanted still finer ones. In order to make sure of the best results they set up a competition between five shortlisted artists, among them Jacopo della Quercia, Filippo Brunelleschi and Lorenzo Ghiberti. Each contestant was to execute a relief representing Abraham's sacrifice of his son Isaac, including the donkey which brought the sticks which made the fire beneath the altar.

Relative merits: Three of the finalists' ef-

ments, and the boy Isaac has a particularly pathetic appeal. Perhaps, ultimately, Ghiberti won because his panel was better technically, cast in one piece instead of Brunelleschi's three, weighing less, using noticeably less bronze and therefore the more economical.

The subsequent careers of both artists proves that if the guild had wanted the work competed speedily, they should have chosen the more prolific Brunelleschi. As it was, Ghiberti, awarded the commission, laboured on the doors for 20 years. Nevertheless, they were so well received that he was almost immediately commissioned, in 1425, without

forts were rejected and melted down, but those of Ghiberti and Brunelleschi survive in the Bargello. Ghiberti's panel was chosen as the winner, but why? What induced the hard-headed merchants to prefer his design to that of Brunelleschi? His design is strongly modelled and action-packed, as Abraham, torn between paternal love and obedience to his maker, delivers the knife to the throat of his son, only to be restrained, at the last moment, by the angel of God.

Perhaps the judges preferred Ghiberti's work because it is the prettier piece: the figures make more rhythmic, delicate move-

competition, to make a third set of doors. This time he was given a freer hand—he abandoned the archaic Gothic quatrefoil frames that the guild had insisted on for the earlier doors—and from the start it was decided they would be gilded.

The result is a glowing, ethereal world of never-never beings, a golden heaven that drew the contemporary epithet "the Gates of Paradise". Ghiberti's doors are the outstanding example of the Early Renaissance taste for the precious, the expensive and the delicate, all of which compete with the impulse for clarity, expression and energy.

Clarity, energy, expression of the human figure—these are qualities specific to the Renaissance and ones that divide it from the Gothic style that went before. But Ghiberti's career illustrates how slowly the Renaissance picked up, and how long, lingeringly and lovingly, the Florentines clung to gold, blue and bright colours, to the soft and decorative, to surface texture and the sensual.

A feast for the eye: For these are the qualities that most characterise the works of the two most successful Early Renaissance painters in Florence, Fra Angelico (active 1420-55) and Fra Filippo Lippi (active 1430-69). However, while continuing to provide for

to his work. As for the passionate Filippo Lippi so in love with life that Cosimo de' Medici would lock him up in order to force him to paint, there is a room in the Uffizi full of his masterpieces. Here the astonishing refinement of the Madonnas he painted at the end of his life can be admired—refinement plus personal oddities, such as the cheeky smiling cherubs that were his hallmark.

Donatello's career: By contrast, the work of two artists, the painter Masaccio and the sculptor Donatello, is so different from that of their contemporaries that they have been hailed as an *avant garde*. Donatello trained briefly in Ghiberti's workshop before mak-

their patrons what they wanted most—a delight for the eye—both painters gradually improvised new effects that, by the end of the century, had completely transformed the look of art.

The work of Fra Angelico can be seen nowhere better than in Florence. He was based at the Dominican monastery of San Marco where, in addition to frescoes that he and his assistants painted in each of the friars' cells, there is now a museum devoted

**Left, Fra Angelico's *Annunciation*: San Marco.
Above, Botticelli's *Judith*.**

ing his mark as one of three sculptors commissioned in 1408 to provide statues of the Four Evangelists for the (still uncompleted) cathedral facade.

All Four Evangelists are now in the Cathedral Museum, the Museo dell 'Opera del Duomo. Donatello's St John is strikingly forceful compared to the other three. The St Matthew, of Bernado Ciuffagni, patently plagiarises Donatello's statue. Such cheating was rife in an age when winning a competition meant great wealth and a stream of further commissions. Aware of this danger, Donatello had applied for a lock to be put on the door to his workshop—for he worked on site, not in a studio.

By the terms of this particular competition, the fourth Evangelist was to be carved by the best sculptor of the other three. In fact it went to a fourth man; Donatello was probably, by then, too busy to care, for he was working on a sculpture for Orsanmichele, another major arena for guild competition during the 1410s and 1420s.

On the outside of the square church of Orsanmichele the guilds had each been allotted a niche, and they vied with one another to command sculptures from the best artists of the age. Ambition and style progressed so rapidly that some even had to remove their first statue and substitute another in order to keep up—this was the case with the Wool Guild's St Stephen by Ghiberti, the second of two colossal bronzes worked by him.

Revolutionary art: The early figures were in marble, including the most famous of them all, Donatello's St George (1417). What was so revolutionary about this statue (now transported to the safety of the Bargello)? Not simply that St George stands with firmness and conviction, of a kind alien to previous Gothic statuary and more akin to classical art; but also that he seems alive and ready for action. With this one work, Donatello had at last stripped off the decorative coating in which Gothic art was wrapped, and exposed a real man, his brows furrowed and his eyes keen as he awaits the sound of alarm.

Donatello's subsequent work punctuates the sightseer's pilgrimage through the city. More works made for the cathedral are in the Cathedral Museum: prophets, still dirty and dusty from centuries of exposure, moved here from their position on the campanile; his singing gallery or *cantoria* with its madly dancing *putti*; and one of his late works, the St Mary Magdalene, shown in all the emaciation of her desert penance.

It is interesting to read what Vasari has to say about this great sculptor. He tells us that even Brunelleschi, whose own sculpture tended to the strong and dramatic, condemned a crucifix by Donatello because its Christ resembled a peasant, not a man. It is extraordinary that, throughout his life, Donatello eschewed the sweet and lyrical,

when that was so much the style around him. Vasari unconsciously acknowledges this when he says that Donatello's work hardly belongs to the second manner at all but, alongside Michelangelo, seems closer in spirit to the third, the age of perfection, the High Renaissance.

The third manner: If Masaccio, Donatello's friend, had not died in 1428 before he reached 30, his painting might similarly have stood out from the rest. As it was, he painted few works, of which the most important are the frescoes of the Brancacci Chapel in Santa Maria del Carmine. These had comparatively little impact in their time yet,

looking back, Vasari saw that they heralded the third manner. Masaccio deliberately imitated his predecessor, Giotto, and his contemporary, Donatello, to create solid, rather grave figures who move little but express much, fixed in a carefully defined light and a clearly understood perspective.

This perspective, applied to painting, sculpture and architecture, is one of the best known achievements of the Early Renaissance. However, it is worth remembering that by the 16th century artists no longer considered it of paramount importance, and that good perspective alone does not make good painting.

In the Early Renaissance, the work of Uccello (1397-1475) proves this. Vasari relates that Uccello would stay up all night working out, mathematically, the vanishing point of the perspective in his drawings, while his wife called for him to come to bed in vain. His major works in Florence, *The story of Noah*, and particularly *The Flood*, in the cloister of Santa Maria Novella (painted about 1430), is a remarkable exercise in perspective but not great art by any standard.

Technical developments: Nevertheless, perspective—or, more exactly, perspective worked out by geometry, rather than by

tion of all the arts, crafts and sciences in one man is Leonardo da Vinci, but he had many precursors, amongst whom Brunelleschi was certainly one. Filippo Brunelleschi, originally a silversmith and sculptor, single-handedly created the style of Renaissance architecture. His success in placing the world's biggest dome over the crossing of the cathedral made him, albeit belatedly, a hero, awarded the unique privilege of burial within the cathedral itself.

Learning from Rome: In the early 15th century, while Ghiberti and Donatello were already at work on the external decoration, the fabric of the cathedral was still incomplete.

guesswork—is a symbol of the comparatively scientific or systematic approach of Renaissance artists. Engineering, in fact, was probably the most essential skill of the Renaissance universal man, and technological advances underpin the more abstract ones. Ghiberti's bronze doors owe as much to the management and techniques of his foundry as to his artistic imagination.

The outstanding example of the combina-

Rivalry, this time between Florence and the rest of Christendom, had led to a revision of the existing plans so as to incorporate an enormous crossing or "tribune". The nettle, which successive architects had avoided grasping, was that an open space of this size could not be vaulted in the usual way, which involved supporting the roof from below, without prodigious expenditure on timber scaffolding. Brunelleschi's solution, which he probably derived from his survey of the Roman Pantheon, was to build the dome from above in concentric rings of brick, laid in such a way that the construction would be

Left, new realism: Donatello's *St George*. Above, Masaccio fresco: Santa Maria del Carmine.

self-supporting.

Though the dome of the cathedral, completed in 1436, was Brunelleschi's most monumental work, his minor works of architecture (Ospedale degli Innocenti, 1419; San Lorenzo; the Pazzi Chapel at Santa Croce; Santo Spirito, 1436) had a great influence on his contemporaries as well as on Vasari and Michelangelo in the years to come.

An enduring style: He evolved a new style which contemporaries believed to be in the Roman manner. It certainly employs some elements taken from classical architecture, but on closer inspection it turns out to be derived more from Romanesque buildings,

death, his style was still popular. Vasari, who begun work on the Uffizi in 1560, was still using Brunelleschi's combination of white plaster walls framed by grey stone mouldings, and echoing his flat, strictly geometric division of the walls, floor and ceilings into squares, oblongs and half-circles.

Botticelli's Venus: About 1460, the Early Renaissance style underwent a pronounced change. A new generation of artists came to the fore, and both painting and sculpture underwent a revolution as profound as that of the beginning of the century. In many ways the most famous of the new generation of artists, Botticelli, was the most traditional,

such as the Baptistry or San Miniato al Monte. The situation is complicated by the fact that Romanesque buildings themselves evolved from classical architecture and the Baptistry was even half-believed, in Brunelleschi's day, to have been converted from the Roman temple of Mars. His style was both new, and yet echoed an older, venerable manner. It was distinctively Florentine, and yet became a national style of enduring influence. The more truly classical, Roman style that later evolved elsewhere in Italy was very much based on Brunelleschi's example and, more than a century after his

continuing the lyricism and the delicacy of line of his master, Filippo Lippi. His two famous paintings in the Uffizi, the *Primavera* (or Spring) and the *Birth of Venus*, which date between 1465 to 1485, illustrate this. Both have been restored: in particular, the Venus has the gold back in her hair, which enhances her beauty and underlines Botticelli's link to Filippo Lippi and Ghiberti.

Before 1460 it is comparatively easy to follow certain main lines of development; after 1460 it becomes harder, because many more excellent artists were active and there were fewer dominant ones. However, certain key characteristics emerge. One is the wider application of drawing. As a result, line dominates in Florentine painting: Florentine art becomes all profile and silhouette, whether it is the exquisite, long contours of Botticelli's Venus or the tense angles and wiry sinews of Pollaiuolo's little bronze of *Hercules fighting Cacus* in the Bargello.

Approaching perfection: Later declared by Vasari as the true basis for Florentine genius and supremacy in art, the ability to draw—*disegno*—was central to all the various skills of Leonardo and Michelangelo and, thereafter, became the cardinal technique in the teaching of the academics.

At the same time, the "study" was born as artists began to analyse their compositions in an increasing number of "preparatory drawings", thus, in Vasari's terms, making them "perfect". Perfectionism had, of course, the unfortunate side effect that many projects were never completed, witness Leonardo's *Adoration of the Kings* in the Uffizi, or the many unfinished works by Michelangelo.

A second important means to perfection was the use of oils rather than tempera as a binder for pigment. Compare the sharp lines of Botticelli, who used tempera, with the work of Perugino (active 1472-1523) who used oils to create softly modelled, sentimental figures in dreamy backgrounds. Oils vastly increased the potential for naturalism because outlines could be blended and contours blurred in infinitesimal gradations.

Thanks to oils, and to the influence of Leonardo and Perugino, artists abandoned their insistence on line, though not the discipline and the chance to experiment that drawing gave. Instead painters sought to create the illusion that their figures were fully three dimensional, by modelling every facet. The newly restored Doni *tondo* by Michelangelo in the Uffizi shows the degree of finish and exactitude of workmanship that Vasari considers the essential ingredients of "perfection" in painting.

Michelangelo's David: In sculpture, Michelangelo arrived on the scene in the 1490s and his best known work in Florence, the statue of David (1504) harks back to Donatello's expressive force and has another quality, which contemporaries called "Roman" or "antique" and which today is called monumental or, better, heroic.

Art in decline: David is one of the last masterpieces of the Renaissance produced in Florence. In 1505 Michelangelo went to Rome to work for the Pope. In 1506 Leonardo returned to Milan, the city in which he spent most of his maturity. In 1508 Raphael, having only come to Florence in 1504, followed Michelangelo to Rome. Florentine art was never better, but the city, in economic and political travail, found it difficult to retain her artists. Vasari even criticised Andrea del Sarto, the best of the artists still working in the city during the High Renais-

sance, for timidity in having stayed in Florence with the result that his art was correspondingly limited.

A brief revival of the arts in Florence was introduced by Mannerist artists, such as Rosso Fiorentino and Pontormo. Their work is fascinating but the sense of striding progress is absent from this 16th-century movement. It produced one genius, Bronzino, but he had no worthy successor. In 1550 it was indeed time for Vasari to write his history.

Left, the Uffizi behind Signoria. Above, Botticelli self portrait.

The Medici family ruled Florence almost continuously from 1434 to 1737 and there is scarcely a corner of the city which does not have some connection with the family.

The Medici coat of arms is ubiquitous: a cluster of red balls on a field of gold. Some say it represents the dented shield of Averardo, a legendary knight from whom the family claimed descent. Others think the balls are medicinal pills—the family name suggests descent from apothecaries. Another theory explains the balls as symbols of money, like the traditional pawnbroker's sign, reminding us of the banking foundations of the family fortune.

Papal banker: The bank was established by Giovanni di Bicci de' Medici (1360-1429), one of nearly 100 financial institutions in the city at the beginning of the 15th century. Its rapid expansion to become the most profitable bank in Europe had much to do with the family's special relationship with the Pope. When the bank secured a monopoly over the collection of papal revenues, the family fortune was made.

Giovanni's son, Cosimo de' Medici (1389-1464) spent his early years travelling Europe in pursuit of new business. Father and son preferred to stay out of Florentine public life, well aware that the price of popularity with one faction was the enmity of another; too many public figures had been sentenced to exile when their party fell from power, and exile was incompatible with running a successful enterprise.

Nevertheless, when Cosimo was arrested and charged with treason in 1433 he was no longer able to stand on the sidelines. Over the previous five years Florence had been involved in a series of inconclusive wars with its neighbours. The cost was bringing the city to the verge of economic crisis.

Cosimo had agreed to serve on the war committee, but resigned in 1430, having

failed to win support for an end to the costly campaign. He left for Verona where, according to rumours spread by the rival Albizzi family, he was plotting to invade Florence and seize power. He was summoned to return to the city, on the pretext that his advice was required, arrested and sentenced to 10 years' exile.

Triumphant return: In the event, Cosimo's absence from Florence was brief. After a disastrous defeat by the Milanese in 1434,

Florence was in no position to pursue its wars. Support for the Albizzi crumbled, the sentence of exile was revoked and Cosimo returned to a tumultuous welcome in September 1434.

Though the people of Florence welcomed Cosimo as if he were a conquering king he himself was characteristically ambivalent about taking up the reins of power. He stayed very much in the background, manipulating, rather than governing, maintaining the appearance, at least, of private citizenship and respecting the city's republican aspirations.

Hence the story that Cosimo turned down

Preceding pages: the Uffizi, home of the Medici masterpieces. Left, portrait of young Lorenzo de Medici. Right, the Medici coat of arms.

a first design by Brunelleschi for the new family palace because it was too ostentatious. Hence, too, the contemporary accounts of Cosimo's cryptic character, the complaint that you could never tell what he was thinking. Both as a politician and as a businessman, running a complex international banking operation, Cosimo was a master of guile, persuasion and discretion.

He was also an enthusiastic supporter of the movement we now call humanism—a name which, though Renaissance in origin, was not used in this sense until the 16th century. In the 15th century the nearest equivalent was "orator".

In its early stages, in Cosimo's time, the movement emphasised the instruction to be gained from studying the classical past. It was nourished by a great belief in the over-riding power of the word: persuasion, knowledge and good sense, leavened by the grace of God, were enough to make the world the way it should be.

The orators were pre-eminently diplomats or statesmen; men like Leonardo Bruni, Chancellor of Florence, Aeneas Sylvius Piccolomini, later Pope Pius II, and Cosimo himself. The origin of the movement can be traced to the period 1397-1400 when the Byzantine, Manuel Chrysoloras, was invited to Florence to teach ancient Greek, a language which had been all but forgotten.

From the start, the humanists were motivated by the excitement of discovery and throughout the 15th century they scoured the world for antique manuscripts. Cosimo himself funded the travels of Poggio Bracciolini who became famous for his discovery of the lost works of Cicero in a remote monastery. Cosimo founded the public library at San Marco to house only a portion of his massive collection of manuscripts—others that he amassed form the core of the Laurentian Library. He also paid for the education of Marsilio Ficino so that he could translate the then unknown dialogues of Plato.

Glory and gout: Cosimo died in 1464 leaving Florence prosperous, peaceful and with just claim to the title "the new Rome"—having given birth contemporaneously to humanism and the Renaissance. Upon him the *signoria* conferred the title once bestowed upon Cicero of *Pater Patriae*, father of his country. Cosimo's son, the sickly Piero, inherited his father's gout and did not long survive. In 1469, Lorenzo was called upon to fill his grandfather's shoes.

Lorenzo was no great patron of the pictorial arts. He owned few paintings and preferred the more princely pleasures of collecting antique gemstones, coins and vases (now in the Argenti Museum). Yet his portrait is familiar to the world through Botticelli's *Primavera* where, as Mercury, he dances with the Three Graces. The picture was painted not for him but for his cousin and namesake.

The youthful and athletic figure in Botticelli's picture is enormously flattering. In reality Lorenzo was strikingly ugly, with a beak nose and a projecting lower jaw that almost engulfed his upper lip. But to portray him as Mercury, god of eloquence, conciliation and reason was entirely just.

Literary talent: Lorenzo was an outstanding poet, writing satirical, often bawdy, sometimes romantic verse in his native tongue. Whereas in Cosimo's time it would have been unthinkable to read or write seriously except in Latin, Lorenzo promoted the study of Dante's work in the universities and encouraged respect for Boccaccio and Petrarch, also writers in the *volgare*. The language of these writers would soon become the standard for all Italian literature.

Moreover, Lorenzo was, like Cosimo, a humanist, much pre-occupied with the new philosophy of neo-Platonism that his grandfather's protégé, Ficino, had begun to develop—and the ethereal quality of Botticelli's painting may also owe something to Ficino's quasi-mystical, half-magical theories as well as Lorenzo's love poetry.

Senior statesman: As for reason and conciliation, although Lorenzo resented being torn from his literary pursuits to deal with affairs of state, he won respect throughout Italy for his attempts to heal old rifts and pacify warring city states. His aim was an alliance of states strong enough to defeat external threats, including the ambitions of the Holy Roman Emperor.

Ironically, it was the Pope who proved to be Lorenzo's greatest enemy, for his own territorial ambitions depended on a divided Italy. It was Sixtus IV who took the papal bank account from the Medici bank, contributing to its near bankruptcy. Sixtus, too, was behind the Pazzi conspiracy of 1478 that aimed to murder Lorenzo and destroy the Medici. Sixtus even sent his allies, the Neapolitan army, to attack Florence, but Lorenzo so charmed the King of Naples that peace terms were rapidly agreed.

The news that his plans had been frustrated probably contributed to Sixtus's death. Lorenzo took care to cultivate his successor, Innocent VIII, and succeeded in having his son, Giovanni de' Medici, created a cardinal, at the age of 16, thus planting a Medici in the heart of the papal domain.

Three weeks after Giovanni's consecration, in 1492, Lorenzo was dead. "The peace of Italy is at an end," declared Pope Innocent, who was himself to die two months later, and his prophecy proved correct. Two years later, in 1494, the French King Charles VIII invaded Italy and marched with a huge army to the walls of Florence. Piero de' Medici, Lorenzo's son, hoping to win the King's

friendship, surrendered the city. Florentines slammed the doors of the Palazzo Vecchio in his face and that night the family fled.

Into the vacuum stepped Savonarola, convinced that Charles VIII was an agent of God, sent to punish the Florentines for their obsession with pagan philosophies, secular books and profane art. He presided over the city for four terrible years, when to wear unbecoming dress was punishable by torture and children were rewarded for reporting their parents' misdemeanors.

Savonarola had both fanatical supporters and equally determined opponents: opinion turned against him when he was excommu-

nicated and the threat of papal interdict fell over the city. His lasting achievement was the new republican constitution adopted in 1494 and, even after Savonarola was executed in 1498, the republic continued to flourish under the leadership of Piero Soderini, assisted by Niccolo Machiavelli.

Return of the Medici: In 1512, the nascent republic suffered heavy defeat at the hand of the Spanish and the Medici forced their way back into the city, led by Cardinal Giovanni. The following year he was crowned Pope Leo X and Florence celebrated for four days. Machiavelli, regarded as a threat by the

Left, Lorenzo as Mercury in Botticelli's *Primavera*. Above, Pope Leo X, by Titian.

Medici, was imprisoned and tortured, then allowed to retire from public life. He began working on *The Prince*, a justification of his own actions in office and a reflection on the qualities that make an effective leader.

Much misunderstood, his work is popularly regarded as a defence of ruthless autocracy. Until now, this had not been the Medici style, but increasingly the family was determined to hold on to power with all the considerable force at its disposal. Two Medici popes, Leo X and his cousin Clement VIII, ruled Florence from Rome for the next 15 years through the agency of Alessandro de' Medici, widely believed to be the bastard

son of Pope Clement.

A brave attempt to re-establish the republic in 1527, when Rome was sacked by imperial troops, was put down by combined imperial and papal forces in 1530. Alessandro was crowned Duke of Florence and proved to be the first of many generations of Medici Dukes who, secure in their power, proved to be corrupt, debauched and tyrannical. When he was murdered by his cousin and occasional bedfellow, Lorenzaccio,

Above: Cosimo I by Vasari: Ceiling of the Palazzo Vecchio. Right, great Italian poet Dante.

Florence was relieved of a great burden.

When the council met to elect a successor, they chose another Cosimo; this time the son of the widely respected Giovanni delle Bande Nere and Maria Salviati, granddaughter of Lorenzo the Magnificent. Those who voted for him perhaps genuinely believed that he would accept constitutional limitations to his power and only act after consulting appointed counsellors. They were wrong—it soon became evident that under his rule, they would enjoy not greater freedom but less. Cosimo I set about systematically destroying all opposition. First he defeated an army of republicans in exile and had the leaders publicly executed, four a day, in the Piazza Signoria. Then he brought the cities of Tuscany to heel, attacking them with such force and brutality that Siena, for example, lost half its population in the defence; to this day many Sienese refuse to set foot in Florence for this very reason.

Unlike former Medici, he was no enlightened patron of the arts. Such work as he did commission—the frescoes of the Palazzo Vecchio—were for his own self-glorification or for practical purposes: the Uffizi was built to bring all the administrative functions, the guilds and the judiciary, under one roof and under his direct day-to-day control.

Cosimo's achievements: He thus created an effective administration, forced Tuscany into political unity and brought security to the region. Where Cosimo de' Medici, in the 15th century, had simply been one of several powerful heads of Florentine families, Cosimo I was truly a monarch, the government his council and his followers courtiers.

Ironically, after his death, Florence achieved something approaching the self-governing status that had so long eluded the city previously. Cosimo's descendants, who nominally ruled Florence for another six generations, proved so indolent, degenerate, drunken and debauched that they had little taste for affairs of state, which was left to the government machine created by Cosimo. Yet no-one again challenged their right to rule and, when the last of the Medici, Anna Maria, died in 1743, there was genuine grief at the passing of a dynasty and the end of a chapter in the city's colourful history.

FLORENTINE FIRSTS

From something as down-to-earth as street paving and eyeglasses to grand concepts such as capitalism and the theory of the universe, it is sometimes hard to grasp the breadth of Florence's contributions to the modern world.

A few of Florence's firsts have a sound historical base. Old records, show that street paving began in Florence in the year 1235, and by 1339 the city had paved all its streets—the first in Europe to do so, And while Florentines had little to do with the actual discovery of the New World, they are quick to point out that one of them, Amerigo Vespucci, provided the word "America", and that Leonardo da Vinci created the first world maps showing America.

A tablet in the church of Santa Maria Maggiore documents another first: "Here Lies Salvino d'Amato Degli Armata of Florence, the Inventor of Eyeglasses, May God Forgive His Sins, Year 1317."

Two developments in music are among the most solidly documented Florentine firsts. The pianoforte was invented in Florence in 1711 by Cristofori, and the origins of opera are traced to the performance, in 1600, of *Euridice*, a new form of musical drama written by Iacopo Peri in honor of the marriage in Florence of Maria de Medici to Henri IV of France.

An earlier marriage was supposedly the impetus for modern table manners. When Catherine de Medici wed the future Henri II and moved to France, she was apparently appalled at the French court's table manners; unlike Florence, no one used a fork. Before long all of Paris society was imitating her.

To the dismay and occasional ridicule of the French, some Florentines also believe that Catherine, equally appalled at French food, sent for her own chefs, and was responsible for the beginning of French grand cuisine.

In the absence of any creditable challenges over the centuries, it is generally accepted that foods such as ice cream and minestrone were also first made and eaten by the Florentines.

Many other firsts, of course, are related to the arts. Donatello's *David* (1430) is regarded as the first free-standing nude statue of the Renaissance. Donatello is also credited with the first free-standing equestrian statue of the Renaissance.

One of Florence's most grandiose claims, that Filippo Brunelleschi is the father of modern architecture, is one of the least contested. He was the first Renaissance architect to evolve the rules of linear perspective, and his approach to his work—detailing specifications in advance, separating design from construction—raised architecture to what the experts call "an intellectual discipline and a cultural dignity".

Machiavelli, through *The Prince* and his many other writings, is credited not just with inventing modern political science, but also modern journalism. Though much of his work was written in exile, Dante's high-brow Florentine language was so admired that it became the basis for modern Italian. Also in literature, Guicciardini is credited with laying the groundwork for modern historical prose, Petrarch for modern poetry and Boccacio for modern prose narrative.

In boasting of "firsts", Florence often overlooks the negative aspects. For example, in the *Inferno*, which did so much to make Florentine the language of all Italy, Dante vilified the city as: "a glut of self-made men and quick-got gain". And though Florentines boast that Galileo popularised the heliocentric theory of the universe, they rarely add that it led to his jailing during the Inquisition of 1633.

In the financial world, it can be disputed whether 13th-century Florentine banks were responsible for modern capitalism, or whether the city's medieval merchants were the first of a new and eventually dominant social class. But there is less doubt that those early Florentine financiers originated credit banking and double-entry book keeping, which both contributed mightily to the success of capitalism.

Finally, it is well documented that in 1252 Florence became the first city to mint its own gold coin, and that coin became widely circulated throughout Europe; indeed, many modern currencies, such as the Dutch florin, still carry the name of the old Florentine coin.

When asked what made life worth living, Harold Acton, the grand old man of letters, recalled Cyril Connolly's words with pleasure: "Writing a book, dinner for six, travelling in Italy with someone you love". As an old man, Acton confirmed that judgement: "I believe Florence has given me all this."

The rich relationship between Florence and its foreign visitors goes back to the 17th century. Before then, foreign visitors were likely to be mercenaries or spies, posing as diplomats. Gradually a few adventurous eccentrics such as Fynes Moryson published their encounters with witty, if outlandish, Florentines and their barbarous architecture.

A century later, the attraction of an alien psyche, a perfect climate, a low cost of living and undervalued works of art made Florence an essential stop on any European tour. The cynical Tobias Smollett decried this new cultural traffic as "an exchange of snobbery, vices and fashions" since travel was an option only open to the aristocracy. As a product of a narrow if leisured background himself, he saw even upper-class Florentines as noble savages at best and horse thieves at worst. Smollett's jaundiced views were perhaps influenced by his unfortunate night arrival in Florence: he and his wife had to trudge four miles round the old city walls before finding an open gate.

Court consuls: By 1737, Horace Mann, the English Consul to the Grand Ducal court, protested against the numbers of English in Florence: "If I had to invite them all to dinner, I'd be ruined." He welcomed the cultivated company of the politician, Horace Walpole, and the poet, Thomas Gray, as a change from the usual "cheesecake" English. Mann himself was part of a noble line of consuls to Florence, an institution dating back to 1456. Although he tolerated his onerous contacts with the rapidly expanding expatriate colony, he was more at ease with Florentine aristocrats.

Left, cathedral façade. Above, Santa Maria Novella, beloved of Shelley and Henry James.

Sadly, his budget would not compete with the splendour of masked balls held by the Corsini and Niccolini in the Pergola theatre. Mann was in fact witnessing the last days of the Medici. After the death of Gian Gastone, Florentine life took on a sedate pace under the bureaucratic rule of the House of Lorraine.tt

Parties   le, Mann was an industrious Consul, a rarity in a British community devoted to merriment and culture alone. The

Anglophile, Mario Praz, put it more bluntly: "For centuries the Italians have gone abroad to work and the English to enjoy themselves."

During the Napoleonic Wars, travel to Florence was suspended, but the unfortunate case of Joseph Forsyth highlights the dangers of idle tourism. After a happy exploration of the region, Forsyth was imprisoned by the French for 12 years and died soon after his release in 1814, the first martyr to tourism. After the British victory at Waterloo, the middle classes joined the aristocratic dilettanti and literati on the road to Florence.

Retired generals, Renaissance scholars, persecuted rebels, demure governesses and eloping couples incongruously filled the ranks. As Samuel Rogers said: "If rich, one travels for pleasure; if poor, for economy; if sick, to be cured; if gifted, to create."

Shelley and Byron: In his famous phrase, Shelley called Florence a "paradise of exiles", an escape from persecution or poverty to art and sunshine. He marvelled at the city, "the white sails of the boats relieved by the deep green of the forest which comes to the water's edge, and the sloping hills covered with bright villas."

Byron was more interested in the people

impassioned plea in 1860; Masaccio and Piero della Francesca were not fully appreciated by visitors until this century. From the 1820s, a clutch of discerning English clergy arrived and promptly carried away some of Florence's greatest Renaissance treasures, including Masaccio's *Madonna and Child*, now in London's National Gallery.

The writer Walter Savage Landor was the only collector ever to own a Cimabue. Landor boasted often: "Nature I loved, but next to nature, art". After an unsuccessful lawsuit in 1858, he fled to Florence permanently and decorated his Villa Gherardesca with paintings by Raphael and Fra Filippo Lippi. For-

than the landscape. "What do the English know of the Italians, except for a few museums, drawing rooms and a little reading?" With a glamorous Italian mistress and active involvement in the movement for Italian independence, Byron challenged English insularity. Most of his contemporaries ignored the natives in favour of Florentine art and architecture.

Now that art was finally on the agenda, foreign visitors flocked to see the Uffizi sculptures and Botticelli's *Medici Venus*; the "Primitives" such as Giotto and Cimabue were not admired until John Ruskin made an

getting his own litigious and unsavoury past, Landor designated Florentines, "Beyond all others, a treacherous, mercenary race". Along with many of his peers, Landor was struck by the contrast between the city's glorious past and mundane present.

After calling Florence "the filthiest capital in Europe", he complained of villas overrun with "tame pigs, rotten grapes, smelly goats' cheese, children covered with vermin." Although comforted to find that the Florentines "have learned the use of carpets... yet they are not afraid of rotting these carpets by spitting on them most prodigiously."

Florence Nightingale would have had little sympathy for the querulous Landor. In 1837 she returned to the city of her birth intending to study language and art in an early Florentine finishing school. Instead, so legend goes, she sealed her fate by nursing a sick Englishwoman back to health.

According to her contemporary, William Cullen Bryant, Florence did well not to be ensnared by the conventional Grand Tour. In his diaries, Bryant perfectly captures the spirit of Victorian Britain abroad. "As the day advances, the English in white hats and white pantaloons come out of their lodgings, accompanied by their hale and square-built spouses, and saunter stiffly down the Arno".

Anglo-Florentines: By the 1850s, escapees from mid-Victorian England made Florence "*une ville anglaise*" according to the Goncourt brothers. In the morning, the English went for a "constitutional" in the Cascine Park; residents and visitors alike met at Vieusseux library for a chat; then it was time for "*i muffins*" at "*i tirummi*" (tea rooms). Italian language and society were forced into retreat as the English acquired shops, paintings and villas.

As Henry James said, from the splendour of Villa Palmieri, "If you're an aching alien, half the talk is about villas". He ruefully pondered on the fate of Florentine villas, not built "with such a solidity of structure and superfluity of stone, simply to afford an economical winter residence to English and American families". Against local custom, the English chose their villa for its view, not for its architecture, function or size.

The Brownings, Florence's most celebrated literary couple, were no exception: the view from "Casa Guida Windows" slipped neatly from reality into Elizabeth Barrett Browning's most famous poem. Since the invalid Elizabeth was largely confined to home, her verandah, "not quite a terrace but no ordinary balcony," was central to her happiness. There among the lemon trees, Elizabeth, the ardent republican, saw the Austrians invade the cowed city. The Florentines had "constrained faces, they, so

prodigal of cry and gesture when the world goes right."

Elizabeth never tired of praising Italy at the expense of England. "Our poor English want educating into gladness. They want refining not in the fire but in the sunshine". Or as Virginia Woolf put it: "So Mrs Browning, every day, as she tossed off her chianti and broke another orange off the branch, praised Italy and lamented poor, dull, damp, sullen, joyless, expensive, conventional England." The improvement in Elizabeth's health and happiness was partly due to the Chianti cure Robert used to wean her off her addiction to laudanum.

Robert loved Florence because, "I felt at home with my own soul there." He channelled his curious erudition into theology, psychology and botany while organising literary salons, writing prodigiously and looking after his "Lyric Love". Although neither poet expressed much interest in real Florentines, both had a genuine passion for the city.

Browning Institute: When Elizabeth died, her last words were for Italy. Today, the Browning Institute is refurnishing Casa Guida in cluttered and eclectic Victorian style, decorated in green and pink, Eliza-

Left, life at Villa Di Belvedere; painting by Adolfo Tommasi. Above, Elizabeth Barrett Browning.

beth's favourite colours. The inscription on the wall is a tribute from "*Firenze grata*", a grateful Florence: "In her woman's heart blended learning and the spirit of poetry and made of her work a ring of gold joining Italy and England."

Florentine literary critics such as Oreste del Buono believe that the prominence and preciosity of the Browning circle have obscured the rest of Florence's foreign community. Precious or not, its members were aware of living in a mythical time. The American community was enriched by Henry James's thoughtful analysis. In the German community, Adolf von Hildebrand surrounded himself with famous painters and composers. One evening Liszt played Chopin at dinner.

Strauss, Wagner and Clara Schumann stayed at Hildebrand's villa on the slopes of Bellosguardo. A stone's throw from the Brownings, Dostoyevsky was finishing off *The Idiot*. The Florentine Slavic community flourished under Count Demidoff's patronage of the arts. Tchaikovsky lived and worked fruitfully in Via di San Leonardo; even Maxim Gorky and Alexander Blok made a late but artistic entrance on the Florentine scene.

Yet not all Florence's visitors were great authors and artists. The obscure epitaph on Arthur Clough's tombstone reads: "Died at Florence November 13 1861, aged 42— came to Florence in search of good health and died of a fever."

Collectors: At the turn of the 20th century, the Anglo-Florentine community was as much a part of the fabric as the Medician villas it inhabited and the art collections it founded. The collections assembled by Acton, Berenson, Horne and Perkins remain a tribute to the enduring effect of the "Grand Tourists" on Florence.

Bernard Berenson was the archetypical collector. Alan Moorhead describes how the penniless young Berenson "had gone over the frescoes in these Tuscan churches inch by inch, riding out every morning on his bicycle with his pockets full of candles." Fittingly, his Villa i Tatti is now Harvard's Center for Renaissance Studies.

World War I chased away most foreign visitors and residents. D.H. Lawrence had a tourist's experience of the political aftermath. He saw the shift from Socialism to Fascism as different forms of "bullying". Under Socialism, "servants were rude, cabmen insulted one and demanded treble fare. Under Fascism, he reported that cabs had a lower price, but so did life; the Socialist Mayor of Fiesole was murdered in front of his family.

In the 1920s and 1930s, the Grand Tour resumed, but for society figures and intellectuals rather than for leisured young aristocrats. Aldous Huxley dubbed Florence "a second-rate provincial town with its repulsive Gothic architecture and its acres of Christmas card primitives". E.M. Forster, on the other hand, was besotted with the city's alien vivacity.

In 1947, Dylan Thomas came to create or vegetate in "the Rasher-frying sun". After initial excitement, he became steadily drunk and shamelessly collapsed in front of Florence's literary elite in the "Giubbe Rosse" café. Undaunted, Thomas damned them all as "editors who live with their mothers, on private incomes, and translate Apollinaire".

Students: Today's successors to the Grand Tourists of old are the sons and daughters of the establishment, in Florence to attend language and Renaissance art courses. The more daring play "pranks": climbing into the Boboli Gardens at dawn with one's beloved is a traditional favourite. The less inspired sit around in Hermes scarves and Gucci moccasins. The "boring" ones actually find time to look at paintings.

For them, *ennui* quickly sets in, and few ever really look at Florence sitting "in the sunshine beside her yellow river... without other industry than the manufacture of paperweights and alabaster cupids, without activity or energy or earnestness or any of these rugged virtues deemed indispensable for civic cohesion". Henry James saw Florence as a frontier town, a survivor in the face of praise or scorn. Others, less romantically, see it as the indifference of a great beauty who has been painted once too often.

Right, passage beside the Arno.

,3)Florence,Nov.5(AP)View of the square in front
lica of Santa Croce with several cars stranded in
after the Arno river swept over it.(AP-Wirephoto

COMUNE DI FIRENZE
FABBRICA PALAZZO VECCHIO
LAVORI DI CONSOLIDAMENTO E RESTAURO
progetto e direzione lavori : DOTT. ARC____O MUCCINI
collaborazione tecnica: RENATO ____DI
Impresa GIUNTINI GIOTTO ____ n.c.
LUNGARNO DELLE GRAZIE, 4/R · FIRENZE · TEL. 24____
OPERA FINANZIATA DALLA CASSA DD.PP. CON I FONDI DEL ____

AFTER THE FLOOD

Shortly before dawn on 4 November 1966, after 19 inches (48 cm) of rain had fallen in 48 hours, the River Arno broke its banks and crashed through the museums, galleries, cathedrals and crafts shops of Florence.

Thousands of works of art were damaged, some dating back to the 12th century—paintings, statues, carvings, frescoes, tapestries and manuscripts, scientific instruments and ancient Etruscan pottery.

Thirty-five people were killed, 16,000 vehicles destroyed and hundreds of homes left uninhabitable as the muddy floodwaters rose to 20 ft (six metres) above street level. Heating oil was swept out of the broken basement tanks. Bella Firenze, Beautiful Florence, the world's cultural capital, the city of art and dreams, was a stinking black morass.

War toll: The city had suffered from past floods—about one really serious inundation each century—but the only other event that caused so much devastation as the 1966 flood came during World War II. After a pitched two-week artillery battle between the Nazis on one side of the river and the Allied forces on the other, the Germans retreated, blocking the Ponte Vecchio with rubble from demolished mediaeval buildings and blowing up the other six bridges across the Arno. It was only hours after the last German left that the reconstruction of the bridges began.

For Florence, the city's unique place in cultural history carries with it the heavy burden of preserving and conserving its treasures for the rest of the world. Consequently, Florence has become perhaps the world's leading centre for art restoration—and one of the perennial focal points for arguments over how, when, whether and what should be preserved of the past achievements of humankind.

Divisive issues: The debate in recent years

Preceding pages: first news pictures of the 1966 flood. Left, restoration continues years after the flood.

has centred on work in the mediaeval Piazza della Signoria, the main city square. Such is the concern for old Florence that it took the city fathers 13 years to decide that the piazza should be resurfaced; the crumbling and chipping of the old gray flagstones had become so pronounced that asphalt patchwork was no longer acceptable.

At this point, Francesco Nicosia, the archaeological supervisor for Tuscany, stepped in and argued that the planned repaving would cover forever the Roman baths and ancient buildings that lay beneath the square. He launched a campaign to excavate the piazza and create an underground museum, dismissing critics by saying Florence "is like a beautiful woman who gets nausea every time someone takes a long look at her".

But the city government wanted no part of yet another museum, especially one with entrances, exits, air ducts and pavement skylights that would disrupt the way the Piazza della Signoria has served Florence for six centuries. A compromise was finally reached: the archaeologists could dig, and document everything but then they would have to cover it back up again so that the repaving could eventually proceed.

Nicosia agreed, but then found that a whole town, including a Roman wool-dyeing plant, lay under the square. He vowed to continue his battle for a museum in the piazza, and city leaders vowed to continue to fight him. It is likely to be at least another 13 years before a final decision is reached, on the basis of past prevarication.

There was no such doubt over what to do in 1966. Florentines did what they have always done when disaster strikes their city. Even as the floodwaters began subsiding, the task of reversing the damage began.

Memories of the flood: Francis Kelly, an American artist who later wrote a book about the restoration, was one of hundreds of art students from all over the world who had gathered that year, as in every other year, to study in Florence. "It was the students who jumped into the mud and pulled out paintings, statues and manuscripts who were the real saviours of Florence", he says. Forming a human chain down into the fetid bowels of the National Library's basement, they passed out old manuscripts that might have been lost in a few hours.

They helped to wrap Japanese mulberry paper over paintings to keep the paint from buckling, and they helped scrape the slime off the base of Michelangelo's famous statue *David*. Living in makeshift dormitories and wearing blue coveralls handed out by the government, many students gave up months of their lives to help with the restoration, to clean up the streets and pump out basements.

Kelly himself remembers walking into a huge hall lined with famous paintings, all damaged. "It was terribly dismaying", he recalls. "Hanging beside each painting was a bag of paint flakes that had broken off."

Money and expertise: When word of the flood spread, millions of dollars in public and private money poured into Florence from governments and individuals all over the world. Art restoration experts arriving from Britain, America and throughout Europe agreed that it could take 20 years for all the damaged art objects—those not completely ruined—to be restored and for Florence to recover.

They were only half right. Florence has definitely recovered, but a quarter of a century later, the task of restoration is far from complete. Thus far, most of the major works that were damaged are back on display, and the shops and galleries have reopened. The banks of the Arno have been re-dug and reinforced, and valuable art objects have moved to higher, safer places.

Yet the Archaeological Museum, so inundated that the curators had to resort to the same digging techniques they had used to recover artefacts from long-buried civilisations, still has some exhibition rooms closed. At the National Library, perhaps the institution hardest hit, students looking for rare old reference books are still told, "That book has not yet been restored from the flood." In all, 1.5 million volumes were damaged. Nearly a million books were damaged beyond repair, including a set of priceless antique miniatures. More than 500,000 modern books

were saved, however, along with 40,000 rare or historic volumes.

Rapid advances: After being dried and treated with chemicals to prevent further deterioration, those volumes were stored—not in the basement this time—to await restoration. Today Fulvia Farfara, the assistant director, estimates that the eighty full-time conservation staff are about half way through the restoration task. She, like many of her colleagues, believes that this sort of restoration effort would have been necessary, even without the flood. Moreover, the resulting scientific advances in restoration now allow all manner of ageing, deteriorat-

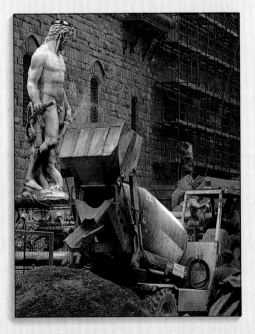

ing or damaged works—not just those rescued from the flood—to be saved.

Benefits of the flood: In the oldest part of mediaeval Florence, among the tiny jewellery and woodworking shops, 24-year-old Paola Lucchesi and 30-year-old Beatrice Cuniberti have a thriving studio restoring antique maps, prints and manuscripts for private collectors. They regard themselves as students of the flood benefitting from techniques which might never have been developed but for that disaster.

Ms. Lucchesi acknowledges that her speciality, paper restoration, was an unknown field before the flood, but developed rapidly as experts gathered in Florence to swap information and work together to develop now-standard drying methods, chemical treatments and rebinding techniques.

Many would echo Ms. Cuniberti's belief that the flood was bad for individual works of art but good for the general field of conservation. New techniques were developed that will preserve important works for many more years.

In the same huge hall where Francis Kelly painstakingly pieced together paint flakes 20 years ago, Marco Ciatti now presides over a laboratory created by the Italian Ministry of

reconstruct damaged areas. Larger paintings, which take up to three years to complete, are painstakingly retouched using brushes and paints that have been re-invented in the style used by the original artist.

Of 3,000 masterpieces rescued from the flood, many of them big canvasses up to 20 ft tall and 10 ft wide (six metres by three), 2,000 are back on display and are still waiting to be restored. At the same time, the techniques developed by the lab are now being used on other, more important works that were not damaged in the flood but nonetheless need restoration. Paintings taken down either earlier this century that

Culture employing 60 specialists in the restoration of paintings. A similar lab on the other side of Florence restores statues and stonework.

Science aids art: Using gamma rays, spectrophotometers, gas chromatographs and other sophisticated equipment, Ciatti's artists work alongside chemists and microbiologists who analyse the canvas and pigment "structure" of deteriorating paintings before deciding on the best way to conserve or

Left, Piazza Signoria under excavation. Above, the Arno: placid here but not always so.

were once thought to have deteriorated beyond repair will soon be back on public display.

Silver lining: Few, perhaps, foresaw that there would be a silver lining to the black storm clouds that gathered over Florence in 1966, but there has been. More than five million people a year now visit the city—10 times the pre-flood record. Despite the frustrations of still-closed galleries and ripped-up paving in the Piazza della Signoria, they can now see works of art in a condition that would make Ruskin, if he only knew, green with envy.

GRANDEUR AND REALITY

People visiting Florence for the first time are frequently disappointed by the crowds and the dirt. Returning visitors, on the other hand, are often pleasantly surprised to find the city neither as dirty nor as crowded as they remember it. Which is to say that things are getting better in Florence, but there is still a long way to go in the search for a balance between the city's past grandeur and everyday humdrum reality.

Important questions: Once again, Florence stands at one of the watersheds that have marked its long and glorious history. Will the city succumb totally to tourism and become little more than an upmarket cultural theme park? Or will changes be made to bolster existing non-tourist based businesses and bring new industry to the town? What can be done to control the dramatic increase in motorised traffic in the twisting, narrow streets where the only pedestrians are the quick or the dead? How many more pizza joints, fast-food restaurants and fashion boutiques will be allowed to replace neighbourhood shops and craftsmen's workshops? Is tourism going to replace culture as the criterion for the future of Florence? Metropolis or necropolis?

The relationship of Florentine citizens to their past is a complex and unusual one. On the surface, there is no mania to conserve, no tensions between old and new. The heritage is not an issue, instead it is part of the very air the Florentines breathe, something so taken for granted that change is almost inconceivable. Thus when change does come, or the force of accumulated problems demands a radical solution, Florentines often stubbornly refuse to accept it or to react.

Prevarication: The historic city centre was enclosed by medieval walls until the 19th century. Those walls were pulled down when Florence briefly served as the capital of Italy after the founding of the republic.

Left, signs of a booming tourist market.

THE POLITICAL MAZE

Florence is no more than a pink patch in Tuscany's "Red Belt". The Florentine preference for left-wing coalitions at local level is a reflection of the old City State's traditional anti-clericalism, hostility to Roman centralisation and also *campanilismo*, "provincialism". More pragmatically, the Communists, and to a lesser extent the Socialists, are seen as untainted by corruption.

Much credit is due to the Socialist Mayor, Massimo Bogianckino, who was chosen for his administrative skills, not his political allegiance. When plucked from the administration of the Paris Opera, he fondly imagined his role to be cultural.

He did not appreciate the myriad of political pressure groups he would need to pacify: the shopkeepers and tour-operators; the Greens and the Masons; the Friends of the Bicycle and the Anti-Hunting League; the Catholics and the Radicals. Not to mention Fiat, the car giant, and Montedison, the chemicals conglomerate, both wishing to build Florence a new satellite city.

However, voting patterns are not class-based but reflect traditional loyalties and a lay/Catholic split. Party membership is also a key to obtaining lucrative council contracts. An aristocrat may well vote Christian Democrat or Liberal because his family has always voted that way. An entrepreneurial hotelier may prefer a left-wing council yet vote for a Christian Democrat government. A conservative leather-worker may vote Socialist because it is a lay party.

A political label says little about life-style or personal wealth: a Florentine Socialist may own a second home and manage a public company. A Florentine Communist may wear Valentino and believe in God.

Covert deals, vote-buying and *clientelismo* (political patronage) are the political facts of life. *Clientelismo* is often the only way of circumventing rigid bureaucracy. Bureaucracy is rife: a driving licence or a residence permit can take weeks to arrange while, despite obvious demand, no local guides to the state galleries can be printed until the correct city authority blesses the venture.

More positively, referenda have helped restore the balance in favour of the individual. The referenda bypass bureaucracy and allow smaller parties to exert political influence disproportionate to their size. Recent referenda have pronounced in favour of hunting, local government de-centralisation, the construction of a metro system and the extension of the experimental Blue Zone ban on non-essential city centre traffic.

The traffic issue has unleashed serious concern about environmental issues, the economy, urban development and Florence's future. Lapo Mazzei, President of Cassa di Risparmio bank believes that Florence "lacks a sense of modernity, accepting the glory but not the responsibility of its role as provincial capital." Harsher critics say that without an airport, a metro system and new hotels, Florence will degenerate into a mediocre tourist centre.

Amidst great controversy, the city council has approved the building of "Firenze Nuova". The new city will be backed by Fiat and by La Fondiaria, Montedison's huge property and services company. It will occupy linked sites between Florence and Prato. The north-western site should be a commercial and industrial centre with a large Fiat factory while the north-eastern site should provide much-needed "green spaces" and leisure facilities. The aim is for "old" Florence to become a centre for craftsmanship, restoration, fashion, culture, commerce and academic study.

The Liberals, Greens, Radicals and resident foreign intellectuals label the plan as a concrete jungle, an American office park masquerading as a rich weave of culture and commerce. They fear "old" Florence will wither or turn into "museumland". However, all the mainstream political parties see the project as a chance for Florence to revitalise the suburbs and experience a second Renaissance.

The American architect in charge of the site goes so far as to suggest that the high-rise blocks will resemble traditional Florentine watch-towers! Social engineering or not, the Mayor has the last word: "We have many doubts, but it is the only way to relieve our terrible traffic problem!"

Though the line of the wall remains well defined in the minds of Florentines they did little to stop the threat to the city and it was foreigners who halted further planned demolition. Despite frequent floods, one or more every century, it was not until the last and most devastating, in 1966, that the easily breached banks of the Arno were given a solid embankment. Many people never returned to their homes and shops after the devastation of the flood. In the 1970s, many others were bought out or driven away—or both—by the booming tourism industry.

Traffic chaos: Today the population of old Florence is estimated at 150,000 compared

lion plus visitors a year, many of whom arrive in cars or exhaust-bellowing buses, the pollution has become a serious problem. Because Florence nestles in the bottom of a bowl formed by the Tuscan hills, the polluted air has no outlet and hangs over the city. Consequently, outdoor sculptures that survived intact for centuries have deteriorated badly in the last 30 years. Many have followed Michelangelo's *David* and have been moved indoors.

Restrictions: In early 1988, Florence instituted an experiment that aimed to reduce the number of vehicles entering the city centre. Each household living in the Blue Zone,

to 400,000 before the flood, and on any given day, especially in the summer, there may be more tourists than Florentines on the streets. Yet this diminishing population is facing a growing number of problems. The first, and most obvious, is the traffic, and the consequent pollution. The growth in tourism has ensured a high standard of living for the Florentine populace, and there are now 2.7 cars for every family living in the city.

Between the Florentines and the five mil-

Left, united in opposition to traffic. Above, excavations in Piazza Signoria.

which encompasses all the area inside the old 14th-century walls, received a permit to drive one car in central Florence; if the family happened to own three cars, only one of them could be driven and parked there.

Commercial vehicles were granted permits to make deliveries during certain hours, but all other cars and trucks had to be left outside the Blue Zone. The city set up large car parks on the edge of the Zone, and provided free bicycles and a fleet of minibuses, running on low-pollution methane gas, to ferry passengers into the inner city. To enforce the new rules, the city increased its police force from 450 to 750. Within weeks, tests showed that pollution and noise had both dropped dramatically and housewives on side streets were hanging their laundry out to dry for the first time in years.

Both visitors and residents have applauded the ban on cars, though it has made things more difficult for many residents. One woman, for example, always used to buy her meat from the butcher just inside the old city; now that she can no longer drive to the shop, she goes to a butcher in the suburbs. It is a small price to pay, she admits, for cleaner air and quieter, less crowded streets.

In a city-wide advisory referendum held cies outside the historic inner city.

In another ballot issue, voters approved, in principle, the construction of a subway system—an idea, like so many others, that has been bandied about in Florence for years. The plan proposes two lines converging from the suburbs on the city centre, with trains every three minutes or so during the rush hour. Given the traditional reluctance of the city council to make such major decisions (it took 13 years to decide to repave the Piazza della Signoria) and the Florentines' inherent abhorrence of any change to their beloved cityscape, it is most unlikely that the system will ever be built, especially in a city

six months later, more than 70 per cent of the city's voters endorsed the ban on private cars and supported the proposal to extend the ban to tourist cars and buses. The referendum serves only to advise the city council, but it appears unlikely that touring motorists will ever again be able to swoop past the Duomo in private cars.

Radical proposals: There were several other important issues concerning Florence's future on that referendum ballot. Approval was also given, for example, to the notion of decentralising the city government and moving some municipal offices and agen-

whose every street covers some sort of ancient Etruscan or Roman ruin.

Satellite city: One of the boldest proposals to keep Florence as a "working" city comes from La Fondiaria, Italy's second-largest insurance group and the only major business concern in Florence not related to tourism, together with Fiat, La Fondiaria has put forward a $500 million, 15-year plan to reclaim marshland on the northwest side of Florence and create what is being called a second city. The plan calls for 3,500 apartments and homes for 15,000 people, several million square feet of office space for 18,500 workers, the first enclosed shopping mall in Italy, three hotels, a convention centre, a branch of the university, a library and a computer communications centre.

Massimo Reale, the La Fondiaria vice-president in charge of the project, says the company intends to reproduce the city effect. "This will not be a suburb or a bedroom community. It will be modern, but it will be similar to downtown Florence in that people will come and go as they live and work there. We want the district to be alive at all hours of the day and night."

Opposition: Reale predicts that the first office buildings and shops would open in the

with the public, nor any figure put on the cost to the city of providing water, sewage, roads, and other services.

The typical citizen does not appear to feel strongly about the project one way or another. Most favour anything that would ease traffic congestion, but fear anything that would change the unique flavour of Florence, the place in which they work and live and play amidst the splendours and the spirit of the Renaissance. Roberto Sabelli, an architect, sums up the views of many when he says, "It would be nice if the La Fondiaria project worked, but another town, a second city centre, would not be Florence. I don't

1990s, but the scheme, which has been approved by the city council, is meeting opposition from environmentalists, who want to preserve the green space, and from the Young Communists who have expressed misgivings about La Fondiaria's motives and the hidden costs of the project.

They believe that the plan is aimed solely at improving the value of a piece of land owned by the insurance company and argue that the plan has not been properly discussed

Left, tourist bus. Above, traffic is now severely restricted.

think Florentines would reognise it as Florence and live or do business there."

Life or death: La Fondiaria's Massimo Reale is convinced, however, that the project will be a success simply because no one else is putting forth any alternatives. "Things cannot go on like this", he says. "Florence as it exists is too old and cramped. Secretaries must share offices with their bosses. There is not adequate space for communications and computer equipment. There is no modern convention or exhibition space. It's a choice between a city that breathes real life and a city of dead monuments."

A Renaissance Florentine standing in the middle of the Piazza Signoria would know exactly where he was. Many of the buildings and the street plan are still close to those of the Renaissance city, despite the neon lights, the *motorini* and *il fast-food*. Moving away from the historic centre, more has changed. The old market area was razed in the last century to make way for the 19th-century monumentalism of Piazza della Repubblica. The city walls are today replaced by a solid wall of encircling traffic.

At the turn of the century, Florence was a residential city of prudent *rentiers*, merchants and minor craftsmen. Only 40 years ago, the city operated a clear class system of landed gentry, solid *borghesia* and poor *contadini*. Today, modern Florence is predominantly bourgeois, despite its left-wing council. The city operates a craft and services economy with industry restricted to the outskirts. Rampant commercialism is kept in check by a sophisticated if provincial culture, and an abiding belief in education, the family and the good life.

Continuity: But ancient and modern Florence often inhabit the same building: a grand *trecento palazzo* may now house a restaurant or fashion showroom run by descendants of the original family. The aristocrats are a small group with a high profile, if only because of the number of streets, squares and palaces named after their ancestors. The nobles have also revived such Renaissance activities as banking, winemaking and patronage of the arts.

On a more humble level, Florence's craftsmen continue their work as cabinetmakers, book-binders or goldsmiths in the city centre. On the edge of modern Florence, the present generation of farmers drive BMWs but still harvest the olives by hand.

The Florentine social elite consists of the political and cultural establishment, led by

the Mayor, the cultural Master of Ceremonies, and by certain ageing intellectuals such as the arcane poet, Mario Luzi. The aristocrats naturally play a starring role. Since the 1950s they have declined in power but continue to see themselves both as Florence's collective memory and as arbiters of taste in modern society: the designer Emilio Pucci makes public proclamations about modern architecture, whilst the Rucellai host literary competitions and photographic exhibitions.

To their credit, the Florentine aristocracy are no longer idle or absentee landlords, but are dynamic entrepreneurs harvesting profits in the wine and food industries. As an early *imprenditore*, Baron Ricasoli "founded" the modern *Chianti* industry. Yet the Frescobaldi and Rucellai have been in the wine trade since the 14th century. These *imprenditori* are matched by the Strozzi in financial speculation, the Pucci in fashion and the Corsini in decoration and restoration. Egalitarian Florentines are not unduly respectful towards the aristocrats, nor do the *nobili* stand on ceremony.

Preceding pages: stallholders in the Mercato Nuovo. Left, students at the Institute of Art. Above, children are indulged.

Although major Italian industrialists have Florentine interests, there is no local industrialist of the stature of Agnelli or De Benedetti, and no tradition of an industrial ruling class. The city's ruling élite consists of top party functionaries supported by influential members of the *sottogoverno*, landowners and entrepreneurs who help set the political parties' hidden agendas in national and regional government.

Nonetheless, the actions of Florentine politicians are influenced by *campanilismo*, the attachment to city roots. Giovanni Spadolini, current President of the Italian Senate, was born near the Medici-Riccardi Palazzo and is as Florentine as the Medici. In 1981, he became the first Florentine Prime Minister since Bettino Ricasoli in 1861. Aware of the honour due to his native town, Spadolini participates fully in Florence's cultural life. In return, Florentines are grateful to him for having kept the political spotlight on their city.

Social mix: The Florentine *borghesia* is equally varied, made up of intellectuals, civil servants and administrative staff.

Today's *intelletuali* are often gatherers not creators: exhibition organisers, theatre critics or art historians. Alessandro Parronchi, the Florentine Post-Impressionist expert, is a dignified member of this circle. He avidly chairs literary committees, collects the works of Lega and Fattori, and will only sell paintings to those who appreciate them. Genuine creators are most active in architecture, sculpture, photography and design. But the intellectuals are not all free thinkers: whether through conviction or inertia, many academics are linked to rigid schools.

The *professionisti* practise law, medicine or architecture and consider themselves refined and hard-working, a cut above the *funzionari*, civil servants trapped in a routine, unadventurous career with the local administration. The *funzionari* are spiritual descendants of the vast class of civil servants who beavered away so efficiently in the Uffizi for the Medici. For their part many *funzionari*, whose salaries are taxed at source, suspect the *professionisti* of tax evasion. As if to refute or confirm such slander, a freelance *professionista* can often be seen on a Sunday

morning closeted with his *commercialista*, the trusted part-time accountant.

The *impiegati*, once low-grade clerical workers in the Medici bureaucracy, are now equally likely to work in the private or public sector, whether for the Regional Administration, the Banca Toscana or the Fondiaria Insurance Company. While such administrative staff are teased about their "employee mentality", the *impiegati* have the last laugh: statutory pay awards and job security ensure a comfortable lifestyle.

The *commercianti* are motivated by profit alone. Florence's shopkeepers, hoteliers and tour operators are the latest incarnation of the

mercantile spirit pioneered by the Medici bankers and Pratesi wool merchants. The *commercianti* are adept at manipulating the black economy to their advantage: nobody suffers but the taxman.

Active, enterprising and often keeping the work in the extended family, cousins and uncles may run offshoots of the main business or work part-time behind the counter. The *commercianti* are a formidable pressure group: the *zona blu* traffic area is constantly under threat from disgruntled shopkeepers who fear a loss of custom.

Work ethic: Florentine capitalism flourishes under a left-wing regime. It is helped by the tradition of family enterprises, whether amongst the great aristocratic families now returning to their mercantile roots, or amongst the thousands of *commercianti*. As to work ethos, there is a fundamental divide between the self-employed and the *dipendenti*, employees of all grades.

In state enterprise and, to a lesser degree in large private companies, torpor and security prevail: fixed income, working hours and responsibilities ensure that more time can be devoted to leisure. By contrast, ambitious shopkeepers and independent professionals display a spirit of enterprise. If job satisfac-

weavers and marble-cutters represent a sacred image of old Florence which modern Florentines are loath to lose.

A newer and more powerful social group are the *operaii*, skilled manual workers who live and work in the industrial suburbs. The Pirelli car company in San Giovanni Valdarno and the textile factories in Osmanorro are amongst the varied local industries.

Concrete jungle: The problems of expansion are clearly visible in the new suburbs. If you miss the autostrada and by some mischance discover the Osmanorro industrial jungle, you may feel that you have wandered onto another planet: roads are pitted with the

tion is greater, so are levels of stress and risk. The two categories may overlap, however: a local government clerk may dash home early to take over from his wife in the family bar.

The so-called lower classes consist of a number of disparate groups with little in common. The *artigiani*, or craftsmen, have an elevated status in Florentine mythology, enhanced by their continuing presence in the city centre. Although small in number, the workshops of shoemakers, goldsmiths,

Left, San Lorenzo market. Above, pilgrims at Santissima Annunziata.

enormous ruts made by transporter lorries; the buildings are universally two-storey concrete blocks and the streets cross each other at right angles before ending abruptly in a plot of half-built concrete. Despite the apparent chaos, however, this does indicate the growth of a modern economy which feeds the city's continuing vitality.

Rural Florence has not been vanquished but has merely retreated to beyond Bellosguardo. The ending of the *mezzadria*, or sharecropping, system coincided with a drift from the land to industry. Depopulation encouraged the spread of the *fattorie*, estate farms, traditional around Florence where they are often still run by landed gentry, perhaps the Antinori or Frescobaldi.

But traditional farmers continue to work the slopes between Florence Observatory and Viale Galileo, within walking distance of the city centre. One such farmer, Signor Parenti, owns a stone villa whose walled grounds conceal old ploughs, orchards, vineyards, and "the only donkey in Florence". Although wealthy, the family works too hard to visit their Forte dei Marmi villa for more than a few days a year.

Some land is still worked by *contadini*, who can be seen shaking the olive trees in November. Appearances can be deceptive, however: Signor Rossi, the gnarled peasant personified, owns a repair shop and is buying a farm with his elderly sister.

Insularity: Towards other Italians, Florentines display anti-social tendencies which in less refined circles might be considered racist. The *meridionali* (Southerners) are made particularly unwelcome, and the *Sardi* (Sardinians), because of their traditional association with kidnapping and family feuds, bear the brunt of Florentine prejudice. Lapo Mazzei, President of the Cassa di Risparmio bank castigates his fellow citizens for their narrowness, insularity and arrogance, but most Florentines are simply contemptuous of *questi primitivi* and avoid suburban residential areas like Scandicci.

The Florentine *borghesia* is served by a foreign underclass of Filipinos. A Florentine Sunday is a *ribollita* soup: little Manila clusters in Santa Maria Novella near the Chinese restaurants. Equally foreign are the motorbike youths on the run from a suburban Sunday. Despite the outsiders, Florence is not a city of immigrants; large numbers of "real" Florentines still live in the city centre.

Newcomers: Although Northern Europeans and Americans receive a better reception, not all Florentines distinguish between *stranieri* (outsiders). Giovanni Koenig, the Florentine architect, dreads descending the Fiesole hills to the cosmopolitan city below because, "Florence has sold out to foreigners". The English have, since the 18th century, formed a numerous and fairly high-profile group. They are still there in force,

sometimes well-integrated but, like the doyen of the community, Harold Acton, fiercely, if rather eccentrically, English.

They are challenged for pre-eminence by the North Americans, aided by research grants and by the local presence of more than 15 U.S. universities. The numbers are swelled during the tourist season by short-stay language and art students. The Germans and Swiss are also there in search of culture but tend to reside out of town in tastefully refurbished country houses scattered amongst the Chianti hills.

Values: Florence's diverse social groups share more than *campanilismo* and a wari-

ness of outsiders. The Florentines attach great value to the home, whether it is a Medicean villa in the Marignolle hills, a bourgeois *appartamento* in Piazza Donatello, a farmhouse outside Fiesole, or a *popolare* Campo di Marte block. Family life is valued: children often live at home until marriage, at which point wealthy parents fund or build the young couple's home.

Doting parents of all classes try to provide their offspring with the latest consumer durables, from a Gianna Nannini album to American loafers or ski equipment. In return, the children dutifully participate in the family business. Even the Conte Rucellai expected his son to work in the family restaurant during the school holidays.

Not that education is ignored, however. Literate Florentines have a high degree of *cultura* in the broad Italian sense and students expect to study hard at various *licei* schools. After *liceo*, Florence University is a magnet for budding architects, economists or lawyers. Lack of grants and accommodation mean that the university is mainly attended by "local" students, who may, however, commute from Pisa or Arezzo.

But university is only one option among a spread of specialist schools. The city offers

academic and practical training in tourism, accountancy, graphics and computing; not to mention the arts and crafts institutes. The traditions of learning and of *cultura* go back a long way in Florence: the *Marucelliana*, one of Florence's great libraries, grew out of a Renaissance noble's collection and still maintains a sense of exclusivity.

Attempting to tap into the tradition, many overseas universities, including both Harvard and Princeton, have established centres

Left, game butcher. Above, University student.

in the city, and it is still a mecca for art and design students. The European University, housed in a former monastery on the slopes of Fiesole, attracts research scholars from around the world.

Second homes: Over the centuries, Florentines have used their mercantile spirit to buy the "good life": education and work are a means to this end. Quality of life is always placed above simple acquisition. In the past, the good life might have meant a villa in the Chianti, away from the summer swamps and malaria. Now it is a *villetta* or an *appartamento* on the coast, for the *borghesia* at Forte dei Marmi, for the *impiegati* and *operai* at one of the less exalted resorts which crowd the Tuscan coast.

The summer beach season is when Florentines reveal their identical love of leisure. From early June, the children begin disappearing from Florence. First the tiniest, accompanied by grandparents or non-working mothers, followed shortly afterwards by all those who do not have the dreaded *esami* to face. By the end of June only the university students are still around, leafing through text books by the open-air swimming pools. As exams finish even these gradually disappear and by mid-July so does the bulk of the working population.

Some shops simply close down for July and August: but not all the shopkeepers are on holiday. Many are both relaxing and raking in money in their second shop, open only during the summer months, at Forte dei Marmi. There, the non-working wives can be seen, scattered amongst the grandmothers, any day from early June to the end of August, decorating the jeweller's and fashion shops with their bronzed and languid presence as they desultorily acquire the compulsory tan.

Common heritage: Both summer leisure and shared culture slice through the social system. Irrespective of class, Florentines flock to the latest sculpture or photographic exhibitions. Although Florence is no longer a world cultural capital, its sophisticated, if provincial, culture has occasional flashes of genius. Above all the city has a strong and enduring sense of its own identity, rooted in its past yet transcending nostalgia.

PUCCI, GUCCI AND FERRAGAMO

Anyone without co-ordinated socks, gold jewellery, a handmade leather belt or a permanent light tan, the ultimate fashion accessory, is not a Florentine. If the visitor wishes to stand out in a crowd it is enough to be in ordinary leisure wear. Anyone in shorts will attract looks of curiosity and concern.

Florentines believe that outward appearances are never deceptive: to be badly dressed is to make a major statement about oneself verging on eccentricity. *Fare bella figura* (looking good) is an instinctive pleasure and a civic duty. To Florentines, fashion has both showy superficiality and intellectual status. Emilio Pucci even avows that, "the aim of fashion is to produce happiness". Florentine quality of life is all the richer for the classic suits in chic Via Tornabuoni, the swirling capes in Bohemian Santo Spirito and the preppy look on *giovanotti* (teenagers) in Piazza Beccaria.

The Florentine fashion industry pre-dates the Renaissance: the merchants of Prato have long woven fine cloth for Florentine tailors to transform into lavish clothes. In the Pitti Palace, the Medici housed one of the richest wardrobes in Europe, sadly auctioned off by the later Grand Dukes.

The products of the modern Italian fashion industry were first revealed to the world in Florence's Pitti Palace in 1945. "Pitti Moda", a series of annual fashion shows is still Florence's grandest showcase. While Milan has taken over as Italy's fashion capital, Giovanna Ferragamo comments that, "Milan is the commercial centre but Florence is still the creative centre". Florentine designers are too good to be modest.

Inspiration: Florentine designers believe themselves the natural heirs to Renaissance painters and master craftsmen. All share a belief in the inspirational nature of Florence. Salvatore Ferragamo, the founder of the great shoemaking firm, was drawn to Florence for its tradition of craftsmanship.

Left, shop in Piazza Santa Croce.

His family, now ensconced in one of Florence's finest Palazzi are more Florentine than the Florentines. Gucci, originally a humble saddlemaker, maintains its creative headquarters in the city. Marchese Pucci runs his international business from his ancestral Palazzo Pucci, a stone's throw from the Duomo. As a believer in Florentine mystique, he regularly visits *David* to capture Michelangelo's fluidity of line.

Pucci, Gucci and Ferragamo represent three different shades of the fashion spectrum. Emilio Pucci represents the aristocratic line while, despite international renown, Gucci is still a firm of humble

to achieve a natural effect.

Pucci is most proud of his invention of silk jersey, "a fabric which never clings, is never vulgar", and of his "signed" underwear, first made in 1957 from scraps of leftover silks. On a recent Concorde flight, an American hostess delighted Pucci by revealing her Pucci panties and gushing: "Thank you for making me feel like a woman again".

A born romantic, Pucci exalts the feminine mystique yet is surprisingly attuned to functional clothes. Florentine *vigili* (local police) wear his neo-colonial uniforms and blue peaked caps. Traditional Florentine craftsmanship is never forgotten: his *bottega*

craftsmen in Florentine eyes. Ferragamo, once a rank outsider, is now a clear winner.

Body moods: From the magnificence of Palazzo Pucci, Emilio Pucci relishes his self-appointed ambassadorial role to Florentine culture. He regularly plays host to visiting dignitaries, including members of the British Royal family and Heads of State. He is the inspiration behind an eclectic empire embracing fashion, textiles, perfume, *objêts d'art* and car design. His talents lie in innovation and craftsmanship. Pucci designs for "a body in motion, a body in all its moods" and is prepared for fifteen to twenty fittings

or workshop is never synonymous with "boutique". Yet Pucci refers to his fashion as "a modest endeavour in the rag trade", an English term he uses to undercut other Italian fashion designers' pomposity.

Rivals: Compared with Pucci, the Gucci clan have never quite shaken off their *parvenu* image. Despite the firm's international renown, the third generation remains a secretive, and often warring, family. The continuing soap opera of cousin against cousin and entanglement with U.S. and Italian tax offices offends against Florentine good taste.

The original firm, Guccio Gucci, maintains its exclusive leather range, made from hides cured with honey according to Florentine tradition. The firm's advertising slogan appeals to international elitism, "Certain people in certain places always like the same thing." Certainly Gucci products are much liked in the backstreets of Hong Kong and Taiwan: a flood of Gucci fakes from the Far East has caused the firm to cease production of those lines that are too easily copied.

Hollywood cobbler: Although founded by a Neapolitan shoemaker, Ferragamo looks and feels Florentine. The 15-year-old Salvatore Ferragamo left his impoverished family to make his fortune in Hollywood. As shoe-

lean war years, he experimented with such materials as rope, raffia and cellophane. At the height of his fame, he once had four Crowned Heads in his salon waiting for handmade shoes. Staunchly apolitical, Ferragamo made shoes for the mistresses of both Hitler and Mussolini. When Claretta Petacci was killed with her lover, Mussolini, she left behind 40 newly-made pairs of shoes at the Palazzo Feroni.

Dreams: While footwear continues to be the cornerstone of the business, Ferragamo is being transformed into a complete fashion house producing leatherware, fashion accessories and men's and women's *prêt-à-poter*

maker to Greta Garbo and Vivien Leigh, he learnt to "read" feet to discover his clients' personality and health. In Florence, he manufactured shoes with consummate craftsmanship and a magnificent reverence for feet. "I love feet—they speak to me," he used to say. His innovative principle that shoes should be light yet support the arch of the foot is still a Ferragamo hallmark.

In 1937 he bought the company's present base in the Palazzo Spini-Feroni. During the

Left, chic in leather. Above, Renaissance-inspired textiles.

collections. Each of Salvatore's six offspring is in charge of a different production line. The Ferragamo hallmark is a simplicity of line offset by decorative details, and bold accessories such as silk scarves printed with oriental or animal motifs. Giovanna Ferragamo, in charge of women's wear, says the firm aims for "the updated classic, a varied and independent look for women over 30".

The top designers serve as an important, if elitist, showcase for Florence's fashion factory. In 1988, the Florentine fashion industry represented 10 percent of the city's income. International buyers flock to Pitti Moda's 12 annual fashion shows held in the elegant Sala Bianca, once home to the Medici grand dukes and princes. The Florentine shoe industry has outpaced other Italian shoe manufacturers in carving out a lucrative overseas market, while at home it is second only to the Veneto and Marche regions.

The home market is just as important as the overseas. The average Florentine spent 820,000 lire a year on clothes. Italy's leading newspaper, *La Repubblica*, suggests that some spend up to a million lire per season. The main retail area lies within a square bounded by the Duomo, Santa Maria Novella, the Ponte Vecchio and Piazza

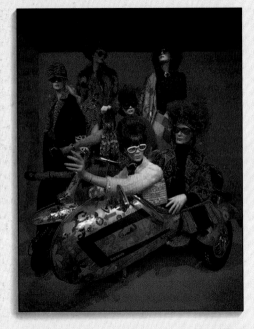

Goldoni. While Via Tornabuoni and Via della Vigna Nuova are the most prestigious places to be seen shopping, Florentines are prepared to don dark glasses and shop in the suburbs or the markets at a fraction of the cost. For clothes, the main production area is in Osmanorro, an industrial suburb favoured by Ferragamo and Coveri.

Small workshops linger on in the Oltrarno while Prato, just northwest of Florence, remains the centre for textile weaving, recycling and dyeing. The traditional rivalry between Florence and Prato has been calmed by the foundation of Polimoda, a fashion training institute designed to promote Florentine fashion and Pratese fabrics.

Exclusivity: Florentine fashion cannot compete with cheap Far Eastern production or even with the efficiency of the Milanese. Instead it relies on traditional quality and craftsmanship. Short production runs mean that exclusivity and variety can go down the catwalk together. Designers only work with the finest materials—jersey, tweeds, honey-cured leather and hand-dyed silks. Firms like Alessandro Pucci's Antico Setificio still practise traditional production methods, specialising in silk furnishings, taffeta and satins woven on ancient looms.

Although Florence lacks London's creative anarchy and Paris' studied elegance, the city's style is striking. Florence itself is a demanding market characterised by its desire to *distinguersi*, to be singled out for one's subtlety not flamboyance. Its quirky style is inspired by Renaissance excess overlaid with classic English sobriety, splashes of Oriental exoticism and Milanese minimalism. Amazingly, it only looks of itself.

Experiments: Florentine diversity is apparent in the smaller fashion houses and boutiques. At the bizarre end of the spectrum, the young designer, Samuele Mazza recently presented his "sado-masochistic" collection in a deconsecrated church in Florence. Such sacrilege enraged high society but was good for sales of his unremarkable minimalist designs. At the artistic end of the spectrum, Lietta Cavalli produces timeless designs which are not quite clothes but are more like embroidered butterfly wings or metallic-looking sculptures.

Florentines are rarely the victims of fashion and their artistry does not depend on social status, wealth, taste or even the beauty of the wearer. The chic executive and the young preppy look-alike are equally at ease with their image and with their setting. Fine clothes and artistry against a Florentine backcloth make a perfect genetic mix and match. Even for the extras, living in a Renaissance film-set is real life.

Above, fashion bizarre. Right, haute couture in Via Tournabuoni.

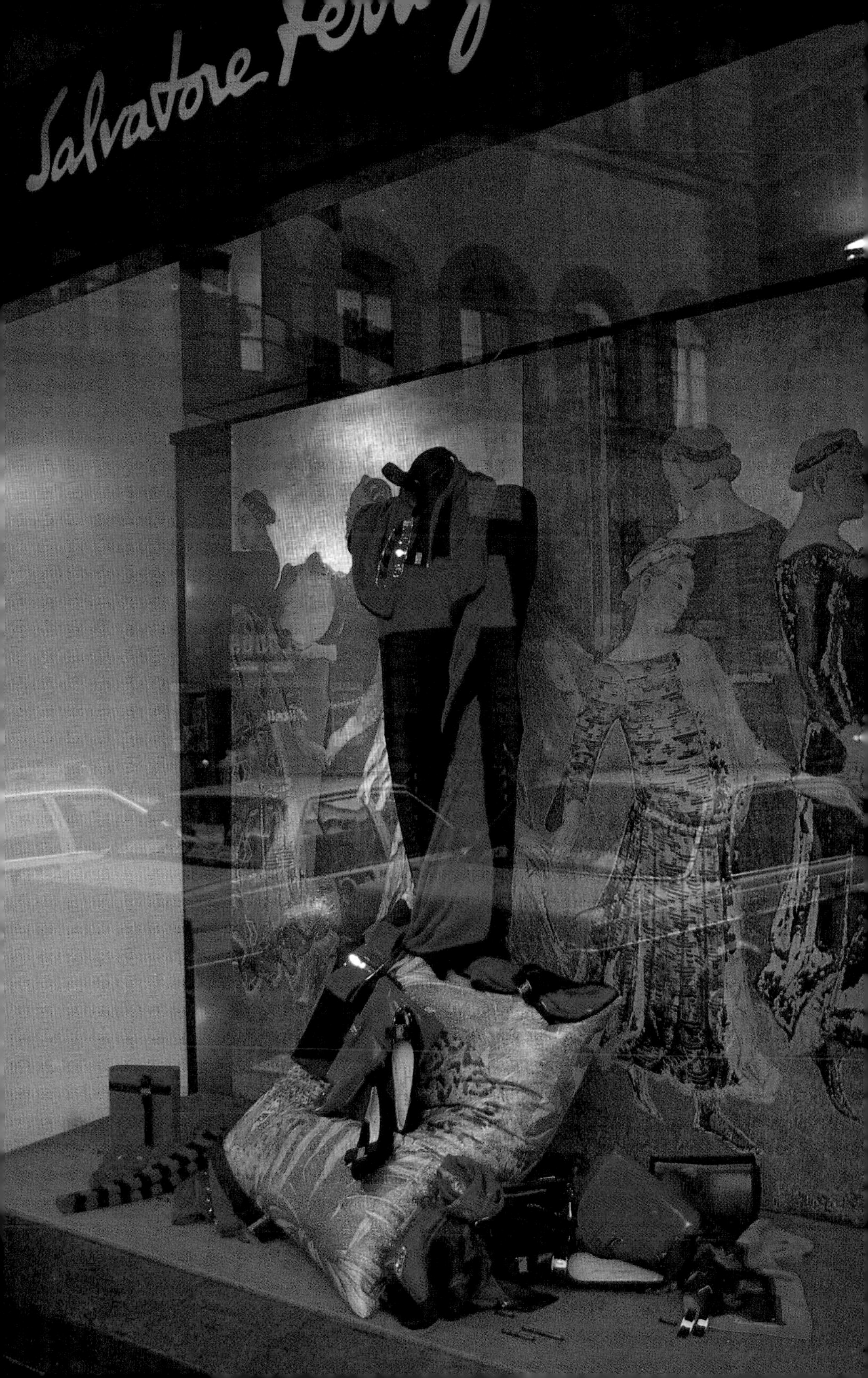
Salvatore

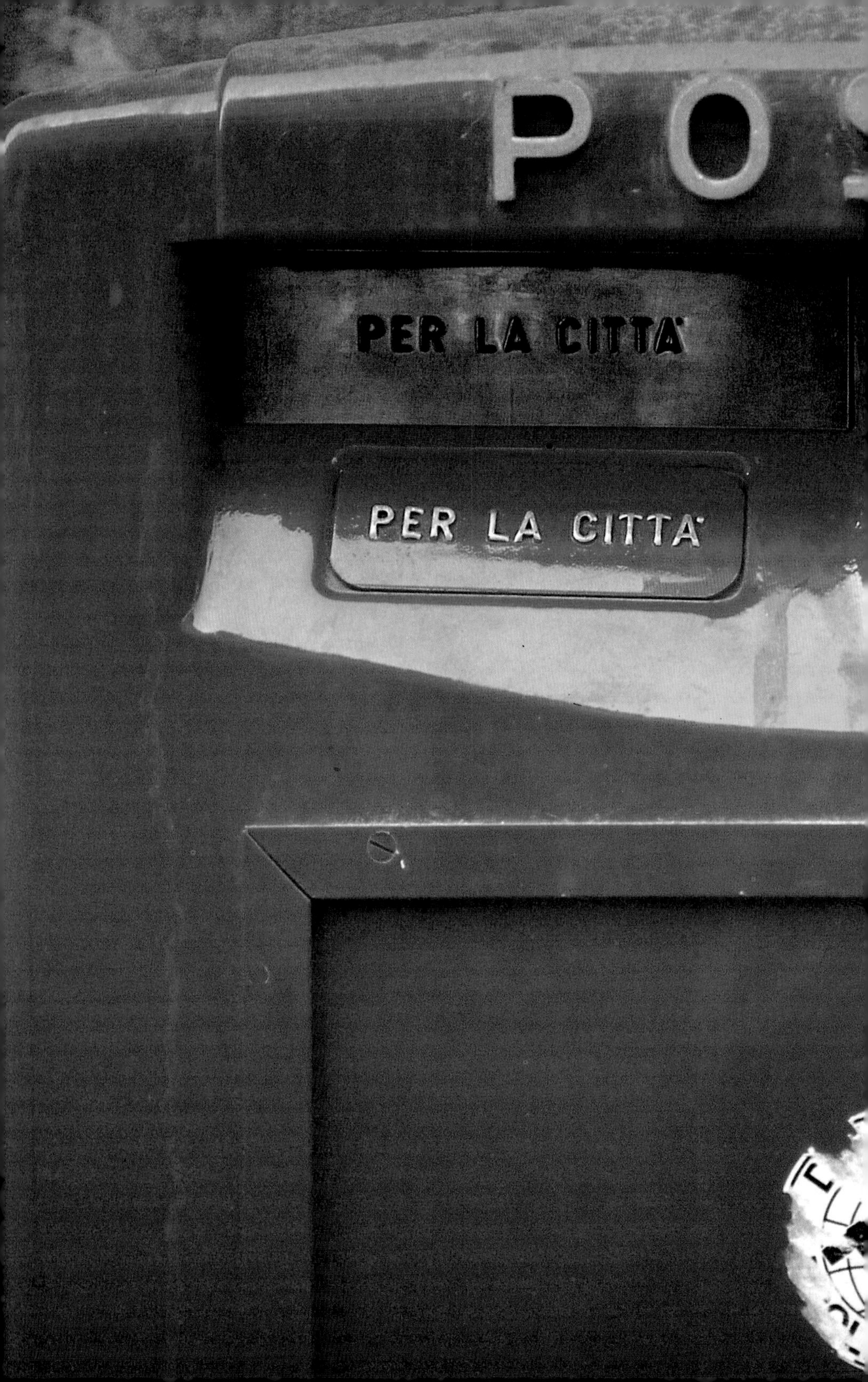
PO
PER LA CITTÀ
PER LA CITTÀ

STE

PER TUTTE LE ALTRE
DESTINAZIONI

PER TUTTE LE ALTRE
DESTINAZIONI

CONTEMPORARY ART

On a recent trip to Florence, David Hockney remarked that he preferred to paint in Los Angeles, "because there are no ghosts there—it would be difficult not to feel burdened by the weight of history in a place like Florence". But it is this weight which makes modern Florentine art distinctive.

The Modern Art Collection in the Pitti Palace is the right place to begin the modern art trail. The luminous paintings by the *Macchiaioli* group of Florentine Impressionists—artists such as Signorini, Fattori and Lega depict naturalistic Tuscan landscapes. The next chronological jump is to the painter Primo Conti whose collection of early 20th-century paintings, left to the city on his death in 1988, is on display in Fiesole.

Florentine painters had a bad year in 1988. Pietro Annigoni, a Florentine by adoption, was mourned in a moving ceremony in Santissima Annunziata church. Annigoni achieved fame with his timeless portraits of Queen Elizabeth, the Kennedys and other world figures yet his work was always snubbed by intellectual Florentines.

Annigoni felt his work was closer to that of Breughel and Dürer than to Masaccio or Michelangelo. Although his studios in Santo Croce and Borgo degli Albizzi were often filled with modern celebrities, his mind was in the 16th century. As he said, "I am a man who lives, survives even, through a nostalgia which links me to the past".

Romantic painters: The Raccolta d'Arte Contemporanea in Piazza della Signoria is a quiet, coherent collection of Tuscan art between the wars. Ottone Rosai is particularly well-represented in his later work, which is too romantic to be called Futurist. His *Via di San Leonardo* depicts his home street, a shadowy, winding road, tinged purple in the evening light. The dark figures in such paintings as *Omino di Strada* represent veiled fears of Fascism.

Preceding pages: Florentine Communism is pink rather than red. Left, iconoclastic art students. Above, *Stones* by Alberto Magnelli.

The painter Bruno Rosai followed his uncle's rich path until his own death a few years ago. Enzo Fargoni, Ottone Rosai's favourite pupil, now paints equally mysterious scenes from his studio in Piazza Donatello.

The Florentine Abstract tradition owes much to the avant-garde work of Alberto Magnelli, a cosmopolitan Florentine whose centenary was recently celebrated with a retrospective in the Palazzo Vecchio. Al-

though Magnelli is considered one of the founders of European Abstractionism, his highly individualistic work transcends labels.

Magnelli, who claimed his only belief was in "the reality of beauty", is justly celebrated for his fusion of form and colour. His *Lyric Explosion*, exalting colour to the level of content, achieves a formal purity that has no parallel.

Florentine contemporary painters are not easily classifiable, as can be seen in the new Modern Art Museum in Prato, just outside Florence. Sandra Brunetti is a mysterious portraitist who shuns publicity. Her anachronistic paintings portray Florence as a bemused city unable to come to terms with its mundane present. Her *Lorenzo consiglia* shows Lorenzo de' Medici advising an American tourist in Piazza della Signoria. The young painter, Claudio Sacchi, echoes Brunetti's concerns in his *Calcio in costume* painting, an intermingling of medieval and modern footballers.

Florentine sculpture has moved on since Michelangelo but remains powerful, classical and often naturalistic. The new San Pancrazio Museum, housed in a deconsecrated church, just off Via dei Spada, is a

homage to Marino Marini, one of Italy's greatest modern sculptors. Marini's bronze nudes are introspective, pure and rooted to the spot. By contrast, his euphoric horses and riders strive for release.

The octogenarian Quinto Martini is still producing classically-inspired sculptures, many of which shelter amongst trees in the Parco Museo di Seano outside Florence.

Architecture: In 1826, William Hazlitt called Florence, "a town which has survived itself" but this is only partly true architecturally. Since then, much has been destroyed and much rebuilt: the old city walls were torn

down to create wide *Viali* and medieval streets were widened. Poggi, the city's town planner at the time of Unification, redesigned the city in the "new" Parisian or Viennese mould.

At best, Poggi's school was inspired by Renaissance models to create such dignified buildings as the present American Consulate (Lungarno Amerigo Vespucci 38). At worst, Piazza della Repubblica stands as an ugly reminder of academic classicism at its most provincial.

More positively, restoration was born in 1870, motivated by posthumous guilt at such wanton destruction and fuelled by the anger of the foreign press at the disappearance of the *mercato vecchio*.

From this point on, standards of Florentine architecture could only rise. In 1911, Michelazzi, Florence's finest exponent of Art Nouveau, designed the tall, graceful building in Borgo Ognisanti. Its narrow façade, decorative arches and vertical lines are worthy of Victor Horta. The finest remaining example of the 1920s is the Odeon Cinema (Via Sasetti 27) with its refined cupola of coloured glass.

During Fascism, Florence proved that, despite its long architectural tradition, it could build offices and flats as shoddily as anyone. The Campo di Marte stadium and Santa Maria Novella station are remarkable exceptions, however. Nervi's stadium is a daring early application of reinforced concrete: the sense of weightlessness is sustained by a curvilinear staircase. Amidst controversy, the interior has been rebuilt by Gamberini for the 1990 World Cup.

Florence railway station is often called the first Functionalist building in Italy and is the most coherent example of modern architecture in the city. It was built by Giovanni Michelucci's Gruppo Toscana according to Gamberini's original design. As Florence's greatest modern architect, Michelucci continued to influence modern architecture well into his nineties, giving his blessing at the age of 98 to the plans for an extension to the station. Toraldo de' Francia will add a Tourist Terminal, complete with reading rooms, shops, restaurants and a small inner courtyard. The use of such precious materials as red marble, crystal and copper indicate the importance of tourism.

Reconstruction: Contemporary Florentine architecture embraces restoration, transformation, Post-Modernist experimentation and "memory architecture", new building inspired by a glorious Tuscan past. Faithful restoration can be seen all over Florence. The Ponte Santa Trinità, mined in 1944, was lovingly reconstructed. Its stone was fished out of the Arno and the ancient quarry in the Boboli Gardens was re-opened to complete the task.

Sensitive transformation has changed the function of some Florentine palaces while

But Florentine architects are also capable innovators under the Modernist umbrella. The Palazzo degli Affari, opposite the railway station, is a suitably business-like congress centre. It was built by Pier-Luigi Spadolini, an influential figure in Florentine architecture (not just because his brother is President of the Italian Senate), and recently awarded the first Italian professorship in Industrial Design. Many of his buildings have been criticised as staid, but his current project, a *Carabinieri* college, is a successful blend of military training complex and ancient villa set against the lovely Marignolli hills.

preserving their integrity. Gamberini's Monte dei Paschi Bank headquarters (Via dei Pecori 626) is a successful combination of old and new: a grand modern interior complements a 15th-century fountain and inner courtyard. Ferragamo, based in the 13th-century Palazzo Feroni (Via Tornabuoni), has conserved the magnificent della Robbia fresco in the entrance; the modern partitions within the store do not detract from the original cross-vaulted ceiling.

Left, Marino Marini's *Pomona*. Above, exuberant nude at the Pitti Palace.

Nostalgia: "Memory architecture" has attracted many humanistic Florentine architects who re-interpret the past through such vernacular elements as Tuscan-arched windows. In Via Guicciardini, the Casa Torre is a modern interpretation of a medieval watchtower all the more remarkable for being the work of Michelucci, architect of the functionalist railway station.

Many projects never leave the drawing board, however, since opportunity for new architecture is scarce. City bureaucracy blocks many projects and the *Comune* is accused of political bias in the allotment of public contracts. The architectural establishment is dominated by such major firms as Superstudio who win the plum contracts.

The open competition system of *concorsi* discriminates against those without political connections. The *Comune* is often illogical: while in theory ardently conservationist, it often breaks its own urban blueprint. Shoddy public building and urban sprawl in Florentine suburbs often result.

Florence's estimated 3,000 architects are currently interpreting Post-Modernism as a supermarket of pragmatic ideas. Elio di Franco, a young independent architect, uses smooth curves reminiscent of Art Deco to

Florentines have proved to be photographers not film-makers. The Florentine photographic tradition is the richest in Italy. In 1852, the Alinari brothers founded a photographic studio which continues to have an impact today. The brothers used new photographic techniques to capture a dramatic time in Florentine history.

The city, unchanged for centuries, had fallen into economic decline and architectural stagnation. The transformation of Florence into the capital of Italy provoked a flurry of demolition and rebuilding. Giacomo Brogi, the Alinari's finest photographer recorded the disappearance of Florence's

create an individual style. His majestic Papal throne at Prato was created for the Pope's recent visit.

The future of Florentine architecture is exciting if controversial. The new city, *Firenze Nuova*, is being created to the north of Florence. It will require an industrial zone, a huge Fiat factory, new law courts, leisure complexes and parks. The 300-strong architecture faculty is eager to advise on the new project. No wonder architecture has been the most heavily-subscribed subject at Florence university.

Photography: Unlike the Romans, the

dilapidated beauty. He later captured the contrast between the unchanging countryside and the new cityscape. In 1988, the Alinari's leading photographer, George Tatge, retraced Brogi's steps and found the surrounding countryside surprisingly unchanged.

Florentine photography reflects different images: humanistic and ironic, portraiture and landscape. These strands are united in the work of the great Florentine photographer, Mario Nunes Vais. Until 1984, his successor, Gino Barsotti, continued to photograph local landscapes, people and works of art. Representative examples of the work of all these photographers can be seen in the noble Rucellai Palace, Via della Vigna Nuova, which now houses the History of Photography Museum; the modern temporary exhibitions are often at odds with the ancient frescoed ceilings.

Occasionally, too, exhibitions are held in various locations of the work of George Tatge, who sustains the Alinari's romantic tradition, and Pietro Nardi, whose humanistic lens captures Florentine amusement at tourists munching sandwiches under *David*'s watchful eye, or the plight of a local drug addict in Santa Croce.

minted the original florins, decorated with the head of San Giovanni, the city's patron saint. Today, Franco Torrini is still proud of his medieval sign-board bearing the symbol of the four-leafed clover, testimony to the wizardry of his craft. He now produces jewels for princes and popes; the Vatican has recently bought a silver altar while a musician has ordered a gold flute encrusted with jewels. The goldsmiths still work in the old city centre but prefer to do so in the privacy of the *botteghe* beside San Stefano church, only a precious stone's throw from their shops on the Ponte Vecchio.

Florentine artisans are natural entrepre-

The goldsmith's art: A great Florentine tradition is to make no distinction between the artist and the artisan: an artist has no false snobbery and an artisan has no false humility; both are natural entrepreneurs. Often the artist and the artisan are literally one and the same: Annigoni happily turned his hand to producing gold medallions in memory of the original Florentine coinage, the florin.

The Torrini, the oldest line of goldsmith's, have worked in Florence since 1369. They

Left, the Academy of Sculpture. Above, modern sculpture at the Congress Palace.

neurs: after wars and floods the jewellers on the Ponte Vecchio are always the first to open their doors for business. Florentines believe in a closed shop in one sense only: the craft is better passed from father to son to keep the magic within the family. Many of the tools and techniques remain unchanged since Medici times: the crucible is still used even though the hare's paw no longer sweeps up the gold dust.

Furniture: In the Oltrarno, the leather and cabinet-making firms continue, albeit on a small scale, to produce specialised, often unique commissions. The Santo Spirito

FESTIVALS

The New Year is celebrated with fireworks and shots fired into the air by enthusiastic amateur hunters. The visitor now runs a low risk of being knocked out by a flying vase: a law has curtailed the Florentine habit of hurling crockery onto the street in symbolic rejection of the old year.

Epiphany is heralded by the appearance of unpleasant charcoal-shaped sweets in shop windows. Naughty children are "rewarded" with these supposed "gifts" from the Befania, the wizened old woman who was too busy cleaning her house to give presents to the Christ child.

Florence's pre-Lenten *carnevale* once rivalled

ers' parades or processions to mark the Anniversary of the 1945 Liberation. Any similar gathering of massed groups singing or waving red flags is likely to be a transport workers strike.

The *Festa del Grillo*, (Cricket Festival) celebrates the Ascension and spring. Cascine Park is full of families buying roast pork, pastries and crickets in tiny cages. To bring good luck, the crickets must be released before nightfall.

The major festival is *Calcio in costume*, a rough football game played on 24 June in honour of Saint John the Baptist, patron saint of Florence. This cross between football and rugby, introduced by Roman soldiers, was perfected in Medici times. Each game begins with a procession of drummers, flag-bearers, soldiers and nobles on horseback, led by Marchese Emilio

the Venetian carnival, but secretive Florentines now indulge their hidden desires in private balls. Still, enough Medici princesses and chained bears dash over the Ponte Vecchio on the way to the ball to intrigue uninvited visitors.

The oldest religious festival is the Easter *Scoppio del Carro* or "Explosion of the Carriage" held in Piazza del Duomo to celebrate the Resurrection. White oxen pull the 18th-century gilded carriage to the cathedral doors where it awaits the end of High Mass. At the intoning of the *Gloria*, a mechanical dove fizzes along a wire from the High Altar and ignites the carriage full of hidden fireworks. As the church bells chime and fireworks explode with holy fire, adults see a mechanical dove and children see a miracle.

Civic displays are restricted to May Day work-

Pucci, aristocratic fashion designer, conservationist and personification of Florentine pride. They march, in mediaeval costume, from Santa Maria Novella to the Duomo, then to the Piazza della Signoria "field" or the Boboli Gardens.

Matches are played over three days by four teams, one from each of the old city *rioni* (districts). The teams wear distinctive mediaeval costumes: blue for Santa Croce; white for Santo Spirito; red for Santa Maria Novella and green for San Giovanni. Hitting and biting are allowed, and players occasionally lose an ear or break a leg.

The winning team is rewarded with a *palio*, a printed silk banner. An all-night party is held in the victorious *rione* and a magnificent firework display in Piazzale Michelangelo brings the Feast of St John to a close.

Leather School was opened in 1950 to bring traditional work back to a poor area. Housed in Franciscan cloisters, the school runs the sort of apprenticeships which appealed to Prince Charles on a recent visit to the school.

Although Luciano Fiorentini's successful cabinet-making business has moved out of the Oltrarno, traditional standards prevail: Tuscan walnut is carved and planed by hand. The resultant furniture can be seen in the Medici-Riccardi Palace or in the Palazzo Vecchio.

The craft tradition, deeply-ingrained in Florentine culture, is now institutionalised in the Istituto per l'Arte e il Ristauro. In three

historic *palazzi*, students select from courses in the restoration of ceramics and stone, fabrics and manuscripts, gold, wood and paintings.

Restoration of paintings is also taught at the Università Internazionale dell'Arte. The University was created in 1968 in response to the flood and aims to provide research into the preservation and restoration of works of art. Even the Corsini, aristocratic entrepreneurs, now offer courses in restoration, de-

Left, mediaeval costume to celebrate the Feast of St John. Above, traditional Tuscan band.

sign and interior decoration—naturally held in the family Palazzo. Florentines claim that everything in the Uffizi can be bought in miniature in Florence. If equally entrepreneurial Renaissance artists knew, they would not turn in their graves but leap from them to join in.

Theatre: The Florentines are enthusiastic, if conservative, theatre-goers. Members of trade unions and professional bodies as well as most civil servants and teachers hold discounted season tickets. To accommodate the local preference for lengthy summer holidays and extended dinners, the theatre season only runs from September to April and the curtain only rises after 9 p.m.

The theatre offers standard Italian classics from Goldoni to Pirandello together with the occasional traditional Florentine play such as *La Strega* (The Witch) by Il Lasca. These are supplemented by American, British and French classics. Florentines are noted for their wit and irony. Their appreciation of humour is borne out by the popularity of all comedy from Pirandello Absurdity through light reviews to Dario Fo's modern satires.

Anyone interested in more experimental theatre must currently travel to Prato where the Teatro Metastasio specialises in new productions. It may not be long, however, before Florence can compete—several newly opened theatres offer scope for avant-garde drama alongside the city's safe and conservative repetoire. Teatro della Compagnia, built by the renowned architect Natalini, has also been renovated. The Teatro Comunale, badly flooded in 1966, has been repaired, but may soon be replaced by a new theatre complex at Porta al Prato.

Music and opera: The official opera season runs from October to March but open air performances grace the *Estate Fiesolana* summer festival. Although Florentines are quite happy to listen to operas by Puccini, a fellow Tuscan, there is even greater enthusiasm for Tchaikovsky, helped by his status as a token Florentine.

Under the direction of Zubin Mehta and Riccardo Muti, the Tuscan Regional Orchestra has played to full houses and the *Maggio Musicale* attracts international stars. World fame has plucked Muti from Florence and left the city proud but disappointed at its protégé's departure. Recent artistic direction has passed to Bruno Bartoletti, former artistic advisor to the Chicago Opera.

The winter concerts in San Stefano church near the Ponte Vecchio attract crowds drawn to the Baroque music or to the *aperitivi* that accompany the concerts. In summer, open-air concerts are held in numerous city *piazze*, or church cloisters or in the grounds of the Badia Fiesolana. The Luigi Cherubini Conservatoire is a bastion against modernity. Vinicio Gai, music professor, so loves ancient instruments that he even studied woodworm in order to kill the offending insects. During the flood, he rowed to work.

Dance: Florentine ballet is bounding forward with the expansion of the *Maggio danza*, the May dance spectacular. An ambitious repertoire covers classical, modern and experimental ballet from Tchaikovsky to Ballanchine to Mario Piazza, the promising local choreographer. International stars lured to Florence recently have included Rudolf Nureyev.

Literature: Once a year, the cream of Florentine literary society gathers in the Rucellai's *Il Latini* restaurant to present a huge ham to a lucky Florentine writer. Giovanni Spadolini, President of the Senate and occasional writer, recently received the prize from Florence's mystical poets, Mario Luzi and Piero Bigiongiari, and from the lawyer-turned-novelist Giorgio Saviane. Saviane, a Florentine by adoption, is proud to follow in the footsteps of Petrarch and Goldoni by embracing both law and literature. As he says, "Both lawyers and writers are defenders of mankind". His new book, *Casa degli uccelli*, gives his latest defence.

Mario Luzi is the Grand Old Man of Florentine poetry, linked to the arcane "hermetic" school of Italian poetry. In 1986, he addressed a world poets' congress during the city's year as cultural capital of Europe. He told fellow poets that in such a dramatic city it was impossible not to believe in the power of poetry. In mystical vein, Luzi recently reminisced about wartime Florence. In October 1944, he found himself caught in crossfire on the Lungarno. A sudden burst of light illuminated the city, soldiers and falling masonry. Luzi, overcome with a sense of the "fragility of the city's ancient history", composed a poem on the spot, reflecting on the city's past.

Piero Bigiongiari also captures the intensity of Florence in his poetry. In his book *Frammenti del poema*, he uses travels through time, space and Florentine streets to express the fragmentary nature of life. Nostalgia is a Florentine literary drug, even experienced by mere journalists such as Vittorio and Maria Brunelli. The couple live in Via di San Leonardo, the idyllic link between town and country. After a long absence, the Brunelli sighed "once cranes used to fly overhead but now there are only planes".

The two most typically Florentine writers are Aldo Palazzeschi and Vasco Pratolini, both recorders of a disappearing Florence: the Oltrarno population of artisans, weavers and tripe-sellers. In *Le sorelle materassi*, Palazzeschi, the son of a Florentine shopkeeper, tells a story of two elderly sisters whose lives are spent embroidering wedding trousseaux for the wealthy while reminiscing about their youth. In 1974, Palazzeschi was buried in his beloved Settignano olive groves on the edge of Florence.

Pratolini, describing the Florence of 50 years ago, pays tribute to the "people of Sanfrediano, the toughest and liveliest of the Florentines... the only ones who retain the spirit of a people who have always been able to make something graceful out of clumsiness". In the Florentine sense of the word cultura, such humble people are "cultured".

In a city which abounds with such contagious artistic beauty, it is only natural to seek echoes in modern art, architecture and literature. Indeed, Florentines pity outsiders unused to *le cose dell'arte*, those unfortunates who were not brought up with the *David*, Dante's verses, the Roman theatre and Pratolini's novels. When narcissistic Florentines are not brooding over past glories and missed opportunities, they sometimes live up to their heritage.

Right, Maggio Danza, the May Arts Festival.

WINE AND FOOD

"I believe no more in black than in white, but I believe in boiled or roasted capon, and I also believe in butter and beer... but above all I have faith in good wine and deem that he who believes in it is saved."

—Luigi Pulci

Whether Pulci is now being gently grilled on some infernal spit or plays his harp perched on an angelic soufflé, in life the 15th-century Florentine poet had a characteristically healthy appetite. In the city that sired the "mother of French cooking", Catherine de Medici, the Renaissance heralded a new interest in food as an art.

The claim that Gallic cuisine dates from the marriage of Catherine de' Medici to Henry II in 1535, is based on the similarity between characteristic French and Tuscan dishes: *canard à l'orange* is not unlike the Florentine *papero alla melarancia; vol au vents* are found in Florence under the name *turbanate di sfoglia*.

Whatever the truth, the Medici were renowned for their multi-course banquets and the Florentine's renowned preoccupation with his stomach increasingly got him into trouble with the Church. "You are great gourmands," railed one preacher, "when you eat ravioli it is not enough for you to boil them in the pan and eat them with broth, but you must put them in another pan together with cheese."

Simple fare: And yet sobriety rather than sensuality was, and remains, an important element in the Florentine character and, despite their love of food, Florentines never really warmed to the complex recipes of the saucy Medici. Popular Renaissance dishes tended to be simple and robust, with plenty of vegetables and plainly grilled meats, eaten for utility as much as enjoyment. Busy people in a thriving commercial environment, they had little time for over-sophistication.

This solid element persists to this day.

Left, simple food presented with flair.

A Night Out

A typical Florentine evening begins with a *passeggiata*, perhaps a riverside walk along the Lungarni, a leisurely stroll around Piazzale Michelangelo, or a more ambitious climb around Fiesole. In the summer, quiet crowds gather in cool Fiesole bars and sip *aperitivi* whilst admiring the views over the city below. In winter, the elegant central bars are preferred. Unless Piazza della Signoria is under excavation, Rivoire is the best bar for people-watching.

The meal, the centrepiece of any Florentine evening, is often informal but always civilised. Busy Florentines appreciate the friendly atmosphere of a hectic *trattoria* run by the owner's underaged family. Florentines are equally at home in a rustic *osteria* with a doleful wild boar's head surveying the scene. The young opt for a *pizzeria* with a wood-fired oven, good beer and slightly singed pizza.

Those with three hours to spare choose a classical *ristorante* with white linen table cloths and a serious wine list. A quiet meal at the aristocratic Cantinetta Antinori precedes a night at the opera or theatre. The trendy congregate in the Oltrarno, especially in the Santo Spirito area.

Arty intellectuals favour expensive restaurants in poor areas such as Cibreo which offers excellent Tuscan and *nouvelle cuisine* in a politically correct *popolare* environment.

No matter how light, the meal is taken seriously. The relative "weight" of wines and even mineral waters is discussed at length. If Chianti is drunk, it must bear the *gallo nero* (black cock) or *putto* (cherub) seal of excellence. Galestro, a simple white wine, is popular on summer evenings while smooth red Brunello warms a Florentine winter. Local aristocrats have cornered the wine market: according to taxi-driver lore, the Frescobaldi are losing out to the Antinori.

As for the food, Florentine taste consistently favours the simple but robust. Tuscan *antipasti*, such as *crostini* (a paste of liver, anchovies and capers served on bread) or cold meats are typically followed by a *primi* of pasta, asparagus

risotto or *ribollita* soup. *Secundi* could be game or a mammoth *bistecca alla fiorentina*, accompanied by Tuscan beans, *fagcoli all ucelletto*.

For those with any space left, Florentine *dolci* take the form of *zuccotto*, a soft ice-cream dessert, *schiacciata*, a dryish cake, or *mascarpone*, a sweet, creamy cheese. Almond *biscotto di Prato* are often dunked in sweet Vinsanto wine.

Few restaurants have good espresso machines so coffee is usually drunk elsewhere, perhaps with a *digestivo*. The borghesi are faithful to the piano bars in the grand hotels or the established bars such as the ceremonious Giacosa in chic Via Tornabuoni, or Paszkowski's where the orchestra enlivens stuffy Piazza della Repubblica.

An after-dinner stroll provides an excuse to watch the talented street performers in Via Calzaiuoli and to indulge in window shopping. A small crowd around a cardboard box suggests the arrival of another delivery of fake Lacoste T-shirts or Vuitton bags. In summer the cognoscenti flock to the Vivoli in Via Isola delle Stinche for the best ice-cream, before going into Florence's cinema d'essai (avant-garde cinema) opposite.

Tourists pay over the odds for ice-cream concoctions in Piazza della Repubblica gelaterie while the youth crowd roar past on noisy motorini. Piazza Beccaria will be their first stop on a circular *giro* (tour) of flashy ice-cream parlours, video bars and discothèques.

If culture not food is the centrepiece of the evening, a quick pizza is followed by a baroque church concert or by a play at the newly-restored Teatro della Compagnia. A stylish alternative is the jazz club Riflessi d'Epoca. In May, meals are sacrificed to the yearly Maggio Musicale, the popular music and opera festival.

On summer evenings, everyone wants to escape to the cool hills around Bellosguardo or Fiesole. Queues of all ages form to see ballets and concerts in the floodlit Roman theatre at Fiesole. *A Midsummer Night's Dream* is a Florentine favourite. Open-air films are shown in the Forte di Belvedere and are an excuse to bring rugs, picnics and one's favourite companion. After an evening under the stars, the crowds wander down to a riverside bar for a final *digestivo*.

Florentines have been nick-named the *Mangiafagioli*, the great bean-eaters, and they specialise in thick soups, large steaks and heavy wines. Though there are culinary extravagances to be discovered, Florentine food is healthy, down to earth and draws on the raw wealth of the Tuscan countryside.

Morning markets: The most colourful introduction to the city's food is morning amid the vegetable stalls of the Mercato Centrale. Here the fruit of the hills, courgettes, tomatoes, mushrooms, peppers, potatoes and aubergines (the speciality *melanzane*) form a bright tapestry of potential tastes. Florentines will happily eat any of these on their own,

are rarely disappointing on their own but together they make two of the city's great specialities, *ribollita* and *minestrone*. Ribollita means reboiled and the naturally thrifty Florentine will put any spare vegetable in the pan to make this filling potage, served on bread. But Tuscan vegetables seem most at home in minestrone soup. Florentines are compulsive soup eaters and, though they share a little of Italy's faith in pasta as the all-purpose dish, they really prefer their own rich and nutritious vegetable stews.

Florence may seem a vegetarian's idea of Eden but the Florentine is undeniably a red-blooded carnivore. For a start and a starter try

fried or served raw in Tuscany's purest *extra vergine* olive oil; emerald green and on the table of any good Florentine restaurant.

But among these gaudy fruits, the undisputed aristocrat is the humble white bean or *fagioli*. Like the potato, the bean was introduced from the Americas by Florentine merchants and it is now a staple of the city. In a soup or mixed with tuna fish, the little fagioli is a marvellously simple beginning to any Florentine meal.

Satisfying stews: Fresh Tuscan vegetables

Left, dusk over the Arno. Above, traditional pasta.

crostini di fegato, chicken liver paté on fried bread and delicious with a young white wine. A feast to follow is *frito misto*, mixed meats fried in batter, or the peasant dish *stracotto*, beef stewed for several hours and especially satisfying in winter.

Feast of meat: But, above all, Florentines specialise in plain roasted meats, *arista*, which can either be of pork or beef, lamb at Easter and even wild boar in season. Tuscany's fertile pasture feeds some of the richest flavours in Italy and Florentines refuse to clutter these tastes with over-adornment. Just as simple is their treatment of chicken, pheasant and another speciality, rabbit.

However, the master of meats and as much a symbol of the city as the florin, is the famous *bistecca alla fiorentina*. A huge and succulent rib-steak from Tuscany's alabaster Chianina cattle, the *bistecca* is charcoal grilled, salted and served with the Florentine's characteristic lack of fuss. It is quite the most delicious meat in Italy and if you can get a seat, the best in the city is said to be served on the marble table-tops of the Ristorante Sostanza (Via Porcellana). But beware, the price on the menu is per 100 grammes of raw meat and you are thought mean if you order less than a kilo.

fruit and water ice, compete for attention with endless pastries and hand-made sweets; huge slabs of nougat, chocolate "Florentines" and *bacci*—the angel's kiss.

But no visit to the city would be complete without a taste of its ice-cream. You can see why Florentines claim to have invented *gelato*, for the city is awash with a rainbow of flavours. Always look for the sign *Produzione propra* (home made) and before you try anywhere else, make for Vivoli on the Via Isola delle Stinche. It remains unrivalled for flavour and variety and here you'll find yet another soup, *zuppa inglese* or trifle ice-cream. Virtually a meal in itself, *gelato* is

At the cheaper end of the culinary spectrum and in their rational desire not to waste, Florentines have even made a speciality out of tripe. *Tripa alla florentina*, cooked with tomatoes and parmesan, is a favourite and inexpensive dish, though its rubbery texture and acrid flavour make it an equivocal choice for the uninitiated.

Sweeteners: If Florentine food tends to be filling, full of flavour but unsophisticated, Florentine *dolce* (sweet) makes up for any lack of imagination. In the city's bars, cake shops and *gelateria* there is a constant carnival of colour. *Copie varie*, bowls of mixed

Florence's most delicious fine art.

Wine: In the region where soil and sunlight nurture Italy's most famous wine, Chianti, Pulci was not alone in extolling the virtues of the blushful Hippocrene. "I believe," wrote Leonardo da Vinci, "that where there is good wine, there is great happiness for men." Happiness may be harder to find, even in Tuscany, good wine certainly isn't.

This is the kingdom of Sangiovese, the little grape that gives heart and strength to Tuscan classified reds, while innumerable other vines serve as royal subjects and even vie for the crown. This is the first lesson to be learnt about Tuscan wine—the subject is enormous. Quite apart from the diversity of growths and strains, Tuscany shares Italy's vast proliferation of vineyards and labels.

Quality: This viticultural promiscuity makes standards hard to control and quality does vary greatly. Stricter quality controls are now enforced, especially after the 1986 methanol scandal. DOC proscribes methods of production, while DOCG guarantees the authenticity of certain favoured wines. These markings will help to identify Tuscany's best, but never take the region's ability to surprise for granted. Tuscany has many remarkable Vino di Tavola and one in par-

to Florence's popular wine-bar, the Enotecca Murgia, will discover.

The heartland of Chianti lies either side of the road connecting the two cities, the Via Sacra of wine. This is the home of Chianti Classico where the Chianti league was first formed in the 13th century. Usually identified by the proud black rooster (Gallo Nero), Chianti Classico produces more consistently good wine than any other zone, except Rufina.

Heavyweights: This, the most important region near the city, and one to be reckoned with throughout Tuscany, lies east of Florence in the hills above the Sieve river. It

ticular, Sassicaia, has become a contemporary legend.

Many wines: Chianti is grown in seven regions surrounding Florence and Sienna. Perhaps Italy's most potent symbol, Chianti is not in fact one wine but many. In its seven zones, the variety of climates, producers and vineyards is staggering, ensuring a huge breadth of quality and complexity as a writer

Left, Bistecca Fiorentina. Above, vineyards of Chianti. Following pages: traditional straw-wrapped Chianti; products of the Tuscan countryside.

is a tiny zone that yet manages to produce some of the giants of Italian wine: Selvapiana, Castello di Nipozzano, Fatoria di Vetrie and the new heavyweight Montesodi.

The region surrounding Florence itself, the Chianti Coli Fiorentina, is the source of many of those characteristic straw-covered bottles that fill the city. Its wines tend to be heavy and coarse but they can also be splendid with Florence's simple food.

After you have enjoyed the pleasantly enervating effects of a heavy Chianti and a large Florentine steak, a delightful way to end the meal and ease the stomach has also become a Florentine ritual: *biscotti di Prato*, almond biscuits dipped in the dark gold Vinsanto. Made from grapes picked late into the harvest, at "the time of the saints", Vinsanto seems to liquefy the Tuscan sunlight and unleash the complex tastes of the land.

Eating out: Whether for business or for pleasure, and invariably for both, dining is an important event for the Florentine. The main meal is lunch, a languid affair which explains the comparative hiatus in the city between one and three o'clock. In the evening Florentines eat around eight and, lacking the Spaniard's nocturnal enthusiasm, the best restaurants close early. The visitor

should also be warned that because so many Florentines take their holidays in high summer, to avoid the city's heat and its glut of tourists, many good restaurants are also closed throughout the month of August.

The very best: However, finding somewhere to eat is rarely a problem in the city and choice is enormous. For haute cuisine, Florence has several extremely fine restaurants. The elegant and world-famous Enotecca Pinchiori invites an extravagant sally into the delights of *nouvelle cuisine*, while Harry's Bar and the Sabatini serve first-class Florentine food. Mamma Gina's

falls into a more affordable bracket, while La Loggia promises a wonderful view from the Piazzale Michelangelo.

As you begin to sample these restaurants you realise that Florentine taste is far from international. Despite a few crêperie and some lonely Chinese restaurants, menus are consistently and proudly Italian. Within these pre-set guidelines, the only rule of thumb is to concentrate on Tuscan and Florentine specialities.

Ones to avoid: If it is easy to fill the stomach in Florence, it is also easy to empty the pocket. This is acceptable in good restaurants, but around the Ponte Vecchio and the main piazzas, too many pizza parlours and trattorie prove mediocre and exploitative. The best food in Florence is often served in the least ostentatious restaurants, among local people. These rarely display the tourist menus that cover the city and between meals often hide behind iron grills, in small side streets east and west of the Signoria or across the river, on the Oltrarno. The Da Benventuo and Sostanza are both wonderful examples of authentic home-cooking and Florentine food at its most gloriously unsophisticated.

For snacks in Florence there is a growing contingent of noisy self-service restaurants, but a better bet are *Rosticceria*, where cheese and meats are batter fried and served over the counter.

Al fresco: But a culinary and aesthetic delight not to be missed is a Florentine picnic. Return to the central food market or stop at Da Vera on the Borgo San Jacopo and choose your own fare. Florentine salami, the creamy Pecchorino da Sienna, Mortadella, figs and a bottle of Pomino can be enjoyed against a thousand and one different backdrops: on the steps of Santo Spirito, in Fiesole's miniature amphitheatre with its wonderful panorama or along the river, in the Parco Della Cascine. But, above all, eating *al fresco* takes on its own magic amid the climbing terraces and shaded groves of the Boboli Gardens. Here, above the noisesome city, with a clear view across Florence's terracotta roofs to the hillsides beyond, strong wine and simple cheese help to celebrate the land and the light—the lifeblood of the Florentine imagination.

STREET MARKETS

Under the Uffizi's elegant colonnades, along the banks of the Arno and beside the Repubblica's cafés, Florentines peddle anything from postcards and prints to second-hand tapes, carved sundials and the ubiquitous plastic "Davids".

If there isn't a stall to be had, hawkers set up shop on the pavement, eyes alert for potential customers and for the police foot patrols. Some call out their wares while others, Libyans and Ethiopians from Italy's former colonies, retire into shop doorways, lacking the self-confidence and showmanship of the born street trader. Dusk on the Ponte Vecchio brings out a shadowy array

mountain of junk. In the Piazza San Ambrogio, an early morning vegetable market also sells clothes, while every second Sunday sees crafts and antiques on sale in front of Santo Spirito.

Whereas these markets cater for tourists and locals alike, Tuesday's fair in the Parco della Cascine is a truly Florentine occasion; the stalls stretch for miles beneath the shade of the poplars and this huge outdoor "department store" sells everything from food to cheap clothes.

But of Florence's many markets, the biggest and the best is the Mercato Centrale by San Lorenzo. In reality two markets in one, this is the city's skin and its guts. In the streets outside, traditional canvas and wooden chests serve the surface traffic of tourists, offering wool, silk, linen and, of course, Florence's stock-in-trade,

of those famous Florentine imitations; beguiling bargains until the Valentino sweater runs or the Lacoste crocodile goes for a swim!

More interesting and a better bet than the fly-by-nights are Florence's various permanent markets. The huddled Mercato Nuovo offers yet more souvenirs but here, too, you are likely to find museum guidebooks which are, inexplicably, rarely for sale in the museums themselves, and scores of "naughty postcards" focussing on the genitalia of Renaissance statues and accompanied by homely greetings such as "missing you".

The little-known flea-market of the Piazza Ciompi is the best place to search for "near antiques" and just occasionally you might uncover a fascinating treasure concealed beneath a

leather work; wallets, shoes, gloves, bags and jackets sway like pendant hams. But inside the great cast-iron palace of the central food market beats the heart of the living city.

This is Florence in the raw. Traders, housewives and shopkeepers try and buy the wealth of the Contado. Everywhere counters groan with meats: huge slabs of Florentine steak, chickens, rabbits, boar, brightly coloured pheasants and tripe like coral. There are whole counters of cheese, *antipasti*, wine and even stalls to stop at for a bowl of boiled rice, pork and Chianti Rufino. Upstairs, amid the shouts of vegetable salesmen and the piles of swollen *porcini* mushrooms, outsized potatoes, dried fruit and, of course, beans of every conceivable shape and size, you quicken to the pulse of Florence's main artery.

PLACES

The motorcars snort in your lanes,
your houses fill me with disgust;
you have given yourself to the stains
of Europe's bilious dust.
—Alexander Blok, *The Twelve and other poems*, 1909

Over such trivialities as these many a valuable hour may slip
away, and the traveller who has gone to Italy to study the tactile
values of Giotto, or the corruption of the Papacy, may return
remembering nothing but the blue sky and the men and women who
live under it.
—E.M.Forster, *A Room with a View*, 1908

These two opinions of Florence are not incompatible, for Florence is very much the city you choose to make of it. Some people hate Florence for its heat, noise and tourists, others love it enough to settle there all their lives. Florence accommodates both extremes. It is true you will not stay long if you do not like paintings, for despite Florentine protestations that it is more than a "museum city", that is what sets it apart. On the other hand, a visitor bent solely on an education in aesthetics will be driven to exhaustion, if not madness by the illogical museum and church opening hours.

Virtually nothing is open in the afternoons, so one has a very good excuse for devoting a part of the day to self-indulgence and preparing for the evening, which is the best time of day to see those aspects of the city that have nothing to do with art and everything to do with modern Florence.

That is the time that everyone comes out to shop and chat and see and be seen. Then one discovers what a small community Florence really is, for everyone seems to know everyone else and groups of people fill the newly pedestrianised streets swapping gossip and more serious news.

The visitor need not be excluded from this community. Anyone who stays more than a couple of days, or visits the same shop or restaurant two days in succession is already well on the way to becoming a regular customer. Attempting to speak in even basic Italian wins friends and breaks through the Florentine reserve.

As for the noise, the heat, the cheating stallholders, pickpockets and rude waiters, surely every city has these and the problem has been much exaggerated by those who affect an *ennui* for a city that has, in their eyes, fallen from fashion. Florence is not so easily dismissed, nor will the sensitive visitor want to leap to easy conclusions about such a complex and rewarding city.

Preceding pages: the terracotta roofs of Florence; David's alter ego: copy in Piazza Signoria; fragments from the life of a busy city. Left, the cathedral, glimpsed through mediaeval streets.

118

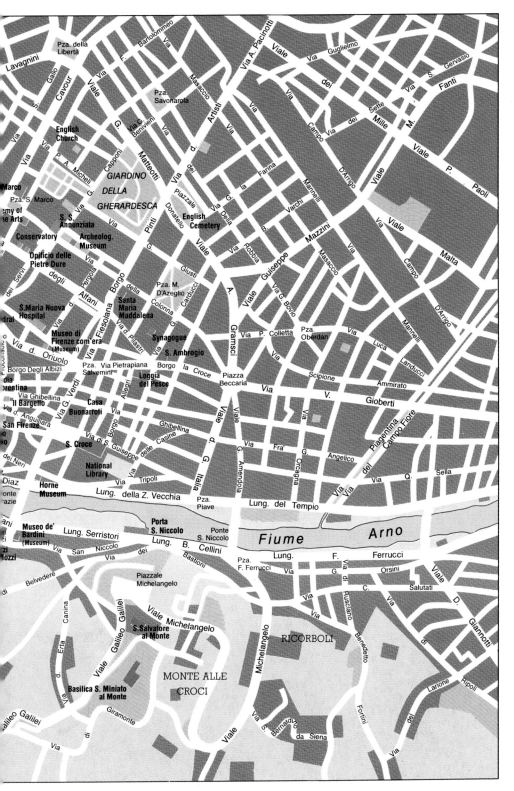

THE RELIGIOUS CENTRE

Piazza del Duomo: The former religious centre of Florence is now the centre of traffic and tourism. Many of the city's bus routes converge on the busy Piazza del Duomo and the road around the square serves as an unofficial race track for youths on their *motorini*. Milling crowds of tourists jostle to get close enough to see the Baptistry doors, their guides shouting to be heard above the traffic's roar.

It is far from tranquil and a leap of imagination is needed to picture the square as it was. Come, if you can, at noon on Easter Sunday for the *Scoppio del Carro* (Explosion of the Cart) for a truly medieval atmosphere.

On this day flints, originally from the Tomb of Christ, are used to spark off a dove-shaped rocket suspended on a wire. If all goes well, the dove swoops through the cathedral door to ignite a cartful of fireworks drawn by white oxen outside, ensuring a good harvest.

For the rest of the year modernity reigns supreme; but persist, for the square contains some of the most important buildings in Florence.

The Baptistry: Dante, in exile, fondly referred to the Baptistry as his *bel San Giovanni* and described it as ancient— a word loaded with meaning. Florentines have always exaggerated its antiquity, asserting that it was originally the Temple of Mars, built by the Romans to commemorate victory over the Etruscan city of Fiesole. In the inter-communal rivalry of the Middle Ages, every Tuscan town claimed to be older than its neighbours and the Baptistry symbolised the Florentine pedigree, its link with the golden classical age.

All the evidence suggests that it was, in fact, built in the sixth or seventh century, albeit reusing Roman masonry. From the 12th century it was taken under the wing of the Calimala, the wool importers' guild which itself claimed to be the first and most ancient trade association in the city.

The guild paid for the beautiful marble cladding of green geometric designs on a white background. This was widely admired and imitated throughout Tuscany, the prototype of many a church exterior, including that of Florence's own cathedral. The interior was reworked between 1270 and 1300 when the dome received its ambitious cycle of mosaics—illustrating the entire Biblical story from Creation to the Last Judgement—and the Zodiac pavement around the font was laid.

Next the guild turned to the entrances, determined to outdo the great bronze doors of Pisa cathedral. They did so, but not for several decades yet. Andrea Pisano's doors, now in the **south portal**, were completed in 1339 and tell the story of St John, the patron saint of the city. They are competent and typical of the best Gothic craftsmanship but it was Ghiberti's north and east doors that really set Europe talking 60 years later.

Left, Giotto's noble campanile. Right, view from the top, to the cathedral dome.

Work stopped on the Baptistry during the intervening period—one of plague, appalling weather, crop failures and famine throughout Europe, as well as bankruptcies and further political turmoil in Florence.

Gates of paradise: The year 1400 was a watershed date. In the winter of that year the guild announced a competition to select a designer for the remaining doors. Entrants were invited to submit sample panels on the theme of *The Sacrifice of Isaac*; only those made by Lorenzo Ghiberti and Filippo Brunelleschi have survived (and are now in the Bargello).

Ghiberti was judged the winner in 1403 but that scarcely matters since art historians, rightly reluctant to award the title of "Father of the Renaissance" to any one artist, have chosen 1400, the year of the competition, as the official starting point of the Renaissance.

Ghiberti's work demonstrates some of the key features of the Renaissance style—the use of deep perspective, realism in the portrayal of the human body and allusions to classical sculpture. He invented none of them, but he did succeed in reflecting brilliantly the artistic preoccupations of his day.

Ghiberti finished the **north doors**, illustrating the Life of Christ, in 1424. The **east doors**, hailed by Michelangelo as the "Gate of Paradise", took almost all of the rest of his life. In their original state, gilded and burnished to a resplendent gold, they must have fully justified Michelangelo's description.

Now the panels are being removed for restoration. Some still remain to be admired; others have been replaced by blank wooden panels. In time, all the doors will be replaced by copies and the originals displayed in the Museo dell' Opera del Duomo.

The Duomo: The Duomo, or cathedral (from *Domus Dei*, House of God), is a symbol of Florentine determination always to have the biggest and the best. It was once the largest in the world, and even now ranks fourth. It was funded by

a property tax on all citizens and is a continuing financial burden on the city and state, requiring constant repair.

It is also a very difficult building to like and looks best from afar, a slice of exuberant colour glimpsed at the end of dark palace-lined streets. It took 150 years to complete, from 1294 to 1436. During that time so many architects had a hand in its decoration that the delicate pink and green marble panelling, copying the restrained Baptistry, got submerged beneath a flurry of Gothic image niches and icing-cake frills.

Worse still is the too-flamboyant neo-Gothic west **facade**, added in the late 19th century. It makes us appreciate Brunelleschi's genius all the more—his dome draws the eye upward from the jumble below to admire the clean profile of the cathedral's crowning glory, 351 ft (107 metres) above the ground.

Scarcely less tall, at 278 ft (85 metres) is the **campanile** alongside, begun by Giotto shortly after he was appointed chief architect in 1331. The climb to the

The Cathedral: left, 19th-century gothic façade; right, marble walls of the nave.

top is worth the effort for intimate views of the upper levels of the cathedral and the panoramic city views.

Stark simplicity: By contrast with the polychrome exterior, the cathedral **interior** is strikingly stark. Centuries of accumulated votive offerings, pews and memorials have been swept away, leaving only those works of art that are integral to the fabric. Even these face an uncertain future for Vasari's *Last Judgement* fresco (1572-9) in the dome has been covered over pending a decision either to restore it or to move it elsewhere.

Thus the highlights are few; at the east end, Luca della Robbia's bronze doors to the **New Sacristy** (1445-69), and the fine wooden inlaid cupboards that line the interior. Here, Lorenzo the Magnificent sought refuge in 1478 after the Pazzi conspirators, in a failed bid to seize power from the Medici, had tried to murder him during High Mass.

In the **north aisle**, there is a painting of Dante standing outside the walls of

Florence, symbolic of his exile. It was commissioned in 1465 to celebrate the bicentenary of the poet's birth.

Close to it is the famous mural of 1436 depicting the English mercenary, Sir John Hawkwood. It is often cited as an example of Florentine miserliness for Hawkwood's services to the city were commemorated not by a real bronze equestrian statue but by Paolo Uccello's *trompe l'oeil* mural. Ucello also painted the fresco clock on the west wall that tells the time according to *ora Italica* which prevailed until the 18th century, whereby sunset marks the last hour of the day.

There are several memorials in the cathedral but only one man—Brunelleschi—was granted the singular privilege of burial within its walls, belated recognition of his genius in resolving the problem of the dome. His grave slab, in the **crypt**, bears an inscription comparing him to Icarus. The analogy is apt for, like the flight of the mythical hero, the dome seems to defy gravity.

The soaring dome: The masterplan for the cathedral had always envisaged a central dome but no-one knew how to erect one of the required height and span without prodigious expenditure on timber for scaffolding. Brunelleschi went to Rome to study the prototype of all domed structures—the Pantheon—and came up with his masterplan: a solution based on classical Roman technology.

Poor Brunelleschi must sometimes have hated the Florentines. Sceptical financiers first made him build a model on the bank of the Arno to prove that his dome would stand up and then appointed the cautious, interfering and incompetent Ghiberti, Brunelleschi's old rival in the competition for the Baptistry doors, to supervise the overall construction.

Always a problem solver, Brunelleschi got rid of Ghiberti by walking out of the project, pretending to be ill. Without Brunelleschi, work ground to a halt and he agreed to return only on condition that he was put in sole charge.

The cathedral in its finished splendour.

Brunelleschi's aesthetic achievement is known to the whole world through countless travel posters. The dome has come to symbolise the city of Florence, an instantly recognisable landmark, rising above a sea of red terracotta roof tiles and seeming to soar as high as the surrounding mountains. To appreciate his engineering achievement it is necessary to climb the **dome**.

The staircase passes between two shells. The inner one is built of brick laid herring-bone fashion, providing a virtually self-supporting structure that could be built from above without support from below. This then provided a platform for the scaffolding to erect the outer shell.

The dome was completed in 1436, the year that the cathedral was consecrated by Pope Eugenius IV. The lantern, planned by Brunelleschi, was not completed until 1461, 15 years after his death. The final touch was the external gallery running round the base. This was begun in 1506 by Baccio d'Agnolo but worked stopped, with only one side finished, when Michelangelo, whose word was law, described it as a "cricket's cage", implying that the design was rustic and childish. Few visitors will agree with his judgement, which has left the base of the dome with no facing to disguise the raw stonework on seven of its sides.

Museo dell'Opera del Duomo: The Opera del Duomo (Cathedral Workshop) was established in the 15th century to maintain the fabric and commission new work—principally sculpture and furnishings to adorn the facade and interior. It was here, in the tiny **courtyard**, that Michelangelo carved his mighty *David*. The workshop premises now serve as a museum of carvings from the Baptistry, Duomo and Campanile brought indoors for protection from pollution and weathering.

On the ground floor a room devoted to Brunelleschi contains his death mask, a wooden model of the dome, and capstans, wheels, pulleys and brick

Gate of Paradise: the Baptistry doors. Next page, the Baptistry: oldest building in Florence.

FORMELLA RESTAURATA
ESPOSTA NEL
MUSEO DEL DUOMO

moulds used in the construction. Another room contains 16th and 17th-century models for the west front, all of which are considerably more handsome than the regrettable 19th-century facade that was eventually built.

A small antechamber is filled with reliquaries, once greatly revered, and containing nails from the Crucifix, several of St John the Baptist's fingers and the arrow that killed St Sebastian.

Penitence and joy: These are all curiosities; the great art treasures lie upstairs. Dramatically positioned on the half landing is Michelangelo's powerful *Pieta*. He began work on it around 1550, intending it to cover his own tomb. Having completed only the expressive body of Christ and the head of Nicodemus (a self-portrait), he broke it up, dissatisfied with the faulty marble and his own work. A servant kept the pieces and a pupil reconstructed it, finishing the figure of Mary Magdalene after the master's death.

The next room contains two delightful **choir galleries**, made for the cathedral but removed in the 17th century. On the left is Luca della Robbia's marble loft, carved 1431-8; on the right, Donatello's work of 1433-9. Both portray boys and girls singing, dancing, playing trumpets, drums and cymbals in a frenzy of joyous celebration.

In stark contrast, Donatello's statue in wood of Mary Magdalene (perhaps carved around 1455) is a striking study of the former prostitute in old age, dishevelled, haggard and penitent.

The room beyond is devoted to early 14th-century **bas reliefs** from the base of the Campanile, some designed by Giotto, most carved by Andrea Pisano. They illustrate the Creation of Adam and Eve and the arts, sciences and industries by which the human race has sought to understand and beautify the world since Original Sin and the barring of the Gates of Paradise. Though Gothic in style, they are Renaissance in spirit, a proud celebration of human knowledge and achievements.

THE POLITICAL CENTRE

The Piazza della Signoria: The main square of Florence evokes strong reactions. Florentines argue furiously about its future, citizens of neighbouring towns are contemptuous of its lack of grace and architectural unity compared with, for example, Siena's harmonious Campo. Visitors from further afield are often disappointed for the same reason: the grim buildings seem to belong to some cold northern climate rather than the city that gave birth to the colour and vitality of the Renaissance.

Worse still, the historic buildings and sculptures are "temporarily" enshrouded in scaffolding and green netting. Dates for the completion of restoration are treated with scepticism.

Meanwhile, prevarication over the repaving of the square threatens to continue for years. Archaeologists, who have been excavating since 1987, want a covering that will preserve the remains of Roman and medieval buildings in an underground museum. A vociferous minority wants the square to be paved in red brick, as it was from 1386 until the 18th century. Others prefer grey flagstones, to harmonise with the streets of Florence, and some do not care so long as they can reopen pavement restaurants and souvenir stalls as soon as possible.

Ancient strife: Such controversy is not new; the Piazza is littered with the symbols of competing ideologies. A plaque marks the spot where Savonarola was burned at the stake as a heretic in 1498. Statues around the square are loaded with political allusions.

Politicians have addressed the public from the front of the Palazzo Vecchio since the 14th century—originally from the raised platform, the *ringheria* (which gave rise to the term "to harangue"), until it was demolished in 1812. Before the archaeologists moved in, mass political rallies in the square were commonplace and they will surely return once the paving is restored.

Indeed, the Piazza was born out of strife. The land was owned by the Uberti, supporters of the Ghibelline (imperial) faction, losers to the Guelph (papal) party in the struggles that tore Florence apart in the 13th century. The property of the exiled Uberti was first left to crumble as a sign of the family's defeat, then chosen as the site of a new palace to house the city government.

The Peoples' Palace: The foundation stone was laid in 1299 and the palace was finished by 1322 when the great bell (removed in 1530) was hung in the tower to ring out danger warnings and summon general assemblies.

The name of the palace has changed almost as often as power in the city has changed hands. From the Palazzo del Populo—the Peoples' Palace—it became the Palazzo della Signoria when the *signori*, the heads of the leading commercial families, began to take over the reins of government.

Left, Palazzo Vecchio: before the restoration. Below, Donatello's *Judith and Holofernes*.

It continued so from 1434, the beginning of Cosimo de' Medici's unofficial leadership of the city until the death of his grandson, Lorenzo the Magnificent, in 1492. The years 1494 to 1537 saw attempts, inspired by the teaching of Savonarola, to establish a republic; the Medici were expelled from the city several times and an inscription was raised above the palace entrance declaring Christ to be the King of Florence.

In 1537, Cosimo I seized control of the city and three years later moved into the palace, which now became the Palazzo Ducale. In 1550, the Pitti Palace became the Duke's new official residence, and from that time to this the building has been known as the Palazzo Vecchio, the Old Palace.

The Loggia dei Lanzi: The graceful little three-arched **loggia** to the right of the palace is named after Cosimo I's personal body guard, the lancers, whose barracks were nearby. It was, however, built much earlier—completed in 1382—to shelter dignitaries from the weather during public ceremonies.

Cosimo considered extending the tall round arches all around the square, at Michelangelo's advice, in order to give the piazza a degree of architectural harmony, but the plan was abandoned as too costly. Instead it came to serve as an outdoor sculpture gallery, housing antique statues and new works, much admired by visitors as the chief adornment of the square.

The statues: The first statue was erected not as an aesthetically motivated decision but as an act of political defiance. Donatello's **Judith and Holofernes** was cast between 1456 and 1460 as a fountain for the courtyard of the Medici Palace. It was brought into the square by the citizens of the newly declared republic of Florence after the expulsion of the Medici in 1494. The symbolism was clear for everyone to read: the virtuous Judith executing the drunken tyrant Holofernes stood for the triumph of liberty over despotism.

Fifty years later, in 1554, another bronze statue depicting a decapitation was erected in the Loggia. This time Cellini's **Perseus** was commissioned by Cosimo I to celebrate his return to power and carries an implied threat—just as Perseus used the head of Medusa to turn his enemies to stone so opponents could expect exile or worse.

Florentines once believed that images had the magical power to bring good or ill upon the city (some still believe that paintings of the Virgin can work miracles). It was not long before the wisdom of displaying *Judith and Holofernes* began to be questioned. It symbolised death and the defeat of a man by a woman and so was moved to a less prominent site (a copy is now back in front of the Palazzo and the restored original is displayed inside).

Enter David: Michelangelo's **David** was erected in its place, a popular decision that transformed the square and gave it a new focal point. Even now, the pollution-streaked copy (the original is in the Accademia) has an arresting force

and exudes ambiguity. David is both muscular and effeminate, between adolescence and maturity, relaxed but ready to fight, a glorious celebration of the naked human body, yet distorted with overlarge head and limbs.

Moreover, the political symbolism was open to numerous interpretations. Those who wished could see David's bravery before the giant Goliath as a metaphor for Florence, prepared to defend her liberty against all who threatened it; or they could read it more specifically and choose the Medici, the Pope, the Holy Roman Emperor, Siena, or Pisa as the particular enemy.

After the success of *David*, more works were commissioned on the same monumental scale, but all were greeted with varying degrees of ridicule. **Hercules** was chosen as a subject because of the legend that Florence was built on swamps drained by the mythical hero. When Bandinelli's carving was unveiled in 1534, Cellini compared it to "an old sack full of melons".

Ammannati's **Neptune Fountain**, an allegory of Cosimo I's scheme to make Florence a great naval power, was carved in 1563-75. Neptune looks as uncomfortable as the artist must have felt on hearing his work dismissed in a popular street cry as a waste of a good piece of marble. The bronze satyrs and nymphs splashing at Neptune's feet are livelier work but the artist, in a fit of piety later in life, condemned his own work as an incitement to licentious thoughts and deeds.

Giambologna's **Rape of the Sabine Women**, in the Loggia, was more popular with the critics when it was unveiled in 1583. The title was suggested as an afterthought—the artist had no specific subject in mind and aimed to portray three different kinds of human body: the old man, the young and the female.

Also by Giambologna is the equestrian **statue of Cosimo I**, commissioned by his son Ferdinando and unveiled in 1594. It is imposing but of indifferent artistic quality—the same could be said of Florence under Cosimo's reign, for though he left it powerful, art went into serious decline.

The Palazzo Vecchio: Nowhere is that decline more evident than in the interior of the Palazzo Vecchio, completely remodelled when Cosimo moved in 1540, having quashed republicanism in Florence and established himself as hereditary Duke.

It is not all bad, of course, and the **cortile** (courtyard) designed by Michelozzo in 1453 as the main entrance, is delightful, even though parts are hidden by the scaffolding of restorers. The little fountain in the centre was designed by Vasari around 1555—copying the putto and dolphin made for the Medici villa at Careggi by Verrocchio in 1470.

The stucco and frescoes are also Vasari's work. On the walls are views of Austrian cities, painted to make Joanna of Austria feel at home when she married Francesco de' Medici (Cosimo's son) in 1565. The ceiling is covered in "grotesque" figures—that is, in imita-

Palazzo Vecchio Watch Tower.

tion of the ancient Roman paintings in the grotto of Nero's garden—a colourful tapestry of sphinxes, flowers, birds and satyrs.

The principal room on the first floor is the **Salone dei Cinquecento**, so called after the 500 council members, was designed in 1495 by Cronaca for meetings of the ruling assembly—the Consiglio Maggiore—of the republic. The vast room, despite appalling acoustics, is now used as a concert hall in which tenors pour out operatic areas, heavy with the romantic vibrato so loved by Italian audiences.

The Duke victorious: Both Leonardo da Vinci and Michelangelo, were commissioned to paint the walls and ceilings, but neither got much further than experimental sketches. It was left to Vasari to undertake the work, executed with great speed between 1563 and 1565. Nominally the paintings celebrate the foundation of Florence and the recent victories over its rivals, Pisa and Siena. The ubiquitous presence of Co-

simo I in all the scenes makes it a vast exercise in ducal propaganda.

It is not unusual for visitors to feel more than uneasy and wonder why the talented Vasari stooped to such overt flattery. By the same token Michelangelo's **Victory** is equally disturbing. Brutally realistic, it depicts an old man forced to the ground by the superior strength of a muscular youth.

It was carved for the tomb of Julius II in Rome, but Michelangelo's heirs presented it to Cosimo I to commemorate the 1559 victory over Siena. The artist intended it to represent the triumph of reason over ignorance, but in this context it seems all part of a gross celebration of war. Even so, artists have frequently sought to imitate Michelangelo's twisted, tortured figures, and it was one of the works most admired by the later 16th-century Mannerists.

Light relief is provided by the **Hercules and Diomedes** of Vincenzo de' Rossi, a no-holds-barred tussle in which the inverted Diomedes takes revenge by

Florence conquers Tuscany: Vasari's fresco in the Palazzo Vecchio.

squeezing Hercules' genitals in an agonising grip.

The lonely alchemist: Off the main hall is the windowless study of the reclusive Francesco I, built between 1570 and 1575. The beautifully painted cupboards were used to store his treasures and the equipment for his experiments in alchemy. His parents, Cosimo I and the beautiful Eleonora di Toledo, are depicted in the ceiling frescoes.

Next in sequence comes the suite of rooms known as the **Quartiere di Leone X**, decorated in 1556-62 by Vasari and named after Giovanni de' Medici, son of Lorenzo the Magnificent, who was created a cardinal at the age of 13 and ended up as Pope Leo X.

Above is the **Quartiere degli Elimenti**, with allegories of the elements, including a watery scene reminiscent of Botticelli, once again by Vasari. The corner room, the Terrazza di Saturno, provides fine views east to Santa Croce and south to San Miniato.

Regal interiors: The **Quartiere di Eleonora di Toledo**, the private rooms of the wife of Cosimo I, includes the chapel with stunning frescoes by Bronzino (1540-45), a rare opportunity to study fresco work from close quarters. The sheer range and brilliance of the colour is most striking—colours rarely seen in modern painting, vivid pinks, luminescent blues and almost phosphorescent green.

Eleonora's bedroom is decorated with a frieze based on her initials, and has a lovely marble wash basin; another is painted with domestic scenes—spinning, weaving and the tasks that correspond to the classical idea of virtuous motherhood; the last with Florentine street scenes and festivities.

A corridor containing the serene death mask of Dante leads to the two most sumptuous rooms of the palace, the **Salla d'Udienza** and the **Salla dei Gigli**. Both have gilded and coffered ceilings, decorated with every conceivable form of ornament. The 16th-century intarsiate doors between the two depict the poets Dante and Petrarch.

The Sala dei Gigli is named after the lilies, symbol of the city, that cover the walls. Donatello's original *Judith and Holofernes* is displayed here with panels explaining how the bronze was cast and, more recently, restored.

A small chamber off, entered through the remains of one of the original 13th-century palace windows, was built as an office, in 1511, for Machiavelli during his term of office as government secretary. A portrait, by Santi di Tito, depicts the youthful, smiling author of *The Prince*, looking nothing like the demonic figure he was later branded when this study of politics and pragmatism was published.

The exit from the palace passes the entrance to the tower (closed for restoration) and through a suite of rooms that temporarily houses the Conservatorio's collection of musical instruments, including violins by Stradivarius and keyboard instruments by the Florentine inventor of the piano, Cristofori.

Left, St John, symbol of Florence in the Sala Dei Gigli. Right, Ammannati bronze, Piazza Signoria.

ART AND NATURE

The Uffizi Gallery: A reading of Vasari's *Lives of the Artists*, or Browning's poems based on them, is a good preparation for an encounter with the greatest works of the Renaissance. Vasari's anecdotes teach us not to be too adulatory, and to realise that many of the great artists were ordinary men, lustful, greedy and always willing to pander to the whims of their patrons.

Vasari himself was one of the arch flatterers. When he designed the Uffizi, he incorporated a continuous corridor, that runs from the **Palazzo Vecchio**, via the **Uffizi** and the **Ponte Vecchio**, to the **Pitti Palace** on the opposite bank of the Arno. Along this elevated walkway, symbolic of their pre-eminent status, Cosimo I and his heirs could walk between their palace and the seat of government without being soiled by contact with people they ruled.

The lower floors served as government offices (*uffici*, hence the name) but the corridor, lit by an almost continuous glass wall thanks to Vasari's innovative use of iron reinforcing, was lined with antique sculptures from the Medici villas and artistic masterpieces that they commissioned, collected or inherited. In 1737, Anna Maria Lodovica, last of the Medici, bequeathed the entire collection to the people of Florence.

Goal of travellers: To visit the Uffizi is to follow in the footsteps of the great. Grand tourists made it one of the principal goals of 19th-century travellers. They came mainly to see and draw the antique statuary and few cared about Giotto, Cimabue, Filippo Lippi or Botticelli until Ruskin began to reappraise the art of the Renaissance and his infectious enthusiasm for the treasures of the Uffizi brought a new set of pilgrims, artists who copied the Renaissance manner, giving birth to the Pre-Raphaelite movement.

Now the bulk of the 1.5 million annual visitors come for the Botticelli, but all the rooms are crowded in summer. Winter (November to March) is quieter and the small café and roof terrace in the west corridor makes a good place to retreat when crowds, heat and sensory overload threaten to overwhelm.

The paintings are arranged chronologically and by school, so it is possible to follow, even without a guide, the development of subject matter and technique over five centuries of artistic endeavour in Florence and Italy.

The quest for realism: Rooms 2 to 4 contain masterpieces of the *trecento*. Cimabue's *Madonna* (c. 1285) is typical of the pre-Renaissance Gothic style, decorative and iconographic, intended to inspire the devout to spiritual contemplation. Duccio's *Madonna* is an early attempt to express the human side of the mother and child relationship and Giotto's *Madonna* (c. 1310) shows how early Tuscan artists were experimenting with the illusion of realistic space, and with *chiaroscuro*, the counterplay

Preceding pages: waiting for customers, the cathedral square. Left, the Uffizi and Vasari's Corridor. Right, tea time in Piazza Signoria.

of light and dark.

The works of the early *quattrocento*, in Rooms 5 and 6, introduce new developments while still being essentially Gothic. *The Life of the Anchorites of the Thebiad* (*c.* 1400-10), by Gherardo Starnina, is striking for the first use of naturalistic blue for the sky instead of heavenly gold, and the real world begins to figure in painting in Monaco's *Adoration of the Magi* (1420), with its cameo view of Santa Croce.

The portraits, in Room 7, of Federico di Montefeltro and his wife, Battista Sforza, by Piero della Francesca (1460) make a new departure. The subjects are living people, not religious symbols, and the background, the watery landscape around the artist's native Arezzo, is painted in loving detail.

Alongside is Paolo Uccello's huge *Battle of San Romano* (1456), a frenetic work, said to have been inspired by della Francesca's treatise on perspective, and betraying a fanatical preoccupation with the problem of depicting receding views realistically.

Religion and lust: Room 8 contains works by Filippo Lippi, including his lovely *Madonna with Angels* (c. 1465). Lippi, a Franciscan monk, was notorious for his lustful passions and Vasari tells us that he painted the women he loved to cool his sexual ardour. This portrait is one of his finest celebrations of feminine beauty.

Room 9 contains early works by Botticelli and the next holds his brilliantly restored masterpieces: the *Primavera* (c. 1480), and the *Birth of Venus* (c. 1485).

The *Primavera* is as strange as it is beautiful and scholars still argue over its meaning. On the right, Zephyr, a personification of the gentle warm wind, brings forth flowers that burst out of the mouth of Spring. In the centre are Venus and Cupid, and beyond the Three Graces. Finally, Lorenzo the Magnificent is portrayed as Mercury, the spirit of eloquence, communication and reason. They all stand in a meadow of

Madonna with Angels, Fra Filippo Lippi.

flowers, a heart-warming evocation of fecundity and the joys of spring.

Just as stunning for its sheer delight in the beauty and sensuality of the female form is Lorenzo di Credi's *Venus*, in the same room. The title is only a pretence, an attempt to justify what is in reality simply a nude, painted without context, background or symbolism, and exactly the kind of purely human and secular work that Savonarola and his followers did their best to root out and destroy.

Prized treasures: Room 18 (the Tribuna) is an octagonal room lit from above, with a mother-of-pearl encrusted ceiling, designed by Buontalenti in 1584, in which the Medici displayed the objects they prized most highly from their collection. The walls are lined with family portraits and the best work is the chaste *Medici Venus*, from the family villa in Rome, a first-century B.C. copy of the fourth-century *Aphrodite* of Cnidos.

Botticelli's Primavera.

A series of linked rooms, containing Dutch, German and Venetian paintings, leads to the south corridor with its fine views of the city and the best of the sculpture, mainly ancient Roman copies of Greek originals. Room 25 contains a rare painting by Michelangelo, the *Holy Family*, painted in 1504, at the same time as he was working on *David*, for the wedding of Angelo Doni to Maddalena Strozzi, uniting two of the most powerful families in Florence. It is characterised by vivid colours, much copied by later Mannerist artists, and the roundedness of the figures, showing the sculptor's natural preoccupation with all three dimensions.

Foul and obscene: In Room 28 is Titian's profoundly influential *Venus of Urbino* (1538), a work that inspired the Impressionists and Picasso as much as it shocked the likes of Mark Twain, who called it, in a fit of puritanical rage, "the foulest, the vilest, the obscenest picture the world possesses", simply because of the attitude of her arms and hand.

The title "Venus" is purely euphemistic, for, like the earlier work of

Lorenzo di Credi, this is a consciously erotic work. It is not, in the final analysis, the ambiguous position of the hand that is so seductive, for it could be read equally as a gesture of modesty as of self-pleasure; it is the knowing, provocative expression on the face of the Venus, her rich lips and the almond eyes that invite complicity in an intimate voyeur/exhibitionist relationship.

Such heady art is followed by a cold shower. There are many works in the remaining rooms, but few of outstanding merit—with the honourable exception of Caravaggio's *Young Bacchus* (*c.* 1589) in Room 43 and Rembrandt's *Self Portrait as an Old Man* (*c.* 1664) in Room 44. On the exit staircase is the famous *Wild Boar*, a Roman copy of a third-century B.C. Greek original that inspired the Porcellino Fountain in the Mercato Nuovo.

Vasari's corridor: The corridor from the Uffizi to the Pitti Palace is lined with pictures, many of them self portraits by artists as diverse as Vasari and Ve-lasquez, Hogarth and Millais; tours take place in the morning, Tuesday to Sunday, and must be booked at the Uffizi the previous day. Otherwise, one can follow the route of the raised arcade along the Arno, across the left-hand side of the Ponte Vecchio and in front of the church of S. Felicita until it disappears behind the Palazzo Guicciardini before entering the Pitti Palace.

The Pitti Palace: Ruskin, and later D.H. Lawrence, argued that the vibrant, colourful, sensual and humane art of the Florentine Renaissance was a re-emergence of the Etruscan spirit that is evident in their tomb painting and sculptures, some 1,500 years after their culture was crushed by the colonial, militaristic Romans. Much the same could be said of many Florentine palaces, and especially the Pitti Palace.

Like the walls of Etruscan Fiesole, the city that Florence replaced, the exterior of this building is gaunt and forbidding, built of massive rough-hewn blocks of stone with little relieving

Titian's shocking *Venus*.

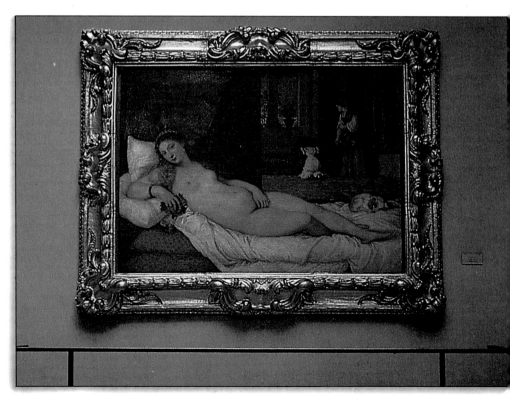

ornament. The exiled Dostoevsky wrote *The Idiot* in the house opposite (No 21, Piazza Pitti), and one can imagine that his view of the palace contributed to the gloom of his novel.

Even so, the palace was regarded as ostentatious in its time, in part because of its great size. The seven central bays of the present building were the first to be built by Luca Pitti, virtually bankrupting the family, from the late 1450s. The aim was to outrival the splendour of the Medici palace.

But the Medici won. In 1549 Pitti's heirs sold the palace to Eleonora di Toledo, and in 1550 she persuaded her husband, Cosimo I, to move the household from the Palazzo Vecchio to the more salubrious Pitti Palace, with its gardens and rural atmosphere, for the good of her health.

Dynasty in decline: The rest of the story was not entirely happy. Eleonora, who had given birth to 11 children, became increasingly sickly. She died in 1562, some say of malaria, others of tuberculosis. Two years later, Cosimo virtually resigned from active government in favour of his son, Francesco. The latter's marriage to Joanna of Austria in 1565 was an occasion of great festivity. Thereafter, Cosimo's own health went into decline: he suffered a series of cerebral haemorrhages that left him paralysed, and he died, aged 54, in 1574.

Francesco I was succeeded by Ferdinand I, and then the sickly Cosimo II, who began to extend the palace, a task completed by Ferdinand II in the mid-17th century. It was at this time that the chief glory of the palace, the ceilings of the private apartments, now the Palatine Gallery, were painted. The two side wings were added at the end of the 18th century (on the right) and in the 19th (on the left), so that the palace was complete in its present appearance by 1828, when it was first opened to the public. It now houses several museums, some of which will be closed for the foreseeable future for restoration.

The Pitti Palace.

They are the **Palatine Gallery**, the **Argenti Museum** and the **Gallery of Modern Art** (all open) and the state rooms and Coach Museum (both closed) within the Palace. The **Porcelain** and **Costume Museums** (both open) are housed in buildings in the **Boboli Gardens**, behind the palace, and the gardens also provide access to the **Belvedere Fortress**, used for occasional open-air exhibitions, principally of modern sculpture.

The Palatine Gallery: The splendid collection of paintings that cover the walls of the gallery were collected by the Medici princes in the 17th and 18th centuries. They are displayed exactly as the princes intended, with the emphasis on decorative effect rather than chronologically or by school.

The richness of the rooms is enhanced by Pietro da Cortona's ceiling frescoes, commissioned by Ferdinand II and executed between 1641 and 1665. They illustrate, allegorically, the stages in the education of the prince.

The rooms are named after the ceiling subjects. Thus, the first room, after the ante chambers, is called the **Sala di Venere**, and the fresco depicts the young prince being torn from the arms of a pneumatic Venus by Minerva (Wisdom) for he must leave behind the joys of adolescent love and begin his education.

In the centre of the room is the very fine statue of Venus emerging from her bath, carved by Canova and given by Napoleon in token exchange for the Medici *Venus* which he took back to Paris (it is now back in the Uffizi). Titian's *Portrait of a Lady* (1536) has justly been nicknamed *La Bella*—the beautiful—and the lady may well be the same that modelled for his *Venus of Urbino* in the Uffizi.

In the **Sala di Apollo**, the prince begins to learn about the sciences and the arts. Titian's delicious *Maddalena* is more lascivious than repentant, with yards of golden hair that provocatively fails to cover her nakedness.

St John the Baptist, **Andrea Del Sarto.**

The horrors of war: In the **Sala di Marte**, the prince learns the "art" of war, and the ceiling is covered in graphic and life-like battle scenes. An interesting counterpoint is Rubens' allegorical painting *Consequences of War*, painted in 1638 at the time of the Thirty Years War. In a letter, Rubens explained that it depicted Mars escaping from the arms of Venus to spread plague and pestilence throughout Europe. It is a profoundly pacifistic work: the figure in black is "unfortunate Europe who, for so many years now, has suffered plunder, outrage and misery".

The **Sala di Giove**, the throne room of the Medici, contains Andrea del Sarto's *St John the Baptist as a Boy* (1523), an effeminate figure with, perhaps, homosexual overtones: the Medici princes were fond of having their portraits painted as the young St John or as St Sebastian. Raphael's *La Valeta* (*c.* 1516) is a virtuoso piece in which the rich detail of the clothing contrasts with the glowing purity and serenity of the subject's face.

The hunting scenes on the ceiling of the **Sala di Saturna** were never completed, so the remaining spaces are filled with gilded stucco. Raphael's *Madonna della Seggiola* (*c.* 1515) depicts an extraordinarily beautiful, naturalistic and gentle mother and child, betraying the influence of Andrea del Sarto in the fleshy lips and watery eyes, but far surpassing the latter in humaneness and vibrant colour.

Beyond, the rooms of chief interest are the **Sala della Stufa**, with frescoes of the Four Ages of Man, the **Sala dell' Educazione di Giove**, containing Allori's dramatic and colourful *Judith*, one of the few great Florentine works of the 17th century, and the **Sala di Bagni**, a 19th-century bathroom and a sybarite's dream, with its erotic stucco bathing scenes and nude statues. The astounding *Pieta* of Fra Bartolomeo, one of the leading painters of the High Renaissance, is displayed in a room of its own with exhibits explaining the

Madonna Della Seggiola, Raphael.

restoration process.

Galleria d'Arte Moderna: The misleadingly named Modern Art Gallery, on the floor above the Palatine, actually contains work dating from the 18th century to the beginning of the 20th; mostly academic work with a few titillating nudes and much heavy furniture. The light amid the general gloom is provided by the paintings, in Rooms 23 to 26, of the *Macchiaioli*, late 19th-century Italian Impressionists.

The Argenti Museum: The "museum of silver" contains much else besides, mostly from the Medici collections and ranging from the antique vases beloved of Lorenzo the Magnificent to the jewel-encrusted baubles of later dukes and princes.

The frescoes alone make a visit worthwhile, in particular the **Sala di Giovanni di San Giovanni**, named after the artist who painted the room for the marriage of Ferdinand II to Vittoria delle Rovere in 1634. The colour and the exuberance compensate for the adulatory subject matter—the assumption of various Medici into the kingdom of heaven.

The Boboli Gardens: These extensive gardens, behind the Pitti Palace, are a great joy, even in their present sorry and neglected state. The predominant colours are the shadowy dark greens of cypress and box, which serve to highlight the numerous statues of amorous nymphs, satyrs and statuesque deities that populate this half-wild world.

It is best to enter from the north wing of the palace, where the path follows the final stretch of the corridor from the Pitti to the Palazzo Vecchio. Beneath its walls is the naked, pot-bellied *Pietro Barbino*, Cosimo I's court dwarf, seated on a turtle, a reproduction of the original carved in 1560 by Valerio Cioli.

Pleasures of the underworld: Next comes the Buontalenti *Grotto*, named after the sculptor who created this frothy, pebble-mosaic cavern in 1583-8. The interior drips stalactites, whilst woodland beasts scurry across the

The Boboli Gardens.

craggy cave floor and the figure of Pan peeps shyly from the limestone walls. Copies of Michelangelo's *Four Slaves*, writhing as if to break free of the stone that entraps them, are set in the four corners.

Oblivious of this, Paris makes love to Helen of Troy in Vincenzo de' Rossi's erotic life-size sculpture. Almost out of sight in the rear of the cave, the equally sensuous *Venus* of Giambologna (*c.* 1565) emerges from her bath.

Grand theatre: From here the carriageway climbs to the terrace behind the Pitti Palace and the great fountain of Francesco Susini (1641). The amphitheatre occupies the site of the quarry used to obtain much of the stone for the palace. In 1630-5 it was laid out as an open-air theatre and used in 1661 for the masques and fireworks that accompanied the marriage of the future Cosimo III to Margaret Louise of Orleans. In the centre is a massive granite basin from the ancient baths of Caracalla, in Rome, and the needle of Rameses II, looted by the Romans from Heliopolis in 30 B.C.

A series of terraces leads up the hill to the Neptune Fountain by Stoldo Lorenzi (1565-8). The path left leads to the frescoed rococo Kaffeehaus (the café only opens in summer) and the entrance to the Belvedere Fortress, built as a private fortification by Ferdinando I in 1590 and now used for outdoor exhibitions. Steps continue from here to the statue of *Abundance*, at the highest point of the gardens, and fine views of the Pitti Palace with Santo Spirito and the rooftops of Oltrarno beyond.

Rural delights: The path follows the crest of the slope to the steps which lead to Michelangelo's enclosed **Giardino del Cavaliere**, constructed in 1529. Ignore the sorry state of this once delightful garden, which is "under restoration" and enjoy the views of San Miniato to the left and the village of Arcetri to the right, rising above a valley dotted with villas and olive groves. The garden is bordered by the Museum of Porcelain containing fine 18th and 19th-century ceramics from the famous factories of Sèvre, Meissen and Vienna.

On leaving the garden, the path continues past gardeners' houses to the top of the **Viottolone**, a long shady cypress alley planted in 1637 and lined with antique statues. A comprehensive tour of the garden would take in the smaller, less-frequented, rose and flower gardens that lie either side of the alley, where nannies take the children of affluent Florentines for walks, or the **Hemicycle** that terminates the avenue, with its Oceanus fountain and circular hedge sheltering the crumbling statues of dancing peasants.

Alternatively, the quicker route continues straight on to the point where the path emerges by the east wing of the Pitti Palace, the smaller **Palazzina della Meridiana**, begun 1776, which houses the **Galleria del Costume**. This well laid-out museum contains a sumptuous display of court and theatrical dress, reflecting the fashions of the 18th to early 20th centuries.

Pitti Palace and Neptune Fountain.

BARGELLO AND SANTA CROCE

The densely populated area on the north bank of the River Arno, east of the Palazzo Vecchio, was the worker's quarter of medieval Florence, its narrow alleys packed with the workshops of cloth dyers and weavers.

The human toll in the 1966 flood was greater here than anywhere in the city, and numerous wall plaques set 20 ft (six metres) up show the level that it reached at its height. After the flood, many former residents were rehoused elsewhere, but it remains an area of workshops, early morning markets, low-built houses and pre-Renaissance towers.

The **Piazza San Firenze**, where seven streets meet, is busy with traffic which everyone manages to ignore as they stop to chat or take a cup of coffee on the way to work. On the west side, a florist's shop occupies one of the most graceful courtyards in the city, that of the **Palazzo Gondi**.

Stone benches running round the base of the palace are used to display the wares of second-hand booksellers. Called *muriccioli*, the provision of such benches for public use was once a condition of planning permission but the ubiquitous pigeon has now ensured that few Florentines exercise their ancient right to sit in the shade of the palace walls and pass the time of day.

Opposite is the baroque church of **San Firenze** (1772-5) now converted to a court of law—though, to the left, **San Filippo Neri** still functions as a church.

Heading north, on the left is the **Badia Fiorentina**, the church of a Benedictine abbey founded in A.D. 978 but much altered in 1627-31. The interior is uninspiring but just inside the door is a delightful painting by Filippo Lippi, painted *c.* 1485. It shows St Bernard and the Virgin; no ethereal vision but a warm-blooded woman accompanied by angels whose faces are those of the children of the Florentine streets.

SVBSTINE
ET·ABSTINE·

151

The little-visited cloister is reached through a door to the right of the sanctuary and up a flight of stairs. This peaceful inner courtyard is adorned with frescoes depicting the miracles of St Bernard by Rossellino (c. 1434-6) and there are good views of the 14th-century campanile, Romanesque below and Gothic above.

Assassination attempt: Opposite the Badia is the grim **Bargello**, begun in 1255 as the city's first town hall but later used as a court and prison. Bernardo Baroncelli was hung from its walls in 1478 for his part in the Pazzi conspiracy, an ill-judged attempt to wrest power in the city from the hands of the Medici.

The story of the attempted coup is one worthy of the pen of Shakespeare. The conspirators, led by Francesco de' Pazzi, aimed to assassinate Lorenzo and Giuliano de' Medici during High Mass in the cathedral, thus removing the two brothers who were next in line to inherit the mantle of Cosimo, their revered grandfather.

The attempt followed a banquet given by the Medici in honour of the Pazzi, and the assassins and their victims embraced as they entered the cathedral—a ploy to check whether the Medici brothers were armed. When the host was raised at the most sacred point in the mass, the assassins struck, killing Giuliano at once. Lorenzo resisted, fought his way to the sanctuary and bolted the massive bronze doors in the face of his attackers.

No escape: The outraged people of Florence took their own swift revenge. Some conspirators were hacked to pieces, others were arrested and hung publicly from the windows of the Palazzo Vecchio or—like Baroncelli who escaped to Constantinople but was captured and returned to Florence—from the Bargello.

Street names around the Bargello recall its former use. **Via dei Malcontenti**—Street of the Miserable—was the route to the gallows in Piazza Piave,

and the **Via dei Neri** refers to the black-robed clergymen who heard the final confessions of the condemned.

In 1786 the instruments of torture were burned and the Bargello was last used as a prison in 1859. Now it serves as the National Museum, containing some of the city's finest sculpture.

The 13th-century courtyard, Gothic with vaulted cloisters and an external staircase, is one of the few that survived the building boom of the Renaissance in its original medieval form. The walls are covered in *stemmae*, stones carved with the emblems of the city wards, magistrates and governors.

Drunken deities: The first room on the right of the entrance contains some of the greatest works of the 16th-century High Renaissance. Michelangelo's *Bacchus* teeters into view as one enters, the epitome of joyful inebriation and carved c. 1497, when Michelangelo was 22, on his first visit to Rome to study classical sculpture.

Next comes a group of animated

Preceding pages: Santa Croce cloister; St Bernard and Madonna, Badia Fiorentina.

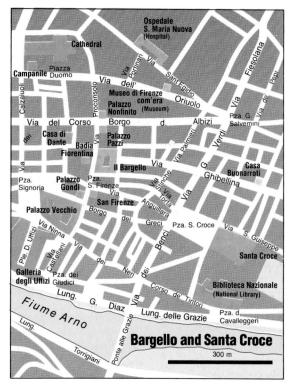

Bargello and Santa Croce

300 m

bronzes by Cellini, who thought of himself primarily as a goldsmith but was an outstanding sculptor as well. His *Mercury* is positioned close enough to the more famous Giambologna *Mercury* to invite comparison.

Giambologna's figure is beautifully poised, floating on a puff of air, with the body of an athlete and superb from every angle. Yet Cellini's fidgeting, restless figure, unable to stand still, seems the more truly mercurial. Equally his *Narcissus* is the quintessence of vanity. The *Perseus* was produced by Cellini as the prototype of his bigger bronze in the Piazza della Signoria, commissioned by Cosimo I to celebrate his triumph over the defeated republic.

The courtyard staircase leads to the first-floor loggia which is used to display a humorous group of naturalistic bronze birds, made by Giambologna for the Medici Villa di Castello on the outskirts of the city.

Innovation in art: On the right, the huge vaulted 14th-century **Salone di Con-** **siglio Generale** is used to display watershed works of the Renaissance, including Ghiberti's winning bronze panel, and that of Brunelleschi, runner-up in the competition to design the doors of the Baptistry.

Of even greater importance is the *St George* of Donatello, a sculptor who many credit with being the first truly Renaissance artist. He went further than most—including Ghiberti, in whose workshop he trained—to break free of the prevailing Gothic style and develop a new classical realism.

The Guild of Armourers chose Donatello to carve St George for their niche on the exterior of Orsanmichele and the finished work, completed around 1416, was hailed as a masterpiece, the first time since antiquity that any sculptor had achieved a lifelike figure, and, moreover, one that is charged with latent energy. No longer contained within the surrounding frame, or *praedella*, it was the precursor of the free-standing statues that became

Bargello sculpture.

the norm in Renaissance sculpture.

His other great work here is the bronze *David* (1430-40), a delicate, almost effeminate figure. By comparison with Michelangelo's strong, muscular warrior, this *David* is child-like and vulnerable, emphasising the mismatch in strength between him and the giant Goliath. It is also the first Renaissance nude, marking a departure from the medieval tradition that only the vicious and the damned were ever portrayed naked.

The 14th-century frescoes in the adjoining chapel illustrate this well, for here the bare-limbed souls in Hell suffer punishments appropriate to their sins while the saved are decorously clothed, including the figure in maroon on the right, thought to be a portrait of Dante.

The remainder of the museum contains a large collection of European and Islamic art and, on the second floor (which is frequently closed when the museum is "short staffed"), a collection of smaller bronzes, terracotta reliefs and works by Verrocchio, a leading sculptor of the later 15th century and teacher of Leonardo da Vinci.

From the Bargello, the **Via del Proconsolo** runs north past the **Palazzo Pazzi**, built 1458-69, before the anti-Medici conspiracy, and unusually handsome, with roses, moons and ball-flowers decorating the upper windows.

Third world art: The next building on the right, across the Borgo degli Albizi, is the **Palazzo Nonfinito** (The Unfinished Palace) begun by Buontalenti in 1593 but still incomplete when it became Italy's first Museum of Anthropology and Ethnology in 1869. Open on the first and third Sundays of the month (or by appointment), it contains native art from the former Italian colonies in Africa as well as objects collected by Captain Cook on his last voyage to the Pacific in 1776-9.

Via del Proconsolo enters the Piazza del Duomo. Via dell' Oriuolo is the first turn right, and a little way down on the left the Via Folco Portinari provides a

Firenze Com'era: the Pitti Palace in 1599.

BELVEDER CON PITTI

glimpse of the **Ospedale Santa Maria Nuovo**, still one of the city's main hospitals. It was founded in 1286 by Folco Portinari, father of Beatrice, the girl whom Dante idolised and made the subject of his early love poetry and his epic *Divine Comedy*.

Further up Via dell' Oriuolo is the **Museo di Firenze com'era** (Florence as it was), housed in a former convent with a graceful loggia surrounding three sides of a green courtyard.

The museum contains maps and topographical paintings that show how little Florence has changed in any essential respect since the first view of the city was sketched in 1470. The painting here, in tempura, is a 19th-century copy of the original engraving now in Berlin and anyone even half-familiar with the city will enjoy spotting the buildings—the majority—that still exist.

It might so easily have been otherwise. Another room contains the 19th-century drawings of the city architect, Giuseppe Poggi, who planned to sweep away the "slums" of central Florence and replace them with the monumental avenues then in vogue.

The city saved: The Piazza della Repubblica was built and the 14th-century city walls demolished before international opposition halted the scheme. Most of Poggi's plans, which included a suspension bridge over the Arno, ended up as museum curiosities, albeit examples of very fine draftsmanship.

The most endearing of the museum's odd ragbag of city views, however, is the series of lunettes illustrating the villas and gardens of the Medici, painted by the Flemish artist, Giusto Utens, in 1599. The view of the Pitti Palace and Boboli Gardens shows them as they were before the extensions were built by the heirs of Cosimo I.

From the museum, Via dell' Oriuolo leads east to the area which, with its handful of Chinese restaurants, approximates most to a Florentine Chinatown. The likeable **Piazza di Pier Maggiore** has a street market most days,

House with *sporti* (stone brackets), typical of Santa Croce.

below the ruined portico of the church that gave the square its name.

This area, and the narrow streets that lead south from it, is different in character to much of the city centre. The low houses and unadorned towers recall the medieval city that existed before wealthy merchants began building grandiose palaces.

Shuttered and silent from noon to three, it is lively for the rest of the day as garulous housewives select from the bunches of spinach and artichokes that are hung from brackets outside the grocers' shops, or wave suggestively shaped marrows at each other and complain about the trials of motherhood and housekeeping.

Via Matteo Palmieri leads to **Via Isola delle Stinche**. Here the **Palazzo di Cintoia** is a solid medieval building with *sporti*, massive stone brackets supporting the upper storeys, jettied out over the narrow street to increase the living space.

Ice-cream interlude: On the left is the **Cinema Astro**, haunt of foreigners and students because it shows films in their original language—often in English. Opposite, the little **Vivoli Geleteria** is regarded as the home of the world's best ice-cream—not their own claim but that of numerous journalists whose framed articles are hung on the walls. Long queues in summer are commonplace but worth enduring for alcoholic zabaglioni or rich chestnut ice cream—just two of many tempting choices.

It is a stand-up only bar, so one might as well buy a tub and move on, south to the **Via Torta**, where the pronounced curve of the street reflects the outline of the Roman amphitheatre, still standing when the medieval houses were built up against its walls, and into the **Piazza Santa Croce**.

Football superstars: Here one can sit and watch young Florentines play football with all the skill and control that will surely make some of them international stars one day. Football has been played here since the 16th century—a

Santa Croce Church.

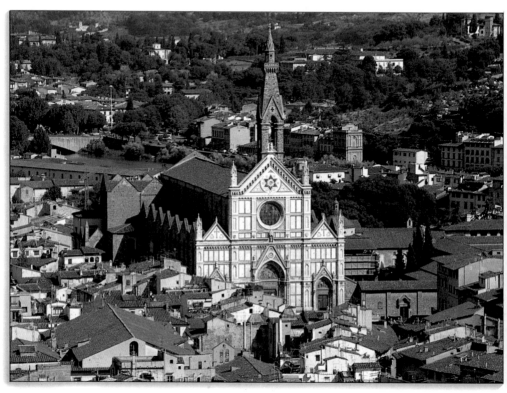

plaque on the frescoed Palazzo dell' Antella (No 21), dated 1565, marks the centre line of the pitch. The square was also used for jousting tournaments between competing teams from each of the city's wards, and for public spectacles, animal fights and fireworks, mounted by the Medici grand dukes. During the Inquisition, heretics were burned here and paintings, mirrors, embroidered clothing and other finery piled on to great "bonfires of vanity".

The church of **Santa Croce**, originally a Franciscan foundation, was one of three—with the cathedral and Santa Maria Novella—that were built and funded by the Commune, the city government, as public buildings and symbols of civic pride. It was one of the largest churches in the Christian world when built and used as a burial place for the great and the good of Florence.

The Florentine pantheon: Monuments to Dante, Petrarch, Boccaccio, Michelangelo and others attracted 19th-century travellers in great numbers, pilgrims to the shrines of the creators of western civilisation. Foreigners paid for the unfortunate 1842 neo-Gothic facade and campanile and the lifeless statue of Dante in the square.

This should not deter, for the interior is a splendid example of true Gothic, huge and airy with a richly painted ceiling and an uninterrupted view of the polygonal sanctuary whose tall lancet windows are filled with 14th-century stained glass.

A series of tombs in the aisles begins, on the right, with Vasari's monument to Michelangelo—an irony here, for the artist who left Florence, refusing to work for the repressive Medici, ended up buried beneath the tomb carved by the Medici's chief propagandist.

Next is a massive 19th-century cenotaph to Dante (who is buried in Ravenna) surmounted by an uncharacteristically crabby and introverted portrait of the poet, flanked by neo-classical female figures. Further on is an 18th-century monument to Niccolo Machia-

Piazza Santa Croce: left, feeding time; right, statue of Dante.

velli and Donatello's partly gilded stone relief of the Annunciation.

Beyond is one of the earliest and most influential funerary monuments of the Renaissance, the tomb of Leonardo Bruni—humanist, historian and eminent politician—by Rossellino (1446-7). It was widely imitated, but rarely so ineptly as in the neighbouring 19th-century tomb of the composer Rossini.

In the floor nearby are numerous *niello* work tomb slabs covering the graves of Florentine worthies. Continuing right, into the south transept, the **Castellani Chapel** is decorated with frescoes (*c.* 1385) by Agnolo Gaddi, and contains the tomb of the Countess of Albany. She was the widow of Prince Charles Edward Stuart—Bonnie Prince Charlie—who fled to Italy after defeat at the Battle of Culloden (1746) and settled in Florence under the spurious title, Count of Albany (Albion is the archaic name for Britain).

Giotto and his pupils: The **Baroncelli Chapel** contains frescoes of 1332-8,

once thought to be by Giotto, now attributed to his pupil Taddeo Gaddi, father of Agnolo. He was no slavish imitator of his teacher's work but an innovator in his own right. The scene in which the angels announce the birth of Christ to the shepherds is one of the earliest attempts to paint a night scene in fresco. A corridor to the right leads to the sacristy with its gorgeous 16th-century inlaid wooden cupboards, and a souvenir shop whose walls are hung with photographs of the 1966 flood. At the end of the corridor a chapel, usually locked, contains the tomb of Galileo, denied burial within the church because his popularisation of the Copernican view of the universe—with the sun, not the earth, at the centre—earned him the condemnation of the Inquisition.

Returning to the church, the two chapels to the right of the high altar were frescoed by Giotto. The **Bardi Chapel**, on the left, *c.* 1315-20, shows the life of St Francis, and the **Peruzzi Chapel**, right, *c.* 1326-30, depicts the lives of St

Santa Croce: night scene by Gaddi.

John the Baptist and St John the Divine. Now restored, they are the best surviving work in Florence of the man who introduced a new clarity, energy and colour into fresco and influenced generations of artists to come.

In the north transept, Donatello's wooden *Crucifixion* in the Bardi Chapel is said to be the one that his friend Brunelleschi dismissed as making Christ look like "a peasant, not a man".

Further up the north aisle, a memorial to Galileo Galilei was erected in the 18th century, in belated recognition of his fundamental contributions to modern science, and in the nave floor nearby is the tomb slab of his ancestor and namesake, a physician of some standing in 15th-century Florence.

Cloisters of serenity: The entry to the cloisters and Santa Croce museum is outside the church to the left (south). The cloister walk is lined with 19th-century monuments, fascinating for their muddled combination of Christian and pagan classical subjects and only just the right side of mawkishness. It leads to the **Pazzi Chapel**, one of the purest works of the Renaissance, a serene composition of grey stone and white walls, of arches, domes, scallops and blank arcading.

Brunelleschi planned it in 1430 but the work did not begin until 1443 and was completed after his death. It shows that even the inventor of Renaissance architecture sometimes faltered, for the fragmentary corner pilasters, squeezed into the angles, are an uncomfortable punctuation of the grand design.

The second cloister is arguably the most beautiful in Florence, completely enclosed by hemispherical arches on slender columns, with a medallion in each of the spandrils.

The **Refectory** houses detached frescoes, removed from the church to expose earlier works, and Cimabue's ruined *Crucifixion*, kept here as a reminder of the tragic consequences of the 1966 flood and a reminder of just how much great art did, in fact, survive.

North of Santa Croce, reached by walking up Via delle Pinzochere, is the **Casa Buonarroti**, the house of the man we know better by his Christian name—Michelangelo. He never lived here, but bought the property as an investment and his heirs turned it into a museum in 1858. It contains one outstanding sculpture—the *Madonna della Scala*, thought to be his earliest work, carved when he was only 15 years old. It is a remarkably humane and noble relief in which the Virgin lifts her tunic to comfort the infant Christ with the softness of her breasts whilst Joseph labours in the background.

As for the rest of the museum, it is best enjoyed as a rare glimpse inside a 16th-century palazzo, frescoed and furnished in the style of the time. Most of the exhibits are of work once attributed to Michelangelo, or paintings and sculpture inspired by his work. They only serve to highlight the difference between a great artist and the deservedly unknown.

Santa Croce: 15th-century tombs.

L'ANTICO CENTRO DELLA CITTA
DA SECOLARE SQUALLORE
A NUOVA RESTITUITO

MDCCCXCV

E' TRADIZION

CENTRAL FLORENCE

Framing the western exit from the **Piazza della Repubblica** is a triumphal arch bearing a pompous inscription to the effect that "the ancient heart of the city was restored to new life from its former squalor in 1895".

With hindsight, the message has the hollow ring of irony. The plan to develop central Florence was conceived between 1865 and 1871 when the city was, briefly, the capital of Italy. The ancient and "squalid" buildings of the former ghetto—a reminder of feudal, divided Italy— were to be swept away and replaced by broad avenues, symbolic of the new age of the United Kingdom of Italy.

Florence in peril: The site of the Roman Forum, at the heart of Florence, was chosen as the appropriate place to begin this transformation. Down came the 14th-century Mercato Vecchio—

then still the principal food market in the city—and along with it numerous cafés and taverns with names like Inferno and Purgatorio (names still preserved in the streets south of the square). These had been the haunt of artists and writers who later adopted the new café in the square, the **Giubbe Rosso** (still one of the best in Florence).

At this point, enter the interfering foreigner, determined that medieval Florence should be preserved. Was it the cries of halt that went up all over Europe that saved the city or simply lack of money to see the scheme through?

In any event, demolition ceased and the square, with its department stores and neon sky signs, remains the only modern intrusion into the heart of the city; useful as a counterpoint to the rest of Florence for, as one turns away and heads for the narrow medieval streets, the sombre old buildings seem all the more endearing for their contrast to the 19th-century pomp.

By means of Via degli Speziale and the Via del Corso, one reaches the part of the city associated with Dante. In **Corso**, opposite the Palazzo Salviati (now a bank) an alley leads to the little **church of Santa Margherita**.

The charming Beatrice: This is where Dante is said to have married Gemma Donati and, where some years earlier, he first set eyes on nine-year old Beatrice Portinari, a girl whose beauty he considered divine. Infatuated, he experienced the most violent passions on the few occasions on which he was able to speak to her, while she, heavily chaperoned and destined to marry a rich banker, regarded him as a figure of fun. Three years after her marriage she died, so that she never read the *Divine Comedy* in which Dante presented her as the embodiment of every perfection.

Nearly opposite the church, on the right, is the **Casa di Dante**, claimed as the poet's birthplace. The tower is 13th-century, the rest an attractive group of old houses restored in the 19th century

Central Florence

and joined together to create a museum of material relating to the poet's work.

A right turn leads into the tiny **Piazza San Martino**, with its 13th-century **Torre della Castagna**, one of the best preserved of the towers that once filled central Florence, soaring to 200 ft (60 metres) or more until the city government imposed a ban on structures more than 50 ft (15 metres) in height. During the turbulent 13th and 14th centuries, the private armies of warring factions organised hit and run attacks on their enemies from towers such as these.

Politics and exile: This particular tower also served, briefly in 1282, as the residence of the *priori*, awaiting the completion of the Palazzo Vecchio, the new town hall. The *priori* consisted of six members of the leading guilds, the Arte Maggiore, elected to serve two-month terms on the city council.

Dante, a member of the Guild of Physicians and Apothecaries (books were, then, sold in apothecary shops), was elected to the *priorate* to serve between 15 June and 15 August 1300. In 1302 he was sentenced to two years' exile on a false charge of corruption during his term of office, part of a mass purge of supporters of the emperor by supporters of the pope. Dante chose never to return to Florence, preferring a life of solitary wandering, during which he wrote his best poetry.

From here, the Via Dante Alighieri and Via dei Tavolini lead to **Via del Calzaioli**. This street, originally Roman, was the principal thoroughfare of medieval Florence, linking the cathedral and the Piazza della Signoria.

Before being pedestrianised, it was such a busy street that anyone who stopped to admire a building was likely to be jostled off the narrow pavement into the road, risking injury from an impatient stream of traffic. Now it is a pleasant shopping street, busy with street vendors, selling leather goods and jewellery, who gather up their make-shift stalls and melt into the back alleys at the first sign of a police uniform.

What now hampers the tourist's appreciation of the buildings is the scaffolding and hoardings of restorers which temporarily cover much of **Orsanmichele**. This eighth-century oratory of St Michael—hence the name—was replaced by a grain market in 1239. When that burnt down it was rebuilt, in 1337, as an open market. In 1380 the arcades were filled in and the ground floor converted to a church, while the upper storey was used as an emergency grain store, to be drawn on in times of siege or famine.

The new aesthetics: A scheme to decorate the exterior was launched in 1339. Each of the major guilds was allocated a niche, to be filled with a statue of their respective patron saints. The Black Death intervened so that the first statues were not commissioned until the early 15th century and they illustrate well the contemporary emergence of the new Renaissance aesthetic.

Donatello's outstanding *St George*, hailed as the first truly Renaissance

Dante's birthplace, Via Dante Alighieri.

164

statue, is here represented by a bronze copy of the marble original, now in the Bargello. Near to it, on the north side (in Via San Michele) is Nanni di Banco's *Four Crowned Saints* (*c*. 1415) with an interesting frieze below illustrating the work of carpenters and masons, whose guild commissioned the work.

The west face is decorated with elaborate Gothic cartwheel tracery and faces the **Palazzo dell' Arte della Lana**, the Guildhall of the Wool Workers, as might be guessed from the numerous Lamb of God emblems that decorate the facade. This building provides access, by means of an overhead bridge, to the splendid Gothic vaulted grain store above the church, occasionally used for exhibitions. The statues on the south side and east front of Orsanmichele (mostly covered for restoration) are still recognisably in the international Gothic style.

The odd arrangement of Orsanmichele's dark interior was dictated by the form of the building. In place of the usual nave flanked by aisles, the central arcade of the original open market divides the church into two parallel naves of equal size.

Miraculous image: The southernmost nave is dominated by Andrea Orcagna's huge tabernacle (1439-59), encrusted with coloured glass. In the centre, scarcely visible behind the cherubs and votive offerings, is a *Madonna* by Bernardo Daddi, painted in 1347 to replace one that appeared miraculously on a pillar of the old grain market before its destruction by fire. The base of the tabernacle is decorated with scenes from the Life of the Virgin.

The **Mercato Nuovo** is reached by taking the Via Lamberti and turning left into the Via Calimala. A market has existed here since the 11th century and the current arcade was built in 1547-51 for the sale of silk and gold.

Later it gained the name "straw market" from the woven goods sold there by peasants from the countryside. Cheap and colourful straw souvenirs are still

Il Porcellino, in the Mercato Nuovo.

sold but, as elsewhere in Florence, leather goods and T-shirts now form the bulk of the market's offerings. At night and at weekends, buskers of varying degrees of talent perform here, deprived of their more lucrative pitches in the Piazza della Signoria for the duration of the excavations.

One seedy and litter-strewn corner of the piazza nevertheless attracts countless visitors. They come to rub the well-polished snout of **Il Porcellino**, the bronze boar copied from the Roman one in the Uffizi, itself a copy of a Hellenic original. It is said that anyone who rubs the snout is certain to return to the city. Coins dropped in the trough below are distributed to city charities.

The southern exit to the square, past a popular tripe vendor's stall, leads to the **Piazza Santa Maria Sovraporta**, completely surrounded by medieval buildings. On the right are two 14th-century palaces, and, on the left, the 13th-century **Palazzo di Parte Guelfa** (open only for the occasional exhibi-

tion), enlarged by Brunelleschi in the 15th century and given its external staircase by Vasari in the 16th.

This was the official residence of the political faction that ruled the city from the mid-13th to the mid-14th centuries, when Cosimo de' Medici's pragmatic leadership put an end to the Guelf/Ghibelline feud that had split Florence for the preceding 150 years.

Just round the corner, in the Via Porto Rossa, is the **Palazzo Davanzati**, a museum that must be visited for an insight into life in medieval Florence—considerably more luxurious than would appear from the dour exterior. This could though, on festive occasions, be gay and colourful, for the long iron poles, bracketed out from the façade, were used to carry banners and flags during feast days and carnival.

Otherwise, the plainness of the façade, as with most 14th-century Florentine palaces, is relieved only by the typically Tuscan depressed window arches that thicken to a slight point at the

Palazzo di Parte Guelfa.

apex, and the coat of arms of the Davanzati family. They acquired the property in 1578 and owned it until 1838 when the last of the family committed suicide.

An antiquarian, Elia Volpi, bought it in 1904 and restored it sympathetically as a private museum, which was acquired by the state in 1951. Most Florentine palaces are still owned by the descendants of the first owners; this one, uniquely, is open to the public.

The vaulted entrance hall was designed primarily for protection, enabling the inner courtyard to be cut off from the street in times of trouble. Later, it was subdivided into three wool shops, much as contemporary owners lease the ground floors of their palaces for use as shops, offices and galleries.

Domestic life revolved around the delightful inner courtyard, a peaceful retreat open to the sky but shaded from the sun by the high surrounding walls. A well in the corner by the entrance supplied all five floors—a rare luxury at a time when most households depended on public fountains for their water supply. From here, a graceful external staircase of banded white and grey stone rises on corbels and wall brackets to the upper floors.

Splendid interiors: The living quarters, with their gorgeous wall hangings, frescoes and painted ceilings, begin on the first floor. The **Sala Madornale** is above the entrance hall and four holes in the floor enabled missiles to be dropped on would-be intruders. The **Sala dei Pappagalli**—Room of the Parrots—is named after the bird motif that covers the walls, in rich reds and blues, imitating, in fresco, fabric wall hangings. The windows, now filled with leaded lights, were originally fitted with turpentine-soaked cloth to repel water and admit some light.

Off the little child's bedroom is one of several medieval bathrooms, complete with lavatory and bath tub. In the main bedroom the sparseness of the furnishings is compensated for by the warmth and splendour of the wall paintings, a running frieze of trees and birds above armorial shields.

The bedroom above is even more sumptuously painted with scenes from the French romance *La Châtelaine de Vergy*. The small room off is used to display exquisite antique lace.

The top floor was the domain of the women, the usual site of the kitchen so that smoke and cooking smells would not penetrate the living rooms. According to contemporary accounts of household management, women were virtual slaves to the kitchen, spinning and weaving when they were not preparing meals, rarely leaving the house except for church and festivals.

Even today, it is said that the daughters of the Florentine aristocracy are accompanied by a chaperone wherever they go. In some respects, little has changed in the city since Dante first caught a fleeting glimpse of his beloved Beatrice and fed his fertile imagination for decades to come on a few equally brief encounters.

Davanzati Palace Courtyard.

FLORENCE OF
THE MEDICI

Cosimo I, Duke of Florence and later Grand Duke of Tuscany, consolidated his grip on the newly created Principality of Florence by moving out of the ancestral palace and into the Palazzo Vecchio in 1540. In doing so, he left behind an area of the city that had been home to the Medici for generations, the place from which an earlier Medici dynasty had been content to rule.

Nevertheless, the family connection with the parish remained so strong that every Medici of any consequence would always return, albeit in a coffin, for burial in the family chapel, attached to the church of San Lorenzo.

Under Cosimo de' Medici (later called Cosimo il Vecchio, the elder), Piero the Gouty and Lorenzo the Magnificent, this area of the city, north of the cathedral, was the centre of power from 1434 to 1492. It is now neither beautiful nor especially imposing. The Medici Palace has become simply the familiar backdrop to the everyday life of the city, the nearby streets littered with the debris of the Mercato Centrale, the central market, while San Lorenzo is obscured by the canvas awnings of souvenir and cheap clothes stalls.

But then again, perhaps it has always been like this—busy, noisy, a mixed-up jumble of the almost splendid and the almost squalid, home to the city's richest and poorest inhabitants. Above all, in the time of the early Medici, it must have seemed one great construction site, with masons, carpenters and tile makers busy on the dome of the nearby cathedral and Cosimo de' Medici himself one of the busiest builders.

Quest for immortality: Cosimo de' Medici has been described as a man with a passion for building, convinced that what he built would, like the monuments of ancient Rome, last 1,000 years or more and immortalise his name. He commissioned scores of buildings, not just in Florence but as far away as Paris and Jerusalem—cities in which the Medici name was associated with the banking empire founded by his father, Giovanni.

Ironically, and perhaps inevitably, he did not always see the finished product. His own palace, the Palazzo Medici, now the **Medici-Riccardi Palace** (incorporating the name of its later owners) was begun in 1444 but was still not complete when he moved in, in 1459, five years before his death.

The simple life: Looking at it now, it seems like any other Florentine palace, but it was the prototype, the one that set the standard for many another family home, and if it looks a little dull, that was entirely deliberate. Cosimo carefully cultivated the image of a man of few pretensions, a man concerned with matters of the mind rather than with material finery. Vasari says that he rejected the first palace plans, drawn up by Brunelleschi, because they were too ostentatious, and, instead, chose his favourite architect, Michelozzo, to design something simpler.

Today it looks more elaborate than it originally was, because the simple arches of the ground floor, once an open loggia, were given their classical, pedimented windows by Michelangelo in the 16th century. The only real concession to ornament are the Gothic-style windows of the upper floors—recalling those of the 13th-century Palazzo Vecchio—and the much simplified classical cornice.

Inside, the main courtyard deliberately evokes the monastic cloister, for Cosimo was a religious man given to taking retreats in the specially reserved cell of the Dominican priory, San Marco, his own foundation. Antique Roman inscriptions and friezes set into the walls recall that he was also a keen scholar of the classical, who hired agents to scour Europe and the Near East for ancient manuscripts.

A small garden beyond the courtyard harks back to the medieval, but, like so

Preceding pages: Dante meets moder Florentines; the church of San Lorenzo; Palazzo Medici-Riccardi. Below, San Lorenzo market.

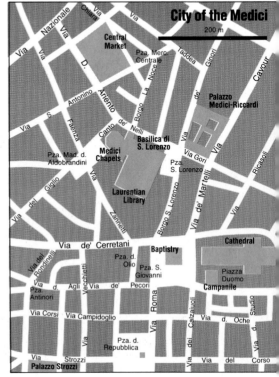

City of the Medici

much of the palace, it looks sparser because it now lacks the antique sculptures and art treasures—including Donatello's *Judith and Holofernes*—that went to the Uffizi and Pitti Palace when the Medici moved out.

Only one room, the **Medici Chapel**, retains its 15th-century appearance—many of the rest were altered after the Riccardi family bought the palace in 1659 and again, more recently, when they were converted into the offices of the Town Prefecture. The chapel frescoes were commissioned by Piero, Cosimo's sickly eldest son (known as the Gouty) and were painted by Gozzoli in 1459.

Piero's liking for rich colours, in contrast to the simple taste of his father, is well reflected in these gorgeous scenes of the *Journey of the Magi*, with their retinue, passing through an idealised vision of the Tuscan landscape. Members of the Medici family are identified by ostrich feather emblems, and the third king is, perhaps, Piero's son,

Procession of the Magi, Palazzo Medici-Riccardi.

Lorenzo (known as the Magnificent), leader of the city from the age of 20 until his death 23 years later, in 1492.

The Medici-Riccardi Palace backs on to the **Piazza San Lorenzo**, where the equestrian statue of Giovanni delle Bande Nere, by Bandinelli (1540), looks out of place amid the bustle of the modern street market. Above the sea of canvas awnings rises the dome of **San Lorenzo**, unmistakably the work of Brunelleschi, cousin to his cathedral dome, and partnered by the smaller cupola of Michelangelo.

Supreme serenity: The façade is rough and unfinished (Michelangelo's design, which can be seen in the Casa Buonarroti, was never built) but the interior is outstanding, a gracious composition of the aptly named grey stone *pietra serena* and white walls. It is one of the earliest and most harmonious of all Renaissance churches, representing a break with French Gothic and a return to an older, classical style.

Giovanni, father of Cosimo de'

Medici, commissioned Brunelleschi to design the church in 1419, but the vicissitudes of the Medici banking empire meant that progress was halting and neither Giovanni nor Brunelleschi lived to see it complete. Thereafter, successive members of the Medici family continued to embellish it, commissioning the greatest artists of their age to add frescoes, paintings and—ultimately—their mausoleum.

The two great tank-like bronze pulpits, in the nave, include reliefs by Donatello (*c.* 1460)—the crowded and realistic Deposition and Resurrection scenes—that are among his last and most mature works.

Beneath Brunelleschi's great soaring dome, in front of the high altar, a massive inlaid marble slab covers the grave of Cosimo de' Medici, buried here in great pomp—despite his characteristic request for a simple funeral—in 1464, after which he was posthumously awarded the title *Pater Patriae*—father of his country.

Harmony of the spheres: On the left, off the north transept, the **Old Sacristy** (often closed) contains the monuments of his parents and two grandchildren, near a dome covered with remarkable rich blue frescoes depicting the night sky and the positions of the signs of the zodiac as they were when the ceiling was painted in 1442.

Nearby, the restored Bronzino fresco of the *Martyrdom of St Lawrence* (1565-69) is a masterful study of the human form in a multitude of contorted gestures, bending to stoke the fire beneath the martyr's gridiron, pumping the bellows and altogether, in their nudity, forming an ironic counterpoint to the notice in the church entrance requesting visitors to "rigorously avoid the wearing of indecent clothes such as mini-skirts and shorts".

The *cantoria* (singing gallery) above the cloister entrance, copying the style of Donatello, is no great work but is one of the few to have survived in its original position. Next to it is another rarity,

San Lorenzo holy water stoup.

a modern painting by Annigoni—perhaps the only truly great artist to have worked in Florence since the 17th century—showing Joseph and Christ in a carpenter's workshop against the hills of Tuscany and a blood-red sky, symbolic of Christ's sacrifice.

The quiet cloister, with its box-lined lawns and pomegranate bushes, gives access to the **Laurentian Library**, designed by Michelangelo between 1524 and 1534 to house the important collection of classical manuscripts begun by Cosimo de' Medici, including the famous fifth-century Virgil codex and the eighth-century *Codex Amiatinus* from the monastery at Jarrow in England.

The books are too precious to be on display, but the library vestibule is open—a dramatic and sophisticated design which shows Michelangelo trying to cram too many elements into a tiny space, brilliantly inventive but needing a room many times bigger for the ideas to be fully worked out. By

contrast, the interior of the library (visible only through the locked glass doors), also by Michelangelo, is deliberately simple and serene, a scholar's room with no visual distractions, lined with lectern-like reading benches.

Grand ducal shrines: The entrance to the **Medici Chapels** is in the Piazza Madonna degli Aldobrandini, behind the church. The plain entrance crypt is floored with simple slabs that cover the graves of cardinals and archbishops, first, second and third wives of Medici princes and those who luxuriated in grander titles—dukes, grand-dukes and electors palatinate—the heirs and successors of this merchant family turned rulers of Florence.

Stairs lead upwards from here to the opulent **Chapel of the Princes**, so ambitious in its use of costly marbles and semi-precious stone that, from its beginning in 1604, it took nearly 300 years to complete. Each of the four great sarcophagi, big enough to contain a score or more burials, is surmounted by

San Lorenzo cloisters.

a crown, a monument to imperial pretensions and a symbol of *nouveau riche* wealth and power.

Two niches contain bronze statues of the deceased dukes, those of Cosimo II and Ferdinando I. The other three, Cosimos II and III and Francisco I, were planned but never executed. The only details that really delight are the 16 colourful intarsia coats of arms, one for each of the principal towns in Tuscany.

These are the tombs of 16th and 17th-century rulers. A passage off, to the left, leads to Michelangelo's **New Sacristy** and his masterful tombs of an earlier generation of the family. On the right, the reclining figures of Night and Day adorn the monument to Giuliano, son of Lorenzo the Magnificent, and, on the left, Dawn and Dusk sit below the meditative statue of Lorenzo, grandson of the Magnificent. Neither of these two minor Medici played any significant role in the history of the city and only the sculpture—some would claim Michelangelo's greatest work—has kept alive their names.

One of the few Medici worthy a monument by Michelangelo, Lorenzo the Magnificent himself, the popular and talented poet, philosopher, patron of the great artists of his day, as well as politician, is buried here in near-anonymity. Above his tomb is Michelangelo's *Madonna and Child*, intended as part of an unfinished monument to Lorenzo.

Michelangelo the rebel: Despite the quality of the work he did for them, Michelangelo never really enjoyed working for the Medici. The New Sacristy was commissioned by Popes Leo X and Clement VII, both of whom were descended, lineally, from Cosimo de' Medici, and Michelangelo resented the manner in which they, and their relatives, were subverting the old republican political institutions which Cosimo and Lorenzo had guided so adroitly. This is reflected in the sombre mood of the sculpture and the incompleteness of the Sacristy—Michelangelo only worked on it by fits and starts in 1520 and again in 1530-33. In the period between these two dates Michelangelo was an active opponent of the Medici. The family was expelled from the city in 1527, but it soon became apparent that they intended to return and take Florence by force, backed by the mighty army of the emperor. Michelangelo supervised the construction of fortifications around the hilltop church of San Miniato and established a battery of cannons in the campanile, enabling the city, briefly, to withstand the seige.

In 1530, however, the city fell to the superior force of the imperial army and Michelangelo went into hiding in this very sacristy. The walls of the small room to the left of the altar is covered in pencil sketches thought to have been drawn at that time. These are not normally shown to the public, but a number of Michelangelo's drawings for column bases are visible on the walls either side of the altar, along with graffiti sketched by his pupils.

Below, *Night* by Michelangelo. Right, the Mercato Centrale.

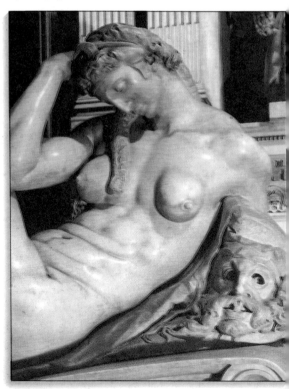

178

THE UNIVERSITY QUARTER

The area north of the cathedral, now occupied by the buildings of Florence's university, was once very much an extension of the Medici domain. The **Piazza San Marco**, where today the students gather between lectures, is named after the convent and cloisters on the north side of the square, whose construction was financed by Cosimo de' Medici.

An older convent on the site was in ruins when Dominican friars from Fiesole took it over in 1436, and the following year, at Cosimo's request, the architect Michelozzi began to rebuild it. The church, remodelled subsequently, is of little interest, but the cloisters and monastic buildings contain outstanding paintings and frescoes by Fra Angelico, who spent much of his life within the walls of this peaceful monastery.

A passionate art: Henry James said of Fra Angelico that all his paintings convey a passionate pious tenderness and that "immured in his quiet convent, he never received an intelligible impression of evil". That may be true of most of his work, but he did not entirely lack the imagination to conceive the horrors of eternal punishment. In the **Pilgrims' Hospice**, the first room on the right of the cedar-filled cloister, his lively *Last Judgement* is one of the most intriguing of the many altar pieces he painted.

The Blessed gather in a lovely garden below the walls of the Heavenly City, but the Damned are being disembowelled and fed into the mouth of Hell, there to undergo a series of tortures appropriate to their sins: the gluttons are forced to eat snakes and toads, the gold of the misers is melted down and poured down their throats.

Gentler by far, and richly coloured, is one of his most accomplished works, the *Tabernacle of the Linaiuoli*, commissioned in 1443 by the flax-workers' guild, and depicting the Madonna enthroned and surrounded by saints.

Across the courtyard, in the **Chapter House**, is Fra Angelico's great and expressive *Crucifixion* (*c.* 1442)—Vasari reports that the artist wept whenever he painted this subject. The angry red sky, reminiscent of Gerard Manley Hopkins's equally mystical sonnet, *The Wrecht of the Deutscheland* ("And Christ's Blood streams across the firmament"), invites comparisons with the paintings of Van Gogh. It throws the pallid flesh of Christ and the two thieves into high relief.

In the small **Refectory**, at the foot of the dormitory stairs, the *Last Supper* is by Ghirlandaio. A small cat occupies the focal position at the bottom of the fresco, adding to the extraordinary naturalism, in which each apostle is individually characterised and the tableware and garden scene reveal much about 15th-century style and taste.

Mystical surrealism: The **Dormitory** is the high point of the museum, consisting of 44 monastic cells under a great

The University Quarter

200 m

open roof. Fra Angelico's *Annunciation* greets visitors at the top of the stairs and, beyond, each cell contains a small fresco, intended as an aid to contemplation, stripped to the essential religious significance, unlike the gorgeous and crowded paintings commissioned by the guilds and rich patrons.

Cells 1 to 10, on the left, are probably the work of Fra Angelico, the rest by his assistants. Cell 7, the *Mocking of Christ*, is typical of his mystical, almost surrealistic style, where, against a black background representing the darkness of night, disembodied hands beat him about the head, and others count out the 30 pieces of silver, the price paid to Judas for his betrayal.

Scourge of the sensuous: Cells 12 to 14 were occupied by Savonarola as prior of the monastery—the man who, according to Harold Acton, brought to Florence a brief and bloodthirsty return to the Middle Ages. It is difficult to separate the man from the deeds that were committed in his name. He him-

self was a sincere believer in the futility of earthly deeds and passions, a man who saw only the afterlife as important.

Yet, after the death of Lorenzo the Magnificent, in 1492, until his execution for fomenting civil strife, in 1498, Savonarola ruled the city with puritanical zeal. He was at first welcomed by the people as a liberator, but their joy turned to revulsion as their pleasures—everything from carnival to the possession of mirrors—became a crime punishable by torture.

The cells contain Savonarola's hair shirt and a copy of a contemporary painting of his execution, an event which caused a riot in the city. Having been struck a mortal blow by the executioner, Savonarola's body was raised on a pile of faggots and set on fire. Suddenly, the flames and smoke cleared and the dead Savonarola was seen to raise his hand in blessing. Terrified Florentines fought to escape from the square and many died in the stampede.

The other wing of the Dormitory

San Marco Dormitory, the *Mocking of Christ*.

184

leads past the **Library** designed by Michelozzi in 1441, a graceful pillared hall built to house the illuminated manuscripts donated by Cosimo de' Medici to create the world's first public library. The cells which Cosimo reserved for his own frequent retreats are at the end of the corridor.

Back in the Piazza San Marco, the Via Cavour, in the north western corner, leads past the **Casino Mediceo**, a pretty house ornamented with ram's heads and scallops. The garden (hidden behind a high wall) once contained Cosimo's collection of antique sculpture (now in the Uffizi) which Michelangelo studied ardently as an adolescent.

Further up, on the left, is the **Palazzo Pandolfini**, a country villa designed by Raphael in 1520, one of his few architectural works to have survived. The entrance provides views of the peaceful gardens and the façade is decorated with playful dolphins, a pun on the name of the owner, Bishop Pandolfini.

On the northeastern side of the Piazza San Marco are the buildings now occupied by the **University** administration. They were built originally as stables for the horses and wild animals, including lions, kept by Duke Cosimo I. The Via Georgio La Pira leads to the **Giardino dei Semplici** (open mornings Mondays, Wednesdays and Fridays), a delightful botanical garden begun by Duke Cosimo in 1545.

On the southeastern side of the square is one of the oldest loggias in Florence (built in 1384). It leads to the **Accademia di Belle Arti**, originally part of the Accademia del Designo (of draughtsmanship), the world's first school of art, established in 1563 with Michelangelo as one of the founding academicians.

The Michelangelo controversy: It is thus an appropriate home for his most famous sculptures, including the original *David*, although art historians have never been happy with the decision to move it here. They argue that it is impossible to appreciate fully, divorced from its original context and hemmed in

Savonarola,
by Fra
Bartolommeo.

by grey walls and low ceilings. Many will find the crowds an even bigger impediment, for this statue attracts more visitors than any other work of art in Florence.

"*Il Biancone*" as he is known to Florentines (the big white one—the reference is intentionally lewd) was commissioned in 1501 to celebrate the new democratic constitution which followed the expulsion of the Medici and then the execution of Savonarola. David, the boy who defeated the giant Goliath, was chosen to symbolise the rebirth of the republic after the 10 years of tyranny that followed the death of Lorenzo the Magnificent.

Completed in 1504, a commission of leading artists was set up to decide on the placement of the statue. The options of the Loggia dei Lanzi and the cathedral steps were rejected in favour of the front of the Palazzo Vecchio, where it stood until 1873, when it was replaced by a copy and the original moved here.

The eternal legacy: The marble from which *David* was carved had been rejected as faulty by other sculptors, but Michelangelo took up the challenge of using the fault lines and discoloration in the block as an integral part of his carving. His belief that the sculptor's job was to liberate the form already in the stone—exploiting naturally occurring cracks and faults—has now become one of the accepted "truths" of art, and idea that has inspired many a subsequent sculptor. A good example is Henry Moore, whose work so often seems to be prefigured in Michelangelo's creations—especially his "unfinished" masterpieces.

Some of these are also displayed in the Accademia, notably the *Four Slaves* (*c*.1519-36) which were intended for the tomb of Pope Julius II in Rome. Many would argue that they are the more powerful for being left in a raw, unfinished state since the figures seem to be caught up in an elemental struggle to free themselves from their stone-bound enslavement.

Michelangelo's *David*, in the Accademia and right, students of the Academy today.

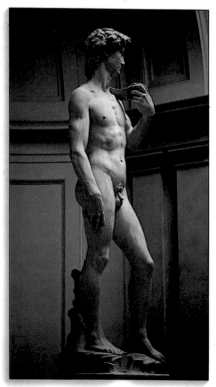

Orgy of nudes: A recently opened room on the left of the Salone di Michelangelo is packed with plaster casts made by 19th-century academicians. Some are dull but many are inspired, especially those of the prolific Lorenzo Bartolini who deserves a museum to himself. They include his renowned *Machiavelli* and numerous nudes, copies of which now fill the art galleries of the Via dei Fossi not to mention the gardens of villas and stately homes throughout Europe.

From the Accademia, Via Ricasoli leads south to its junction with Via degli Alfani and the **Conservatorio**. When its restoration is completed, it will once again house the collection of rare musical instruments currently on display in the Palazzo Vecchio. Midway down the Via degli Alfani, the **Opificio delle Pietre Dure** has a small museum devoted to the art of decorating furniture with semi-precious stone (*pietre dure*).

A left turn into the **Via dei Servi** leads to the **Piazza Santissima Annunziata**, a lovely square almost completely surrounded by a colonnade. The fair held here on the feast of the Annunciation (25 March) fills it with festive stalls selling homemade biscuits and sweets, but for rest of the year it is a peaceful, traffic-free haven.

Miracle of the Virgin: To the north is the **church of the Annunciation** (1516-25), still a living church which has not become a tourist haunt and one which is far more typical of the rest of Italy than it is of Florence. Compared to the rational interiors of so many of the city's churches, this one is heavily ornamented. Devout Florentines come in and out all day to pray before the candle-lit baldacchino that is so cluttered with votive offerings that the object of their veneration is almost hidden; it is an image of the Virgin, said to have been painted miraculously by an angel.

The portico of the church is interesting for its frescoes, several of which were painted by Andrea del Sarto. Though damaged, his *Coming of the*

Innocenti
Orphanage,
Brunelleschi's
Loggia.

Magi is still a rich and colourful scene in which the three kings are accompanied by an entourage of giraffes, camels and splendidly dressed courtiers. The **Ciostro dei Morti** (Cloister of the Dead) to the left of the church contains more of his frescoes and the burial vaults of many leading 16th and 17th-century artists, including Cellini.

To the east of the square is the **Spedale degli Innocenti**, the world's first orphanage, opened in 1445 and still operating as such. The colonnade, built by Brunelleschi beginning in 1419, was the first of the city's classical loggias and the inspiration behind all the others. The glazed terracotta roundels, added c.1487 by Andrea della Robbia, depict babies wrapped in swaddling clothes—the emblem of the orphanage.

The museum within is not much visited and is a quiet, cool retreat in summer. It occupies the upper rooms of the cloister, from which there are views on to the green courtyard and Brunelleschi's slender Ionic columns.

Above, the spandrils are decorated with *sgraffito*—drawings of infants and cherubs scratched into the plaster when it was still wet.

Many of the frescoes in the museum came from nearby churches, removed to expose earlier paintings beneath. Several are displayed with their *sinopia* alongside. These were the sketches roughed out in the plaster using red pigment (obtained from Sinope, on the Black Sea) to guide the artist when the finishing coat of plaster was added and the finished fresco painted.

The former nursery contains paintings commissioned for the orphanage, nearly all of them variations on the theme of the *Madonna and Child*. The most remarkable is the radiantly colourful *Adoration* by Ghirlandaio. The rich nativity scene in the foreground contrasts poignantly with the scenes of slaughter—the Massacre of the Innocents—portrayed in the background of the picture.

To the east of the Piazza, the **Via**

Piazza Santissima Annunziata.

della Collona leads to Florence's **Archaeological Museum**, which contains one of the best collections of Etruscan art in Italy, apart from the National Museum in Tarquinia. Badly hit by the 1966 flood, restoration work is still in progress and a long way from complete; the reconstructions of Etruscan tombs in the courtyard are still closed and, in case after case, outstanding bronzework is poorly conserved and suffering from verdigris.

This deters many visitors, so the museum is rarely crowded. It is a pleasure to browse here peacefully but the fact that Egyptian treasures have been well-restored while the indigenous art of ancient Florence and Tuscany has not is cause for some sadness.

Work has begun, though, and recently restored pieces are displayed on the ground floor. Here two outstanding figures representing Apollo (dated some time between 530 and 510 B.C.) demonstrate both the Hellenic origins of Etruscan art and the astounding similarities between the work of the Renaissance and the Etruscan sculptors, though separated by two millennia.

Heroism and immortality: The Etruscan tomb sculpture on the first floor seems, at first, a mass of hunting and battle scenes taken from the heroic myth of the Greeks. Little by little, though, one discovers the domestic scenes that were carved from real life rather than copied from Hellenic prototypes: banquet scenes, athletic dancers, coffins carved in the shape of Etruscan houses with columns and entrance gates and (see exhibit 5539) an arch that can be paralleled in many a 15th-century Florentine palace. Above the tombs the reclining figures of the dead are all obese and garlanded, a wine bowl in their hands, symbolising the eternal feasting and sensual pleasures of the afterlife.

The room devoted to bronze work shows another aspect of the Etruscan culture that the Florentine artists of the Renaissance later inherited: their skill in bronze casting. Here are delicate mirrors inscribed with erotic scenes, cooking pots, military equipment and harnesses, statues and jewellery.

Two of the most important pieces were excavated in the 16th century when Florentine artists, aware of the brilliant work of predecessors, went in search of the finest examples. The fifth-century B.C. *Chimera*, discovered at Arezzo in 1553, was entrusted to Cellini who repaired its broken foreleg, and the *Orator* (c. second century B.C.) was discovered in Trasimeno in 1566.

The Egyptian collection resulted from the joint French-Italian expedition of 1828-89. It includes a chariot from a 14th-century B.C. tomb at Thebes, but equally compelling is the large quantity of organic materials that survived in the arid, oxygenless atmosphere of the ancient desert tombs: wooden furniture, ropes, baskets, cloth hats and purses, all looking as fresh as if they had been made only recently and throwing an illuminating light on the ordinary life of the ancient Egyptians.

Innocenti
Orphanage
roundels by
Andrea Della
Robbia.

SANTA MARIA NOVELLA

If so many of the sights of Florence are frustratingly "closed for restoration", the compensating pleasure is the revelation that occurs when the scaffolding is removed and the newly restored frescoes are back on view. Details lost under centuries of grime—details that even the great art historians who rediscovered the Renaissance in the 19th century never saw—are exposed again in all their original clarity, and the colours have all the brilliance of freshly applied paint.

It is this which makes **Santa Maria Novella** such a rewarding church, despite its unpromising location. It lies by the **railway station**, the first building that most visitors to Florence see and the first building in Italy to be designed in the Functionalist style. Its appearance was summed up well by the joke that greeted its unveiling in 1935: "I see

Preceding pages: Via Maggio. Left, Piazza Santa Maria Novella.

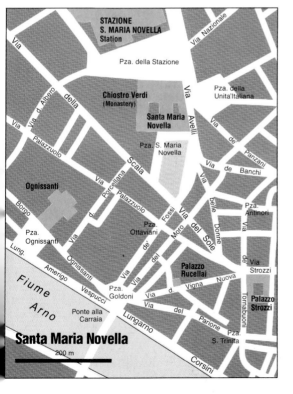

Santa Maria Novella

200 m

the box the station came in, but where is the station?"

As for the square in front of Santa Maria, it could be anywhere in Italy except for Florence. It lies within the 14th-century city walls but the city's population never grew to fill the newly enclosed space. Instead it remained an undeveloped corner on the western edge of the city used, from 1568 on, for annual chariot races: the obelisks supported on bronze turtles either end of the square mark the turning points on the race track.

In the 19th century the square was peaceful and its new hotels were popular with foreign visitors. Henry James, Ralph Waldo Emerson and Longfellow, translator of Dante, all wrote from rooms that looked down on the quiet, green piazza.

Today the foreigners that come to the square are the Filipino housemaids who gather on Sundays to complain about their wages and their mistresses in a polyglot mixture of English, Italian, Tagalog and the multiple dialects of the Philippines. Old ladies scatter bread for the huge flocks of mangey pigeons that infest the square and gangs of youths stand around looking slightly menacing and probably dealing in drugs.

Romanesque style: The church itself, though, is friendly enough, with its delicate white and grey/green marble façade. Building began in 1246, starting at the east end. The lower part of the façade, in typically Florentine Romanesque style, was added around 1360. Another 100 years passed before the completion of the upper part of the façade; the inscription below the pediment dates it to 1470 and includes the name *Ihanes Oricellarius*—the Latinised form of Giovanni Rucellai who commissioned the work from Battista Alberti.

The Rucellai were one of the great Florentine families (their name betrays the source of the wealth since *oricello* was a costly red dye made from a lichen imported from Majorca). They formed a marriage alliance with the Medici in 1461 and symbols of the two families decorate the intricately inlaid façade: the billowing ship's sail, stylised to an abstract pattern, of the Rucellai and the ring and ostrich feather of the Medici.

Fear of plague: To the right of the church, the walled **Old Cemetery** with its cypress trees is lined with the tomb recesses of many a noble Florentine, and the lavishness of the church interior owes much to the wealth of these same families. Frightened into thoughts of eternity by the Black Death that devastated the city in the 14th century they donated lavish chapels and works of art in memory of their ancestors.

It was here, in this church, that Boccaccio set the beginning of *The Decameron* when a group of young noblemen and women meet and agree to shut themselves away to avoid contact with the disease, and entertain each other by telling stories.

The basic structure of the church is Gothic, but not the florid French style—rather a rationalised and toned-down version. Pointed arches and simple rib vaults are supported by widely spaced classical columns. The only architectural decoration comes from the alternate bands of white marble and soft grey *pietra serena*.

The best of the many monuments and frescoed chapels are at the east end. In the south transept (on the right) is the **Capella di Filippo Strozzi**, frescoed by Filippino Lippi, son of Filippo Lippi and Lucrezia—the nun he seduced while painting the walls of the Carmelite convent in Prato.

In style and subject matter, Filippino's work is nothing like that of his father, nor, indeed, that of any of his own contemporaries. His *St Philip*, standing in front of the Temple of Mars with the dragon he has just slain, is full of classical, rather than Christian allusions, and his crowd-filled scenes and remarkable *trompe l'oeil* architecture are brimming with energy.

Artistic vulgarity: Behind the altar the

Santa Maria Novella and the railway station.

late 15th-century frescoes by Ghirlandaio and his pupils (including, perhaps, the young Michelangelo) are among the most vibrantly colourful and entertaining in Florence. The *Life of the Virgin* is set in the Florence of the artist's own time, replete with details of everyday life and many actual portraits of members of the Tornabuoni family who commissioned the work. The stunningly fresh colours are almost gaudy, the pop art of its time, and the work was dismissed contemptuously by Ruskin as verging on the vulgar.

In the north transept, the **Strozzi Chapel** has frescoes by Nardo di Cione, painted 1351-7. *The Inferno*, based on Dante's vision, is a maze of demons and tortured souls while *Paradiso* is crowded with the saved, including portraits of Dante himself and the patrons, members of the Strozzi banking family, being led to heaven by an angel.

The entrance to the cloister is to the left of the church façade. It is called the **Chiostro Verde** after the frescoes (now in the Refectory) of Piero Uccello, painted in green pigment called *terra verde*. Ironically his major masterpiece, the *Universal Deluge* (*c*.1445), was severely damaged by the 1966 flood.

On the north side of the cloister is the **Spanish Chapel**, originally built around 1350 as the chapter house and renamed in the 16th century when the entourage of Eleonora di Toledo (wife of Cosimo I) adopted it as their place of worship. The fresco cycle painted by Andrea di Firenze (1365-7) represents the teachings of St Thomas Aquinas and includes a depiction of Florence cathedral complete with a dome which did not then exist—nor did it for another 100 years.

Venus for sale: From here there is a choice of routes to Ognissanti, of which **Via dei Fossi** has most to offer. It has the greatest concentration of art galleries in the city, some specialising in original paintings and others stacked to the ceilings with reproduction *Davids*, *Venuses* and female nudes, available in

The Old Cemetery, Santa Maria Novella.

every size from mantlepiece ornaments to monumental pieces for the courtyard or garden.

Alternatively, Via della Scala offers one of the few *art nouveau* buildings in Florence (No. 26), with exuberant bronze balconies, lamps and window boxes. The frescoed pharmacy (No. 16) sells fragrant soaps, toilet waters and pot pourri from the former premises of the Officina di Santa Maria Novella.

The **Piazza Ognissanti** is open to the river bank and the hotel buildings either side frame the view of Santa Maria del Carmine, on the opposite bank, and the hills of Bellosguardo beyond. Once the view would have been obscured by the many buildings that were erected across the river at this point, standing on wooden piles, to make use of the water in the processes of washing, fulling and dyeing cloth.

The church of **Ognissanti** (All Souls) was itself built by an order of monks, the Umiliati, who supported themselves by wool processing. It was completed in 1239 but in later years came under the patronage of the Vespucci family, merchants who specialised in importing silk from the Orient and whose most famous member, Amerigo, gave his name to the New World. The Vespucci built the adjoining hospital and several of the family are buried in vaults beneath the frescoes they commissioned.

On the south side of the nave (on the right) Ghirlandaio's fresco of 1472 shows the Madonna of Mercy, her arms reaching out in symbolic protection of the Vespucci family; Amerigo is depicted as a young boy.

The naming of America: He later went to Seville to manage the affairs of the Medici bank in Spain and there taught himself navigation. In 1499 he followed the same route across the Atlantic that Columbus had pioneered in 1492 and realised that the land on the ocean's western shores was an unknown continent—and not, as Columbus thought, Old Cathay. The notes he made enabled Florentine cartographers to draw a map

Ghirlandaio's *Birth of John the Baptist.*

of this new world and they, naturally, named it after their fellow citizen so that it became, for all time, America instead of Columbia.

Further along the south aisle is Botticelli's *Saint Augustine*, companion piece to Ghirlandaio's *Saint Jerome* on the opposite wall, both painted in 1480 and based on the portrait of Saint Jerome by the Flemish artist, Jan van Eyk, then in the collection of Lorenzo the Magnificent. It is thought that both works were commissioned by Giorgio Vespucci, Amerigo's learned tutor.

In the sanctuary off the north transept, recently discovered frescoes by the father and son, Taddeo and Agnolo Gaddi, depict in brilliant colour and realistic detail the Crucifixion and Resurrection of Christ. A similar delight in the realistic portrayal of birds, flowers, fruit and trees enlivens the *Last Supper* of Ghirlandaio (1480) in the refectory of the next door convent.

Borgo Ognissanti leads southeast to the **Piazza Goldoni**, the busy meeting point of eight roads. The Via della Vigna Nuova leads to the **Palazzo Rucellai**, half-way up on the left. This, one of the most ornate palaces in Florence, was built around 1446-51 for Giovanni Rucellai, humanist, author and intellectual and one of the richest men in Europe. In style it blends medieval pairs of lancet windows with classical columns, pilasters and cornice.

The ground floor of the palace is occupied by the offices and photographic museum of Alinari, the firm (founded in 1852) which supplied 19th-century Grand Tourists with prints, postcards and art books. It has one of the best photographic collections in Europe and continues to publish handsome books whose outstanding black and white plates show Florence as it was in the time of George Eliot, the Brownings, Ruskin, E.M. Forster and Henry James.

Florentine fashion: Via dell Vigna Nuova emerges in **Via Tornabuoni**, Florence's most upmarket shopping

Ognissanti: Botticelli's St Augustine. Following pages: Santa Maria Novella cloisters.

street. It is lined with palaces that house the showrooms of Italy's leading couturiers: Giorgio Armani, Salvatore Ferrragamo—names that evoke a world of style and craftsmanship that the Florentines believe is another legacy of the Renaissance. "Only we Florentines", they say, "love and understand the female body. How can we not, surrounded from birth by paintings of glorious nudes!"

Backing onto Via Tornabuoni, but approached from Via degli Strozzi, is the **Strozzi Palace**, one of the last of the hundred or so great palaces built during the Renaissance, and certainly the largest. Filippo Strozzi watched its construction from the house, itself of palatial dimensions, that stands on the opposite side of the piazza.

Bankrupt ambition: Begun in 1489, it was still not complete 44 years later, in 1536, when Strozzi died leaving his heirs bankrupt. The massive classical cornice was added as an afterthought towards the end of the construction when Roman-style architecture came into fashion.

Original Renaissance torch holders and lamp brackets, carried on winged sphinxes, adorn the corners and façade. The interior, by contrast, has been ruined by the addition of a huge modern fire escape, installed "temporarily" when the building began to be used as an exhibition hall.

By then, anyway, most of the arches of the Renaissance courtyard had been filled in with 19th-century windows to create office space for the various institutions that now occupy the upper floors. A small museum on the left displays the original model made by Giuliano da Sangallo, one of several architects who worked on the palace, and exhibits explaining its construction.

On the right of the courtyard, the **Gabinetto Vieusseux**, a public library with an excellent collection of books on the city and its art, is a favourite meeting place of scholars, literati and art historians of every nationality.

ARNO AND OLTRARNO

The Arno is a fickle river. Normally too shallow to navigate, it swells to a torrent in spring, fed by the meltwaters of the Apennines. In summer it shrinks to a trickle and was like this when Mark Twain saw it, causing him to write: "It would be a very plausible river if they would pump some water into it. They call it a river and they honestly think it is a river, do these dark and bloody Florentines. They even help out the illusion by building bridges over it. I do not see why they are too good to wade".

The autumn rains fill the channel again and it is at this time of the year that Florence becomes apprehensive; once a century, typically in November, the river has flooded the city. New embankments are supposed to prevent this ever happening again and the roads that follow the banks, called Lungarni, provide many an entrancing view—especially at sunset when all of Florence, or so it seems, comes out for the evening stroll, the *passeggiata*, and swallows weave and skim the water's surface.

The **Ponte alla Carraia**, the eastern-most of the four ancient bridges across the Arno, was built in 1220 when it was called the Ponte Nuovo to distinguish it from the older Ponte Vecchio. What we see now is a modern reconstruction, for all the bridges, except for the Ponte Vecchio, were blown up during the Nazi retreat from Florence in 1944. Even so, it is a faithful reproduction of the graceful 14th-century bridge, perhaps designed by Giotto, that replaced the first timber one.

Eastwards the view is of the modern Amerigo Vespucci bridge, with the park of **Cascine**, in which Shelley composed his *Ode to the West Wind*, just visible on the north bank.

The Lungarno Corsini, for all its traffic, is lined with some of Florence's top shops, hotels and restaurants, occupying noble palaces. The **Palazzo Corsini**, one of the city's largest, is unmistakable for its villa-like form, with two side wings and classical statues lined along the parapet. Built between 1650 and 1717, it contains the Galleria Corsini, an extensive private art collection with numerous works by Raphael, that may be visited by appointment.

Kings and exiles: Further along, the **Palazzo Gianfigliazza** (built 1459) was the former home of Luigi Buonaparte, King of Holland (died 1846). Next door the **Palazzo Masetti** is now the British Consulate and was, ironically, the home of Bonnie Prince Charlie's widow, the Countess of Albany. She scandalised the Scottish aristocracy by choosing as a second husband the playwright Alfieri, and her salon was the fashionable meeting place of writers and artists, including Shelley and Byron, at the end of the 18th century.

The palace overlooks the **Ponte Santa Trinita**, the most graceful of the four Arno bridges. Some of the original masonry was recovered from the river

Preceding pages: Ponte Santa Trinita. Left, oarsmen on the Arno. Below, Cascine, the Tuesday Market.

after 1944 and the quarries of the Boboli Gardens were reopened to enable the bridge to be rebuilt in the original material and to the original design commissioned by Cosimo I from Ammannati in 1567. The statues of the **Four Seasons**, carved by Pietro Francavilla for the wedding of Cosimo II in 1593, were also dredged from the river bed and restored to their original position.

From the bridge there are fine views of the Ponte Vecchio. The houses leading up to it were all reduced to rubble and used to block the bridge to delay the advance of the Allied troops in 1944. Those on the south bank are a much more successful evocation of the original jumble of medieval tenements that crowded the embankment than the obviously modern hotels and shops on the north.

A left turn into the elegant shopping street of Via Tornabuoni leads to Piazza Santa Trinita. On the right the battlemented and formidable **Palazzo Spini Feroni** is one of the few remaining

13th-century palaces in the city and home to the British Institute.

Opposite, the noble baroque façade of **Santa Trinita**, sadly now peeling, has capitals ornamented with cherubs and the Trinity carved in the pediment above the central door. This façade was added in 1593-4 by Buontalenti, but the inner face retains its almost complete 12th-century Romanesque form, indicating the appearance of the original late 11th-century church. The rest of the church, rebuilt in 1250-60, is a simplified form of Gothic, typical of Cistercian austerity.

The life of St Francis: The frescoes of the **Sassetti Chapel**, in the choir, were painted by Ghirlandaio in 1483 and illustrate the Life of St Francis. The scene above the altar, in which Pope Honorius presents St Francis with the Rule of the Franciscan Order, is set in the Piazza della Signoria. Lorenzo the Magnificent and the patron, the wealthy merchant Francesco Sassetti, are depicted on the right.

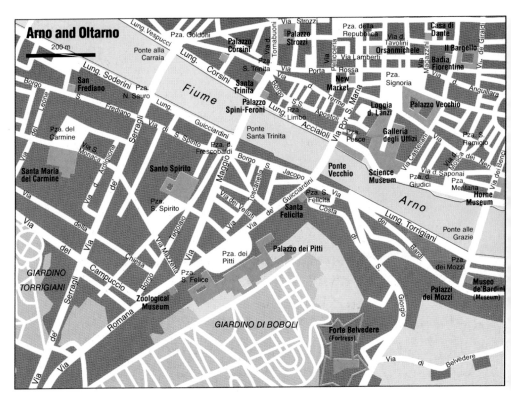

The altar piece itself is a delightful painting, also by Ghirlandaio (1485) of the *Adoration of the Shepherds*. Joseph turns to watch the arrival of the Magi, clearly bewildered by the events in which he is caught up, but Mary remains serene and beautiful throughout.

Instead of a manger, the infant Christ lies in a Roman sarcophagus; this, along with the scene on the outside wall in which the Sybil foretells the birth of Christ to the Emperor Augustus, demonstrates the Florentine preoccupation with establishing continuity between their own Christian civilisation and that of the classical world.

The view, on emerging from the church, is of the Roman column, from the Baths of Caracella in Rome, presented by Pius IV to Cosimo I in 1560 and surmounted by the figure of Justice. Behind it is the **Palazzo Bartolini-Salimbeni**, of 1521, an outstanding building and one of the last of the great palaces to be built in the city.

To our eyes it is a gracious work, especially the delicate shell hood niches of the upper floor. Nevertheless it was ridiculed by contemporary Florentines who thought it over-decorated. The architect, Baccio d'Agnolo, answered his critics by carving an inscription above the door in Latin which translates as, "it is easier to criticise than to emulate." It seems appropriate that this feminine building, with a tiny and endearing inner courtyard covered with *sgraffito* decoration, is now home to the French Embassy.

Behind and to the east of the palace is a warren of narrow alleys lined with medieval towers and palaces and, in the little Piazza del Limbo, one of the city's oldest churches.

Founded by Charlemagne: Santi Apostoli is not, however, as old as the inscription on the façade suggests. This attributes the foundation to "Karolus Rex Roma"—otherwise known as Charlemagne—in A.D. 786, but the church is Romanesque in style and was probably built in the 10th century. The

double arcade of dark green marble columns and Corinthian capitals includes some that were salvaged from the Roman baths of nearby Via delle Terme.

A short walk away, down Borgo Santi Apostoli and across Via Por Santa Maria, is another church of equal antiquity: **Santo Stefano al Ponte**, founded around A.D. 969 and with a fine Romanesque façade of 1233. Open-air concerts are held in front of the church in summer. The narrow lanes east of this secluded piazza lead to buildings used as workshops for the goldsmiths and jewellers whose creations are sold in the kiosks lining the **Ponte Vecchio**.

The oldest bridge: This bridge, as much a symbol of Florence as the cathedral or Palazzo Vecchio, dates, in its present form, from 1345, replacing an earlier wooden structure that was swept away in a flood. Workshops have always flanked the central carriageway and in 1565 Vasari's corridor, linking the Pitti Palace and the Palazzo Vecchio, was built high above the pavement along the eastern side.

In 1593, Ferdinand I, annoyed at the noxious trades that were carried on beneath his feet as he travelled the length of the corridor, ordered the butchers, tanners and blacksmiths to be evicted. The workshops were rebuilt and let to goldsmiths and this traditional use has continued ever since, though no craftsmen work in the cramped but quaint premises any more.

Today it is not just the shop owners on the bridge who earn their livelihood from the million-plus visitors that are drawn to the bridge every year. Hawkers, buskers and portrait painters, artists and souvenir vendors all contribute to the festive atmosphere that always seems to prevail upon the bridge, especially at night. There is no better place in Florence for people watching or taking in the river views.

To avoid the traffic that tears along the embankment past the bridge, it is

The Ponte Vecchio beyond Ponte Santa Trinita.

206

best to take the **Via dei Girolami**, a sombre tunnel lined with medieval cellars, out through the Uffizi and along the embankment to the Science Museum in Piazza dei Giudici.

The **Science Museum** is one of the most absorbing in Florence and a welcome change from an over-indulgence in the arts. The exhibits show that Renaissance Florence was pre-eminent in Europe as a centre of scientific research as well as of painting and sculpture—indeed the humanistic concept of the "universal man" did not recognise any dichotomy between the two.

Reaching for the stars: Much encouragement was given to scientific research by Cosimo II who, it is said, saw the similarity of his own name to the cosmos as auspicious and so he announced a grand scheme to master the universe through knowledge. The best mathematicians, astronomers and mapmakers were hired from all over Europe and the Middle East and their beautifully engraved astrolabes and armillary spheres, showing the motion of the heavenly bodies, are well displayed in this museum.

The genius of Galileo: Ironically, though, the most brilliant scientist of his age, and the one whose discoveries and methodology laid the foundations for modern science, suffered greatly as a consequence. Galileo was popular enough when he discovered the five moons of Jupiter and named them after members of the Medici family. He was appointed court mathematician and his experiments in mechanics and the laws of motion must have given great pleasure to the Medici court, even if their true significance might not have been understood. Beautiful mahogany and brass reconstructions of these experiments, like giant executive toys, are displayed in the museum and demonstrated from time to time by the attendants.

But Galileo fell foul of the authorities when, from his own observations, he supported the Copernican view that the sun, and not the earth, was the centre of

eweller's hop, Ponte ecchio.

the cosmos. Refusing to retract a view that ran counter to the teachings of the Church, he was tried before the Inquisition in 1633, excommunicated and made a virtual prisoner in his own home until his death in 1642.

As if to exculpate their collective guilt for this unjust treatment, Florence has devoted a large section of the museum to his work, and many regard him as the greatest Florentine (though he was, in fact, born in rival Pisa).

Mapping the world: Equally intriguing are the rooms devoted to maps and globes which demonstrate how rapidly the discoveries of the 15th and 16th centuries were revolutionising old ideas about the shape of the world.

The early 16th-century map of the monk, Fra Mauro, still defines the world in religious and mythological terms, with Jerusalem at the centre and the margins inhabited by menacing monsters. Only 50 years later, in 1554, Lopo Holmen was producing a recognisably accurate map of the world

which had to be extended, even as it was being drawn, to accommodate the newly surveyed west coast of the Americas and discoveries in the Pacific, such as New Guinea.

From the Science Museum, Via dei Saponai leads to **Piazza Mentana**, the site of the Roman port. Via dei Mosca follows the curve of this ancient harbour. At the point where it joins the Via dei Neri, cross to the junction with Via San Remigio for the building on the left that has two plaques high up on the wall. One records the level of the flood reached in 1333 and two feet above it is the 1966 mark.

Via dei Neri leads to Via Benci and the **Horne Museum**. The best of the art collection assembled by the English art historian, Herbert Percy Horne (1864-1916), is now in the Uffizi and there are no great treasures here, but the palace, built in 1489 for the Corsi family and latterly Horne's home, has a delightful courtyard. The kitchen on the top floor retains its original form—a simple range, chimney and sink—and is used to display Horne's collection of ancient pots and utensils.

Immediately south, the **Ponte alle Grazie** is a modern bridge built to replace the Ponte Rubiconte, first built in 1237 and destroyed in 1944. Upstream, to the east, the modern stone embankment of the Arno gives way to natural grassy banks, trees and reeds.

Across the Arno: Over the bridge is the district of **Oltrarno**—meaning simply "beyond the Arno"—first enclosed by walls in the 14th century. Florentines persist in thinking of it as on the "wrong" side of the Arno, even though it contains many ancient and luxurious palaces, as well as some of the city's poorest districts.

The first building beyond the bridge is the **Palazzo Bardini**, housing the Bardini Museum, built in 1883 to house the magpie collection of Stefano Bardini. This is a fascinating hotchpotch of art and architectural details, jumbled up together like a vast antique emporium and a great delight to those who enjoy unguided browsing amongst the relics of past grandeur.

Though just a century old, the palace feels medieval, for the gorgeously painted ceilings and many of the door-cases and chimney pieces were salvaged from old buildings being demolished at the time—some say that Bardini encouraged demolition in order to augment his own collection.

This was left to the state by Stefano's son, Ugo Bardini, along with the three 13th and 14th-century palaces at the southern end of the **Piazza Mozzi**. Austere but noble, these hide an extensive hillside garden, and there are long-term plans to restore them all for public enjoyment.

The **Via dei Bardi** leads back to the Ponte Vecchio, past several more unspoiled 14th-century palaces, whose only adornment consists of the sculpted coats of arms of the owners.

Medieval defenses: The southern end of the **Ponte Vecchio** is the more pictur-

esque, for here Vasari's corridor makes several twists and turns, corbelled out on great stone brackets, to negotiate the 13th-century stone tower that guards this approach to the bridge. The corridor then sails over the Via dei Bardi and runs in front of Santa Felicita, forming the upper part of a portico that shelters the west front.

On the opposite side of the busy little **Piazza Santa Felicita** is a charming fountain composed of a 16th-century bronze Bacchus and a late-Roman marble sarcophagus, brought together on this site in 1958.

Santa Felicita stands on the site of a late Roman church, thought to have been built in the third or fourth century A.D. by eastern merchants at a time when Christians were still liable to persecution. It was rebuilt in the 16th century, and again in 1736, making effective use of contrasting bands of grey and white stone.

Hail Mary: The frescoes in the **Capponi Chapel** (by Pontormo, 1525-28)

ia Maggio.
eft, Palazzo di
ianca
appello and
elow, baroque
graffito work.

include a remarkable *Annunciation*. The artist captures Mary as she climbs a staircase, one foot in the air, turning to hear the Archangel's scarcely credible message, with a look of genuine disbelief upon her face. Just as accomplished is the altar piece, a *Deposition*, in which Pontormo succeeds in recreating, in oils, the vivid colours and translucence of fresco, and the deathly pallor of Christ's flesh.

Via Guiccardini is named after the first historian of Italy, who was born in 1483 in the palace of the same name (No 15), part way down on the left. A slice of the fine garden and a relief of Hercules and Cacus can be glimpsed through the gate. Beyond lies the Pitti Palace and the **Via Romana**, a narrow street and yet one of the city's principal thoroughfares leading to the southern suburbs.

On the left, the **Palazzo Torrigiani** (No 17), houses the **Zoological Museum** and its large collection of anatomical wax models, made between 1775 and 1814 by the artist Susini and the physiologist Fontana. They are extraordinarily detailed and realistic and, inevitably, the organs of reproduction attract most interest. On the opposite side of the road is the **Casa Guidi**, the house in which the Brownings lived from 1847, shortly after their secret marriage, until Elizabeth's death in 1861. Their apartments can be visited by appointment through the British consulate, and the Browning Institute intends, eventually, to open a research centre here.

Antique splendour: Via Maggio, despite heavy traffic, is a magnificent palace-lined street whose many antique shops are stuffed with rich and expensive treasures—the sheer quantity is an indication of the past wealth of Florence and how much furniture and art has survived.

At night, when the lights come on, and before the shutters are drawn, it is possible to glimpse richly frescoed ceilings through the windows of many an upper room—revealing the splendour

Santa Felicita, Pontormo's Virgin.

in which those Florentines fortunate enough to have inherited property pass their daily lives.

Immediately west of the Via Maggio, however, the scale and atmosphere changes completely. The homes of the aristocracy give way to the homes of the people in the districts of **Santo Spirito** and **San Frediano**, adjacent parishes that even have their own dialects and were once the areas in which the wool dyers and leather workers worked at their noxious trades.

The **Palazzo Guadagni**, in Piazza Santo Spirito, is one of the few palaces to be built this far west. The pillared upper loggia, open to the air, was an innovation when the palace was built, around 1505, and set a new fashion. Subsequently, many medieval palaces had an extra storey built in the same style, providing a retreat in which to enjoy the cool evening air above the noise of the city.

The piazza itself is an attractive square, planted with trees, with an early morning market on weekdays. **San Spirito church** was designed by Brunelleschi and begun in 1436 but he never lived to see it finished.

Modelled on Rome: Over time, his plan was modified and compromised—not least by the ugly 17th-century baldacchino that dominates the eastward view of the nave and introduces a note of flamboyance into an otherwise measured classical composition. Mentally strip this away and one is left with a building that is secular in inspiration, modelled on Roman civic architecture, and a complete break with the Gothic style that prevailed elsewhere in Europe.

A total of 40 chapels with side altars and paintings radiate from the aisles and transepts. If Brunelleschi's design had been executed in full, these would have formed a ring of conical-roofed apses around the exterior of the church, clinging like a cluster of limpets to the main structure. The one artistic masterpiece, Filippino Lippi's *Madonna and Child* (c.1490) has been removed for restora-

Via Toscanella.

tion but there are many other accomplished 16th-century paintings to enjoy.

From here it is worth taking an indirect route to the church of Santa Maria del Carmine by way of Via Sant' Agostino, left into the Via de' Serragli and right into **Via dell' Ardiglioni**. The latter is the reason for the detour, a simple narrow street which appears to have changed little since Filippo Lippi was born here in 1406. Scarcely wide enough to admit a car, the buildings exclude the city noise and it does not need much imagination to think oneself back into the 15th century. Half way down, an aerial corridor links the two sides of the street and close to it is Lippi's birthplace, number 30.

At the northern end, a left turn into Via Santa Monica leads to the **church of Santa Maria del Carmine**. The original church was destroyed by fire in 1771, but by some miracle the **Brancacci Chapel**, with its frescoes by Masaccio, was unaffected.

Youthful genius: Masaccio lived for only 27 years, and was just 24 when he began work on *The Life of St Peter*, as a pupil of Masolino, in 1425. In 1427, Masaccio was put in sole charge of the work, and the result, painted a year before his untimely death, has been called the first truly Renaissance painting. Masaccio developed the technique of *chiaroscuro* to highlight the faces of Christ and the Apostles and, for the first time, applied the principles of linear perspective, previously developed in architecture and sculpture, to painting.

These alone do not account for the extraordinary power of his work, or the influence it had on leading artists of the 15th century who came to study it. Instead, it is the boldness of the draughtsmanship and the humanity expressed in the faces and animation of the figures. The frescoes' status as one of the city's unmissable sights has been enhanced by comprehensive restoration, a process which kept them under wraps for most of the 1980s.

Across the spacious Piazza del Carmine, spoiled by its use as a car park, lies the **Borgo San Frediano**. This is the principal street of a district full of character, whose tough and hard-working inhabitants are celebrated in the novels of Vasco Pratolini, one of the city's best-known authors. The district is no longer as rough or as squalid as it was earlier this century when rag pickers made a living from sifting the nearby Central Refuse Dump and tripe (for sale all over the city) was boiled in great cauldrons in back alleys.

Cleaned up, it is now a neighbourhood of small shops selling everything from provocative underwear to fishing tackle. The **church of San Frediano** looks unfinished because of its rough stone façade but its fine dome adds a touch of glamour to this part of the city and it looks over the Arno to the tower of Ognissanti on the opposite bank.

At the western end of the Borgo is **Porta San Frediano**, built in 1324 and one of the best preserved stretches of the 14th-century city walls.

Left, portrait artist, Ponte Vecchio. Right sunset on the River Arno.

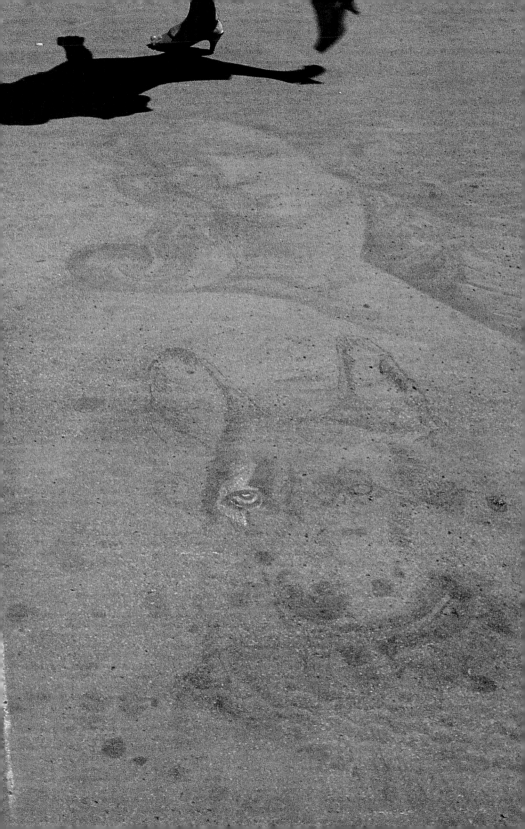

THE FLORENTINE COUNTRYSIDE

One of the great joys of Florence is the proximity of the surrounding countryside. Other cities are ringed by sprawling suburbs but in Florence such developments are limited to the north bank of the Arno, leaving the south side, Oltrarno and beyond, surprisingly rural. Natural landscapes, small farms and fine views are available only 10 minutes' walk from the city centre.

From the Ponte Vecchio, walk south towards the Pitti Palace and turn left at the church of Santa Felicita to reach the **Costa San Giorgio**. This narrow lane winds steeply up the hill and holds out the promise of what lies ahead for several of the houses have quite spacious gardens, including the **Villa Bardini** (on the left, beyond the junction with Costa Scarpuccia) which will, one day, be open to the public.

After a short climb, the granite-flagged lane flattens out at the **Porta San Giorgio**. This is the city's oldest surviving gate, built in 1260. On the inner arch is a fresco by Bicci di Lorenzo (1430) of *Our Lady with St George and St Leonard*. On the outer face is a copy of a 13th-century carving of St George in combat with the dragon (the original is in the Palazzo Vecchio).

To the right of the gate the sheer and massive walls of the **Belvedere Fort** rise to a great height and cause one to wonder what lies behind. In fact, the interior is almost empty and used now for exhibitions of contemporary and experimental art and, on occasions in summer, as an open-air cinema.

Access to the fort is so restricted that, when exhibitions are held, the larger sculptures have to be lifted in by helicopter—an extraordinary sight, if you happen to witness it, as great elemental shapes and Henry Moore-style figure groups sail through the air suspended from the end of a cable.

Ducal paranoia: The fortress was built at the orders of Ferdinando I, beginning in 1590, to Buontalenti's design. It symbolises the Grand Duke's sense of insecurity, for though the structure was explained as part of the city's defences, there was only one means of access—a secret door entered from the Boboli Gardens behind the Pitti Palace. Clearly it was intended for his own personal use in times of attack or insurrection. Now Florentines come to stroll around the ramparts on Sunday afternoons, to walk off lunch and enjoy the extensive views.

Scented alleys: The fort marks the beginning of the **Via di San Leonardo**, a cobbled rural lane that climbs between the walled gardens of scattered villas. Here and there a gate allows a view of the gardens behind and the wisteria and roses grow so vigorously that they spill over the walls, tumbling in fragrant blossoms into the lane. On the left is the **church of San Leonardo**, which contains a fine 13th-century pulpit.

Both Tchaikovsky and Stravinsky lived in this lane. Florence was a favour-

Preceding pages: pavement art, Piazza Signoria; dusk over Fiesole. Left, Porta San Giorgio.

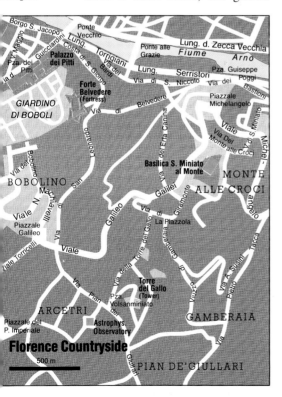

Florence Countryside
500 m

ite resort, before the 1917 Revolution, for Russians seeking an escape from the rigours of their own climate. On the right, the house in which Tchaikovsky stayed in 1878 (No. 64) is marked by a plaque that says, in Italian, that "the sweet Tuscan hills inspired the great Russian pianist and nourished his immortal harmonies".

Cross the Viale Galileo and continue along the Via di San Leonardo, before taking the first left turn to follow **Via Viviani**. This road climbs steeply, with the promise of some fine views ahead, until it levels out at the Piazza Volsanminiato in the village of **Arcetri**. Follow the Via del Pian de' Giullari until, after a few metres, the views suddenly open up.

To the right, the only signs of modernity are the receiver dishes of the Astrophysical Observatory. On the left is its ancient predecessor, the **Torre del Gallo**, once used for astronomical research, and much restored in the 19th century by Stefano Bardini (of Bardini Museum). He used it as a repository for the larger architectural materials that he rescued from demolished buildings.

On the hillside below the tower is the sadly neglected 15th-century **Villa "La Gallina"**. This contains very fine frescoes of nude dancers by Antonio del Pollaiuolo (c. 1464-71) but faces an uncertain future.

Galileo's exile: To the right again, the hillside falls away steeply in a series of terraced gardens, vineyards and orchards. Beyond is a typically Tuscan view of a series of low hills covered in sculptural groups of pencil-thin cypress trees, echoing the shape of the medieval towers and church campaniles, rising above the red-tiled roofs of villas and simple village homes.

This is a view that Galileo enjoyed, by force, in the last years of his life. He lived at the **Villa il Gioiello** (No. 42 Via del Pian dei Giullari) from 1631 until his death in 1642, virtually under house arrest, though permitted to continue his work and receive a stream of distin-

Via di San Leonardo.

guished admirers. Some say that Milton came to visit Galileo some time between 1637 and 1639 and later, in his great poems, *Paradise Lost* and *Regained*, did so much to reconcile Galileo's discoveries with Christian theology. The villa and gardens have been under restoration since 1986 and will, eventually, be opened to the public.

At the crossroads in the village of Pian de' Giullari there is a choice of routes. **Via Santa Margherita** leads to the early 14th-century village church and some far-reaching views up the Arno valley. **Via San Matteo** leads to the monastery of the same name. An inscription on the nearby house (No. 48) forbids the playing of football within the vicinity of the monastery—a rule which local children joyfully flout.

The route back to Florence involves backtracking as far as Arcetri and taking the Via della Torre del Gallo downhill to the **Piazza degli Unganelli**. As the road descends, there are fine views of the cathedral glimpsed across olive

groves, a reminder of just how small and rural a city Florence is. Only the occasional sounds of traffic, echoing up the Arno valley, disturb the rural peace and this is drowned out by the pleasing sound of church bells at midday or, if you are out on a Sunday, at regular intervals throughout the morning.

Villas of the great: Cypress trees, like beautiful clusters of green pillars from some ruined temple of antiquity, tumble down the hillside. Many villas have marble plaques recording that they were once the home of philosophers, artists, poets and architects, so many has Florence produced over the centuries. Sunlight warms the scene and, even in winter, lizards and the occasional butterfly bask on the warm garden walls.

At the Piazza degli Unganelli, ignore the main road that bends to the left and look instead for the narrow **Via di Giramonte**, an unmetalled track that leads off to the right between high walls. This cool and shady path follows the sheer walls of the city's 16th-century fortifi-

cations and eventually climbs up through trees and oleander bushes to the **church of San Miniato**.

This, in the opinion of many, is one of the most beautiful and least spoiled churches in Italy. St Minias was a merchant from the east (the son of the King of Armenia, according to one story) who settled in Florence but was executed around A.D. 250 during the anti-Christian purges of the Emperor Decius. A church was probably built on the site of his tomb soon after, but the present building was begun around 1018 and completed around 1207.

Roman origins: Like the cathedral Baptistry, the delicate geometrical marble inlay of the façade was much admired by Brunelleschi and his contemporaries who believed, or at least claimed it to be the work of the ancient Romans. Certainly some of the columns of the nave and crypt, with their crisply carved Corinthian capitals, are re-used Roman material. Again like the Baptistry, the Calimala guild was responsible for the maintenance of the church and the guild's emblem, of an eagle carrying a bale of wool, crowns the pediment.

The interior has, remarkably, survived in its original state, except for 19th-century repainting of the open timber roof and an attempt to line the walls with marble, copying the motifs of the façade. Frescoes on the aisle walls include a large 14th-century St Christopher by an unknown artist. The nave floor has a delightful series of marble intarsia panels depicting lions, doves, signs of the Zodiac and the date: 1207.

At the end of the nave, between the staircases that lead to the raised choir, is a tabernacle made to house a miraculous painted crucifix (now in Santa Trinita) that is said to have spoken to Giovanni Gualberto, the 11th-century Florentine saint and founder of the Vallambrosan order of Benedictine monks. The tabernacle is the collective work of Michelozzo, Agnolo Gaddi and Luca della Robbia and was made around 1448.

San Miniato

On the left of the nave is the **Chapel of the Cardinal of Portugal** who died, aged 25, on a visit to Florence in 1439. The very fine tomb is by Rossellino, the glazed terracotta ceiling, depicting the Cardinal Virtues, by Luca della Robbia, the *Annunciation* above the Bishop's Throne by Baldovinetti and the frescoes by the brothers Antonio and Piero Pollaiuolo.

The highlight of the church is the raised choir and pulpit, all of marble and inset with intarsia panels depicting a riot of mythical beasts. The mosaic in the apse, of 1297, shows Christ, the Virgin and St Minias. The combined effect is distinctively Byzantine in feel.

The martyr's shrine: The choir was elevated in order to accommodate the 11th-century crypt below, in which the remains of St Minias were placed beneath the altar for veneration by visiting pilgrims. The vaulted crypt roof, with frescoes of saints and prophets by Taddeo Gaddi, is held up by a forest of pillars and capitals from diverse sources—many of them Roman—with delightful disregard for match and even less for symmetry.

To the north of the church is a small graveyard, opened up in 1839, full of rewarding 19th and early 20th-century monuments. Family tombs, like miniature houses, are supplied with electricity to light the "everlasting lamps" of Etruscan form, and there are numerous highly accomplished figures and portraits in stone and bronze of former Florentine citizens.

Florence under siege: Towering above the graveyard is the massive, but incomplete, campanile, built in 1523 to replace the original one that collapsed in 1499. This played a strategic role during the 1530 siege of Florence when the Medici, expelled in 1527, returned to take the city, backed by the army of the Emperor Charles V.

Under Michelangelo's direction, the tower was used as an artillery platform and wrapped in mattresses to absorb the impact of enemy cannon fire. Mich-

The cemetery, San Miniato. Following pages: Piazzale Michelangelo.

elangelo also supervised the construction of temporary fortifications around the church, later rebuilt in stone and made permanent. Later they were incorporated into the grand cascade of terraces and staircases laid out by the city architect, Giuseppi Poggi, in 1865-73.

Photogenic views: These descend the hillside to the broad **Piazzale Michelangelo**. This viewpoint, decorated with reproductions of Michelangelo's most famous works, is crowded with visitors at all times of the year who come for the celebrated panorama over the red roofs of Florence to the green hills beyond. Despite the milling hordes, and the sellers of tacky souvenirs, the sight is awe-inspiring, and never better than on a clear Sunday in spring at around 11.45 a.m. when the bells of the city's churches all peal to call the faithful to midday mass, and the surrounding peaks are sharply delineated against the pale blue sky.

The best route back to the Ponte Vecchio is the steep descent, through acacia groves and past overgrown grottoes, along the Via di San Salvatore to **Porta San Niccolo**. This imposing gateway of *c*. 1340 has recently been restored.

Turn left along the Via di Belvedere to **Porta San Miniato**, now little more than a hole in the wall. A poignant plaque on the wall opposite records that several members of the Florentine Resistance were shot in August 1944 in a final vindictive act as the Nazis fled the city and the advance of the Allied troops.

From here there is a choice of routes. **Via dei Bardi** offers the most direct return to the bustle of the city. Alternatively, the **Via dei Belvedere** offers a final taste of rural Florence. This tree-lined lane follows the high walls and bastions of the city's 14th-century defences, marking a sharp division between town and country. It climbs to the Porta San Giorgio from where the Via della Costa San Giorgio leads directly back to the Ponte Vecchio.

FIESOLE

Fiesole is the hilltop town of Etruscan origin that preceded Florence and was once the most powerful city in the region. Founded perhaps as early as the eighth century B.C., it was colonised by the Romans around 80 B.C. and later became the capital of Etruria. The growth of Florence overtook that of Fiesole but it remained sufficiently important as a competitor to Florence in the 11th and 12th centuries for the two towns to be constantly at war with one another.

Violent conquest: In 1125 Florentine troops stormed Fiesole and won what was, perhaps, the easiest victory in a long campaign to dominate the whole of Tuscany. Not content merely to subjugate Fiesole, the Florentines razed the village, sparing only the cathedral complex. With hindsight, this destruction of a whole community had its benefits. Few buildings were erected in succeeding centuries and important Roman and Etruscan remains were thus preserved relatively undisturbed beneath the soil.

Much of Fiesole has now been declared an archaeological zone and, despite the snail's pace progress and incompetence, typical of Italian archaeology, excavation is proceeding and the results throw new light on the origins and achievements of the Etruscans.

An English colony: The rejuvenation of Fiesole began in the 19th century. A handful of villas had been built in the 16th and 17th centuries, but the main impetus for growth came with the adoption of Fiesole by the Anglo-Florentine community. The Brownings praised its beauty in their poetry and here, unlike in Florence itself, there was space for the English to indulge their passion for gardening.

Nearly 1,000 ft (295 metres) above sea level, Fiesole was considered altogether more salubrious than the furnace of Florence. This belief that the town is cooler than the city below (in fact the difference in temperature is marginal) still attracts refugees attempting to escape from the summer's heat.

Provincial hill town: The best way to reach Fiesole is by No 7 bus from Via de' Cerratani, just west of the Florence cathedral. In a matter of minutes the bus is climbing through semi-rural countryside where villas with trim gardens are dotted amongst the orchards and olive groves. Psychologically, at least, the air feels fresher and when the bus reaches **Piazza Mino**, the main square of Fiesole, there is an atmosphere of provincial Italy which seems miles from urbane Florence.

Just off the square, to the north, is the **Teatro Romana**, the Roman theatre, which is still used during the *Estate Fiesolana*, the arts festival that takes place every July and August. The larger blocks of stone represent the original Roman seats, the smaller ones modern replacements.

Left, Badia Fiesolana. Below, San Francesco cloisters.

Tuscan landscapes: The great and noble views from the amphitheatre are as dramatic as anything that takes place on the stage. The theatre, originally built at the end of the first century, was excavated out of the hillside which drops steeply away, revealing the beautiful Tuscan landscape. To the left, the river Mugnone cuts a deep valley while, in the middle distance, an endless succession of hills and peaks stretches as far as the horizon, dotted with villas and clusters of cypress trees.

The excellent **Museum Faesulanum**, next to the theatre, was built in 1912-14. The building is an imaginative reconstruction of the first-century B.C. Roman temple, whose excavated remains are in the northwestern area of the theatre complex; parts of the original Roman frieze are incorporated into the pediment.

Treasures of the ancient world: Exhibits on the ground floor consist principally of finds from local excavations and illustrate the development of the Florence region from the Bronze Age onwards. The upstairs gallery is used to display early medieval (seventh to 13th-century) jewellery, coins and ceramics as well as Etruscan treasures of unknown provenance donated by Florentine families. The last room contains a very fine torso of Dionysius and early Roman funerary monuments.

Tangled ruins: Much of the rest of the site is overgrown and neglected, which makes exploration something of an adventure, but the exact form of the various structures difficult to interpret.

Below the museum, to the right of the theatre, is a first-century A.D. bath complex with furnaces, hypocaust system and plunge baths. Next, a terrace follows a stretch of the third-century B.C. Etruscan town walls. This leads to the ruins of the first-century B.C. Roman temple built on the foundations of an earlier Etruscan one.

Opposite the theatre complex, in Via Dupre, is the **Museo Bandini**, recently closed for restoration. It contains Ren-

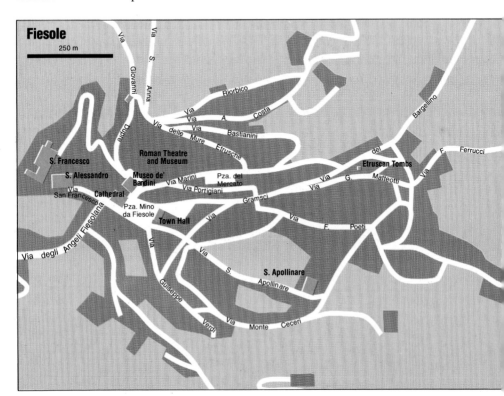

aissance paintings, furniture, architectural fragments and a small, but remarkable, collection of Byzantine carved ivories.

The Piazza Mino, the main square, occupies the site of the Roman forum. At one end is the town hall, at the other **Fiesole cathedral**. This looks uninviting from the outside due to over-restoration in the 19th century but the interior retains something of its original Romanesque form. Begun in 1028 and extended in the 14th century, the original nave columns survive (some with Roman capitals) leading to a raised choir above a crypt. The altar piece by Bicci di Lorenzo (1440) and 16th-century frescoes are under restoration.

City views: The Via San Francesco, west of the cathedral climbs steeply to the **church of Sant' Alessandro**, originally sixth-century and built on the site of earlier Roman and Etruscan temples. The *cipollino* marble columns of the nave are Roman and there are splendid views back over Florence from the nearby lookout point.

Further up, on the summit of the hill, is the friary of **San Francesco**, unattractively restored in neo-Gothic style, but with an intriguing small museum of objects brought back from the Orient by missionaries.

Back in the main square, one has to decide whether to spend an hour or two over lunch in one of the town's inexpensive *trattorie*, or summon up the energy for further walks.

Anyone who chooses the latter option is almost bound to get lost in the maze of lanes and footpaths leading east off the square. This only adds to the pleasure, and sooner or later one is bound to find lovely open views that help to re-establish one's orientation.

Via Marini leads to the **Piazza del Mercato**, which overlooks the valley of the River Mugnone. A little further, on the left, the **Via delle Mura Etrusche** follows the best preserved stretch of Etruscan town wall, composed of monolithic blocks of stone.

Fiesole, Roman theatre. Following pages, the wooded hills of Fiesole.

From here, steep lanes lead back up to the main road, Via Gramsci, and the first fork left, Via del Bargellino, leads to an overgrown plot between two houses where two third-century B.C. Etruscan underground tombs have been preserved. A short way further on, take the right turn for Borgunto to reach the Via Adriano Mari which joins the Via Monte Ceceri to return to Piazza Mino in the centre of Fiesole.

The stones of Florence: Along the route there are excellent views of Florence and of the wooded slopes and disused quarries of **Monte Ceceri**, source of much of the beautiful dove-grey *pietra serena* used by Renaissance architects to decorate the city's churches.

From the southwestern corner of the main square, Via Vecchia Fiesolana descends to the **Villa Medici**, one of the first Renaissance country villas, built by Michelozzo in 1458-61 for Cosimo de' Medici, and deliberately sited to make the best of the views.

Take any of the downhill paths from here to reach the hamlet of **San Domenico** after about half a mile (800 metres). The church here dates from 1406 and contains a recently restored *Madonna with Angels and Saints* (1430), an early work of Fra Angelico who began his monastic life here before transferring to San Marco.

Opposite the church the Via della Badia dei Roccettini descends to the **Badia Fiorentina**, a monastery that now houses the European University Institute, founded in 1976.

The façade of the little church is an exquisite and jewel-like work of inlaid marble. It is all that has survived of the original Fiesole cathedral, rebuilt around 1028 and again in the 15th century when Brunelleschi, it is thought, was responsible for the cruciform plan.

The relatively isolated position of the Badia, with views south to Florence, west to the Mugnone valley and northeast to Fiesole, is superb. The No. 7 bus can be caught in San Domenico for the return to Florence.

SUBURBS AND EXCURSIONS

Bellosguardo means "beautiful view" and that is what attracts walkers up the steep paths to this hilltop village south of Florence. The No. 13 bus goes as far as the Piazza Torquato Tasso and from here it takes no more than 20 minutes to reach the summit by way of Via San Francesco di Paolo and Via di Bellosguardo.

A plaque in the **Piazza Bellosguardo** records the names of the many distinguished foreigners who have lived in the villas on this hillside, including Nathaniel Hawthorne, Aldous Huxley, the Brownings and D. H. Lawrence. At the very summit, enjoying the best views over Florence, is the **Villa dell' Ombrellino**, the home, at various times, of Galileo, the tenor Caruso, Edward VII's mistress Alice Keppel and her daughter, Violet Trefusis.

On the opposite bank of the Arno, **Le**

Cascine is a pleasant park that runs along the embankment west of the city for two miles (three km). *Cascina* means "dairy farm" and that is what it was until it was acquired by Duke Alessandro de' Medici and then laid out as a park by his successor, Cosimo I.

A large market is held here every Tuesday morning and there are open-air concerts and firework displays in summer. At most times a place of innocent pleasure, it is also the haunt of transvestites and prostitutes and best avoided after dark.

Ancient fortifications: From the Cascine, the **Viale**, laid out in 1865-69 along the line of the 14th-century city walls, now forms a busy inner ring road around the city. It leads northeast to the **Fortezza da Basso**, built by Alessandro de' Medici in 1534 as a symbol of the family power. Ironically he was assassinated within its walls by his cousin, Lorenzo, in 1537.

After the 1966 flood, it was used as a centre for the restoration of damaged works of art. An international exhibition centre, used to stage prestigious fashion shows, was constructed within the walls in 1978.

From here, the No. 1 bus is the best means of avoiding the dull modern suburbs that stretch the mile or so (two km) to the **Villa Stibbert** and its park. Frederick Stibbert (1838-1906) inherited two adjoining 14th and 15th-century properties from his Italian mother and converted them into one vast museum whose 64 rooms are stuffed with antiques from all over the world.

The central great hall is filled with an army of knights on horseback in 16th-century battle dress, just a small part of a collection that ranges from Etruscan and Roman military equipment to an important group of Japanese Edo period armour. All the rooms are heavily decorated with tapestries, paintings, furniture and porcelain.

Back in the Viale, the northernmost point is marked by the **Porta San Gallo**, the ancient gate that defended the old road to Bologna. The Via Bologna itself heads north to **La Pietra**, the villa home of the distinguished art historian Sir Harold Acton with its splendid Italianate terraced garden full of statues and urns (Agriturist organises tours of this and other villas in summer, bookable through most hotels).

Tree-shaded tombs: The Viale turns south to reach the Piazza Donatello. Here, on an island in the midst of a major traffic intersection, is the **English (or Protestant) Cemetery**. Opened in 1827, it is the burial place of numerous distinguished Anglo-Florentines, including Elizabeth Barrett Browning, Arthur Hugh Clough, Walter Savage Landor, Frances Trollope (authoress and mother of Anthony) and the American preacher Theodore Parker. Sadly, the noise of traffic prevents this being the romantic and restful spot it should be, despite the beauty of sheltering cypress trees.

Borgo Pinti leads south from here, back towards the city centre. Just after the junction with Via della Colonna, on the left, is the entrance to the **church of Santa Maria Maddalena dei Pazzi**—dedicated to the Florentine nun and descendant of the anti-Medici conspirators. She died in 1609 and was canonised in 1685 when the church was renamed in her honour.

It originally dates to the 15th century and has a lovely quiet cloister of 1492 formed of square Tuscan columns with flat, rather than rounded, classical arches. The fresco of the *Crucifixion* in the chapter house is one of Perugino's masterpieces, painted in 1493-96. The figures kneeling in adoration of their Saviour are glimpsed, as if through a window, between a series of *trompe l'oeil* arches. The cross of Christ is set in a delightful landscape of winding rivers and wooded hills, and the whole scene is lit by a limpid blue light.

From here it is a short walk left, down Via dei Pilastri and left again up Via Farini, to the **Tempo Israelitico**, the huge synagogue (built 1874-82) whose

Loggia Dei Pesci.

green copper-covered dome is such a prominent feature of the Florentine skyline. It is sobering to think that, had the 19th-century planners had their way, a significant section of the city from here west to the Piazza della Repubblica, would have been demolished and redeveloped.

The nearby **church of Sant' Ambrogio**, at the southeastern end of Via dei Pilastri, was built in the late 13th century and contains several beautifully restored frescoes, including a 14th-century *Martyrdom of St Sebastian* attributed to Agnolo Gaddi. To the south is the **Mercato di Sant' Ambrogio**, the second largest produce market in the city, after the Central Market, housed in a cast-iron market hall of 1873, now deteriorating.

Fish market: To the west, in Piazza dei Ciompi, is the **Loggia del Pesce**, designed by Vasari in 1568. The delicate arcade is decorated with roundels full of leaping fish and crustacea, but it is no longer used as a fish market. It was moved here in the 19th century when the Mercato Vecchio was demolished to create the Piazza della Repubblica. By day it is a market for junk and "near antiques". By night it is a rendezvous for transvestite prostitutes and their clients, and the pillars are covered in lewd graffiti.

Further out of town (a mile/1.5 km to the east) is the 14th-century church of the former **San Salvi** monastery (No 16 Via San Salvi). This houses one of the most famous of all Renaissance frescoes, the lively *Cenacolo* (Last Supper) of Andrea del Sarto. Nearby is the huge **Stadio Communale**, one of the city's few modern buildings of any architectural merit, capable of holding 66,000 spectators and designed by Pier Luigi Nervi in 1932.

Of the sights further out of Florence, the newly restored **Medici Villa** at **Poggio ai Caiano** is the most rewarding (10 miles (17 km) west of Florence; the bus from Piazza Santa Maria Novella takes 30 mins). The villa was built for

Villa della Petraia.

Lorenzo the Magnificent by Giuliano da Sangallo in 1480-85. The architect's innovative design was based on antique Roman prototypes, known from the treatise *De Architectura*, written by Vitruvius in the first century A.D. and, perhaps, from extant Roman villas still standing in the Tuscan countryside.

The result, much copied subsequently, is a handsome two-storey building rising from a broad colonnaded terrace. In 1802-07, the curving staircases were added, totally out of keeping with the original simple design but adding a note of grace and femininity to the façade.

Instead of an open atrium, or central courtyard, the space is occupied by a covered *salone* rising the full height of the building and covered with frescoes by various artists, including Andrea del Sarto and Pontormo, illustrating events from the lives of Cosimo and Lorenzo de' Medici, paralleled with events in classical history. The villa is surrounded by an extensive park and a

splendid orangery of 1825.

Two other villas, of interest principally for their gardens, are located in the northern suburbs (bus No. 28 from the Railway Station). About three miles (five km) out, in the suburb of **Il Sodo**, is the **Villa della Petreia**, built in 1575 by Buontalenti for Ferdinando de' Medici and incorporating the tower of an older castle. The moated garden and park are exceptionally well maintained, though the delicious statue of Venus wringing out her hair, by Giambologna, has been removed for restoration.

A short walk away, along Via della Petreia to Villa Corsini and then down Via di Castello, is the **Villa di Castello**, seat of the Accademia della Crusca, founded in 1582 to monitor the development of the Italian language and publish definitive dictionaries.

Castello was acquired by the Medici in the 15th century, but it was Cosimo I who restored it and commissioned Tribolo to design the allegorical garden, begun around 1537. Cosimo I later retired here, having handed over the reins of power to his son, and for the final three years of his life, during which he became increasingly irrational, devoted himself to the garden.

As with many grandiose Medici schemes, this one was never completed; but, even so, visitors from all over Europe came to marvel at its lavish scale and opulent ornamentation.

At the top of a series of terraces is the colossal figure, by Ammannati, of a chilly Apennino emerging from a pool. Below is a shell-encrusted grotto; Giambologna's bronze birds (now in the Bargello) were made for this, and visitors exploring the labyrinthine inner recesses were likely to be doused by trick fountains, triggered by false stones in the floor.

Secret gardens, an enormous Orangery and a fountain (under restoration) with bronze figures of Hercules crushing Antaeus all contribute to an atmosphere of ostentatious but enjoyable theatricality.

Villa Della Petraia: left, the Ballroom; right, history of the Medici family.

TRAVEL TIPS

GETTING THERE
242 By Air
242 By Rail
242 By Bus
242 By Car

TRAVEL ESSENTIALS
243 Visas & Passports
243 Health Tips
243 Money Matters
243 Customs Formalities
243 What to Wear

GETTING ACQUAINTED
244 Time Zones
244 Climate
244 Culture & Customs
245 Language
245 Business Hours
245 Electricity
245 Holidays
245 Festivals
246 Religious Services

COMMUNICATIONS
246 Media
246 Telephone
247 Postal Services
247 Telegrams & Telexes

EMERGENCIES
247 Security & Crime
247 Medical Services
248 Loss of Belongings
248 Left Luggage

GETTING AROUND
248 From the Airport
248 Orientation
249 Recommended Maps
249 Buses
249 Taxis
249 Walking & Cycling
249 By Car
250 Getting out of Florence
250 Hitchhiking

WHERE TO STAY
250 Hotels
252 Camping
252 Youth Hostels
252 Villas

FOOD DIGEST
253 What to Eat
254 Where to Eat
256 Drinking Notes

THINGS TO DO
256 Lectures
257 Libraries
257 City Tours

CULTURE PLUS
257 Museums & Art Galleries
257 Key Sights
258 Music, Opera & Ballet
258 Theatre
258 Cinema

NIGHTLIFE
259 Night Spots

SHOPPING
259 Shopping Hours
259 What to Buy
260 Markets
260 Export Procedures

SPORTS

SPECIAL INFORMATION
261 Children
261 Disabled
261 Students
262 Parks & Gardens

FURTHER READING

USEFUL ADDRESSES
263 Consulates
263 Airlines
263 Tourist Information

GETTING THERE

BY AIR

Florence itself does not yet have an international airport. The closest you can get by air is Pisa airport, 50 miles (80 km) west of Florence and linked to the city by train. British Airways and Alitalia operate regular scheduled flights from London. These are heavily booked in summer and advanced reservations are essential. Charter flights are also available, chiefly through tour operators who specialize in "flight only" packages to Italy. Alitalia also operates regular scheduled flights from Frankfurt and Paris in addition to direct internal services from Rome, Milan, Sardinia and Sicily. Visitors from outside Europe can fly direct to Milan or Rome, then take a connecting flight or train to Florence.

Peretola Airport, 2½ miles (4 km) northwest of Florence handles daily flights to and from Milan and Rome only, but the runway is being extended and, despite resistance from the Pisan authorities, the airport may open to European traffic soon.

BY RAIL

Two trans-European trains call at Florence—the Italia Express from London, which can also be picked up at Lille, Strasbourg and Basel, and the Palatino from Paris. Both cost more than a charter flight and involve a 24-hour journey. Reservations are obligatory on both services. Cars can be conveyed on special trains which operate during the summer season. Information from the European Rail Travel Centre, P.O. Box 303, Victoria Station, London SW1V 1JY or tel: 01-834 2345.

Florence railway station (Stazione di Santa Maria Novella) is located in the centre of the city. It is one of the busiest stations in Italy, with excellent connections to the rest of the country. Facilities include a small tourist office, with a hotel booking service, and a bank with long opening hours. The station is well served with buses but there are often lengthy queues for taxis in the summer.

BY BUS

National Express Eurolines operates a coach service from London to Florence (and Rome) via Turin, Genoa, Milan, Venice and Bologna. This is undoubtedly the most uncomfortable way of getting to Florence and, outside of the peak summer season, can cost more than a charter flight. You set off from London on Day 1 at 21.20 and arrive on Day 3 at 05.30. Details from National Express, Victoria Coach Station, London SW1. tel: 01-730 0202.

BY CAR

A determined driver could reach Florence from London in 24 hours using French and Italian motorways, though in summer one can expect long delays on the principal north/south routes. Visitors are entitled to buy petrol coupons from motoring organisations such as the AA, and the RAC, Italian tourist organisations such as Citalia, or at the frontier points. These allow a 15 percent discount on current petrol prices. They cannot be purchased in Italy.

To drive in Italy, visitors must carry a current driving licence (an international licence is not necessary), vehicle registration document and international green card (insurance certificate) and a warning triangle for use in the event of an accident or breakdown.

TRAVEL ESSENTIALS

VISAS & PASSPORTS

Citizens of the USA, EEC and Commonwealth only need their passport for a stay of up to three months. Citizens of most other countries must obtain a visa in advance from Italian embassies or consulates.

HEALTH TIPS

If you are going to Florence in high season, take mosquito repellent and some sort of protection against the sun. Tap water is safe provided there is no warning sign *ácqua non potabile*. Most visitors prefer to drink bottled mineral water, either fizzy (*gasata*) or still (*naturale*).

All EEC residents are entitled to medical treatment on the same basis as Italian nationals. Before departure you should obtain an E111 form from your local social security office. Officially the E111 form should be taken to the Local Health Unit (*Unita Sanitoria Locale*) in Italy before you seek treatment. The form covers free treatment by a doctor and free prescribed medicines, but not trip cancellation fees or cost of repatriation. If you want full cover you should take out separate medical insurance.

MONEY MATTERS

Traveller's cheques are the safest way of carrying around large amounts of money. The best rates of exchange are those of banks and bureaux de change which are generally open Mon-Fri 8.30-13.30 and 15.30-17.00. Commission rates for traveller's cheques vary considerably from bank to bank so it is worth shopping around. Eurocheques and major credit cards (Mastercard, American Express, Diner's Club, Visa) are accepted in the main hotels, restaurants and smarter shops—but not in petrol stations.

CUSTOMS FORMALITIES

Personal possessions are not normally liable to duty or tax if you enter Italy as a visitor, provided you intend to take them out again. A maximum of 400,000 lire can be taken into Italy but there is no restriction on the amount of foreign currency imported. Duty free allowances vary according to where you bought the goods. Goods obtained duty and tax paid within the EEC: 300 cigarettes or 150 cigarillos or 75 cigars or 400g of tobacco; 1.5 litres of alcoholic drinks over 22 percent volume or 2 litres of fortified or sparkling wine plus 4 litres of still table wine, 75g (3 fl oz or 90 cc) of perfume and 375 cc (13 fl oz) of toilet water.

Goods bought duty-free or in non-EEC countries: 200 cigarettes or 100 cigarillos or 50 cigars or 250g of tobacco; 1 litre of alcoholic drinks over 22 percent volume or 2 litres of fortified or sparkling wine plus 2 litres still table wine; 50g (2 fl oz or 60 cc) perfume and 250 cc (9 fl oz) toilet water.

WHAT TO WEAR

Casual wear is acceptable in all but the grandest hotel dining rooms and restaurants. Clothing should be as light as possible for summer but take a light jacket or sweater for the evenings which can be surprisingly cool.

If you go in spring or autumn, it's worth taking a light raincoat or umbrella. In winter, November to March, the temperature frequently drops to freezing or below, and warm clothing is essential for the outdoors. A pair of comfortable shoes is invaluable for sightseeing and walking the cobbled streets. Shorts and bare shoulders are frowned upon (and frequently forbidden) in churches.

GETTING ACQUAINTED

TIME ZONES

Italy is one hour ahead of Greenwich Mean Time (GMT) in winter and two hours ahead in summer (last weekend of March to last weekend of September). During Standard Time periods, when it is 12 noon in Florence, it is 12 noon in Bonn, Paris and Madrid; 13.00 in Athens and Cairo; 14.00 in Moscow and Istanbul; 16.30 in Bombay; 18.00 in Bangkok; 18.30 in Singapore; 19.00 in Hong Kong; 20.00 in Tokyo; 21.00 in Sydney; 01.00 in Honolulu; 08.00 in San Francisco and Los Angeles; 05.00 in Chicago; 06.00 in New York and Montreal; 08.00 in Rio de Janeiro; 11.00 in London.

CLIMATE

Enclosed in a ring of hills, Florence can be unbearably hot and humid in summer. Winters are wetter and not much warmer than London, but sightseeing without the crowds can be very pleasant at this time of year. Overall the best months to visit are May, September and early October when the temperatures are not too hot for sightseeing. The worst periods for crowding are Easter and June to the end of August.

CULTURE & CUSTOMS

Other Italians characterize the Florentines as miserly and hostile to strangers. Most visitors today will wonder where this patently untrue reputation came from. Though less demonstrative and histrionic than Romans or southern Italians, Florentines are welcoming and friendly, particularly to those who travel with children, or who attempt to communicate in Italian. They do not, rightly, tolerate boorish or drunken behaviour, but—on the other hand—they respond warmly to people who show a love and appreciation of their city.

Some Florentines are always bad-tempered—especially museum attendants and church custodians who take out their boredom on visitors. It is forbidden to use flash photography in any church or museum, and (in a city which abounds in sensual and erotic art) anyone who attempts to enter a church in shorts or with bare shoulders will be rudely ejected. Museum opening hours are notoriously unreliable. Strikes, union meetings and "staff shortages" frequently result in the closure of all or part of a museum without notice.

Tipping is expected even though restaurants include a service charge in the bill. Waiters and taxi drivers expect 10 percent, porters around 2,000 lire, and in cafés and bars it is usual to leave the small change.

LANGUAGE

English is very widely spoken but Florentines, like any other Italians, will appreciate even the feeblest attempt to speak their language. A phrase book is useful for translating menus in some of the smaller restaurants and shops.

BUSINESS HOURS

Virtually all offices, shops and banks close between 13.00 and 15.30 all year round. Office hours are usually 08.30-12.30 and 15.30-18.30. Banks open 08.20-13.20 Mon-Fri, but some open for an hour or so in the afternoon for foreign exchange transactions—times vary from bank to bank but there are usually several open 15.00-16.00. The bank at the railway station is open 08.20-19.00 mid-June to mid-September.

Shops are open from 08.30/09.00 to 12.30/13.00 and from 15.30/16.00 to 19.30/20.00. Off-season, food shops are closed on Wednesday afternoon, other shops on Monday morning. From mid-June to mid-September most shops are closed on Saturday afternoon; and throughout the year all of them are closed on Sunday.

ELECTRICITY

The standard current is 220 volts AC. Plugs have two round pins and an adaptor will be necessary for most razors, hair dryers, computers, etc, though the better hotels will usually supply these.

HOLIDAYS

Shops and banks close during the days listed below:

Capodanno	1 January
Lunedì dell'angelo	Easter Monday
Anniversario della	
Liberazione	25 April
Festa del Lavoro	1 May
Ferragosto	15 August
Ognissanti	1 November
Immacolata	
Concezione	8 December
Natale	25 December
S. Stefano	26 December

Many shops in Florence also close on 24 June, festival of the patron saint of Florence, San Giovanni.

FESTIVALS

Like most Italian cities, Florence has its fair share of festivals, some religious, others cultural or commercial. Exhibitions, many of them high fashion and crafts, are organised throughout the year. The following are the main events held in the city or close by.

Shore Tuesday: *Carnevale*. A low key

event in Florence, but many nearby villages celebrate with fireworks and processions. The most elaborate is at Viareggio.

Easter Day: *Scoppio del Carro* (Explosion of the Cart). A firework in the shape of a dove is sent from the high altar of the Duomo to ignite an oxen-drawn cart laden with fireworks, which awaits outside.

April: June Flower display in Piazza Signoria and Uffizi.

May: Iris festival in garden just below Piazzale Michelangelo.

Mid-May to late June: Maggio Musicale (see Music, Opera and Ballet section).

24 to 28 June: Feast of St. John the Baptist, patron saint of Florence. Fireworks displays in the Piazzale Michelangelo. The *Gioco del Calcio*—a traditional football game played in 16th-century costume—is played in the Piazza Sigonia or in the Boboli Gardens.

2 July, Siena. The famous *Palio* festival—a frenzied bareback horserace around the Piazza del Campo, following a day of pageantry and parades.

15 August, Assumption Day: *Festa del Grillo*. Large fair in the Cascine park where caged crickets are sold.

7 September: *Festa delle rificolone* (Festival of Lanterns). Children run through the streets with coloured paper lanterns—an ancient festival celebrating the eve of the Birth of the Virgin.

September—November: Antiques fair at Palazzo Strozzi held biennially in odd numbered years.

RELIGIOUS SERVICES

Services are held in English at the American Episcopal Church of St. James, Via B. Rucellai 9 (tel: 294 417), and the Anglican church of St. Mark, Via Maggio 16 (tel: 294 764). Catholic mass in Italian is celebrated at 12.00 on Sundays and at the same time on weekdays in most churches. The Duomo holds a Mass in English every Saturday at 17.00. The Synagogue is at Via L.C. Farini 4, tel: 210 763.

COMMUNICATIONS

MEDIA

The national daily newspaper read by most Florentines, because of its coverage of local events, is *La Nazione*. The English language *International Courier* covers local as well as world news. The fortnightly listings magazine *Welcome to Florence* is a useful guide to local events and is available free from tourist offices and larger hotels. Most foreign newspapers and magazines are available at city centre newsstands.

Televisions in the larger hotels usually carry cable and satellite TV, including English-language news, sports and entertainment channels, in addition to local stations.

TELEPHONE

There is no shortage of public telephones. You can find them at post offices, bars and tobacconists. Some of the new phones take cards, which you can buy at newsagents and tobacconists. Other public phones take 100 lire or 200 lire coins except the oldest among them and those in cafés which still take *gettoni* or metal tokens. These cost 200 lire and you can buy them from a tobacconist or at the bar.

For long distance calls the cheapest method is to use the SIP telephone offices where you can talk for as long as you like and pay after making the call. The offices are at Via Pellicceria post office (open 24 hours), or at Via Cavour 21r—close to San Marco (open 09.00 to 20.00), and at the railway station. Making a long-distance call from a hotel will cost you a good deal more.

POSTAL SERVICES

The main office, open 24 hours, is the Palazzo della Posta in Via Pellicceria. The other head office is at 53, Via Pietrapiana. Stamps are sold at tobacconists (look for the black sign with a white "T"), post offices and some hotels. At the time of writing, letters weighing up to 20g cost 600 lire within the EEC, 700 lire elsewhere; postcards 500 lire to all destinations. You can receive *Poste Restante* mail at the post office in Via Pellicceria; this should be marked "Fermo Posta" and you will need to produce a passport or similar form of identification in order to collect mail.

TELEGRAMS & TELEXES

Telegrams and telexes can be sent from the main post offices. The telegram office at the station is open 24 hours. Alternatively you can send a telegram message on a private phone by dialling 186.

EMERGENCIES

SECURITY & CRIME

For all emergencies telephone 113 and ask for police, fire or ambulance. Florence is one of the drug centres of Italy. Terrorism and kidnapping have also loomed large in recent years. For tourists, however, the major problems are pick-pocketing, bag-snatching and robbery. These can usually be avoided if you follow a few basic rules: leave large amounts of cash or jewellery at your hotel (preferably in a safe deposit), avoid deserted areas of the city after dark and always keep an eye on handbags.

If driving, be sure to lock your car and never leave valuables inside; in particular, you should never leave the vehicle registration or rental documents in the car because proof of ownership is required before the police will assist in cases of theft.

MEDICAL SERVICES

There are 24-hour emergency departments at the following hospitals: Ospedale Santa Maria Nuova, Piazza Santa Maria Nuova 1, tel: 27581 and Generale di Careggi, Viale G.B. Morgagni 85, tel: 43991. The Tourist Medical Service, at Via Lorenzo Il Magnifico 59, tel: 475 411 is a privately run organisation which provides an emergency service (including dental treatment) for foreigners.

Pharmacies (farmacia) open at night according to a rota, copies of which are posted on the door and published in La Nazione. There is a 24-hour pharmacy—The Farmacia Communale—in the railway station tel:

263 435. The International Pharmacy, Via Tornabuoni 2, has multi-lingual staff.

LOSS OF BELONGINGS

The lost property office is at 22 Lungarno delle Grazie tel: 367 943. The loss or theft of valuables should be reported to the local police at once, as it is usually a condition of insurance policies that you do so and obtain a police report. You should also report the loss of a passport immediately to the police and your consulate.

LEFT LUGGAGE

There is a left luggage office, and coin-operated lockers, at the railway station.

GETTING AROUND

FROM THE AIRPORT

At Pisa's Galileo Galilei airport, taxis are available for the one-hour journey to Florence, but they are expensive—allow 100,000 lire. Most visitors use the excellent rail link. Tickets cost 4,400 lire and can be purchased at the kiosk in the airport arrival hall. The station is just outside, and to the left of the terminal exit. Trains leave at hourly intervals taking 50 minutes to reach Florence. Florence railway station is in the heart of the city and most hotels are a short taxi journey away. There is no bus or coach link between Pisa airport and Florence—at least until the completion of the Pisa/Florence motorway—but the major car rental firms all have offices at Pisa airport.

ORIENTATION

In such a compact city the easiest way of getting around is on foot. Most of the streets of Florence run north/south or east/west and landmarks, such as the Duomo, provide a visible reference point from most points in the city. None of the main sights is more than 15 minutes walk from the Duomo.

During the day the city centre is prohibited to all motorcars except those of residents who own a special permit. Most of the principal streets are now pedestrianised.

If you are looking for a particular address, bear in mind that every street has a dual numbering system. Commercial premises are numbered in red and the written address has a small "r" after the number (e.g. to find the Post office at Via Cavour 21r you should look for a white plate with the number 21 in red). Residential addresses have blue numbers on a white plate. In the principal streets there are many more commercial than residential addresses, with the result that number 21 (blue) may be a considerable distance further down the road than number 21r.

RECOMMENDED MAPS

The free tourist map is adequate for individual principal sights. The Hallwag map, sold at all city centre newsstands, is comprehensive and the easiest to use.

BUSES

The bus network, run by ATAF, provides an efficient and fast means of transport in the city and out to suburbs such as Fiesole. But it takes a while to master, thanks to the complexity of one-way streets. Tickets are bought from tobacconists, newspaper stands, bars or from the ATAF offices at main points throughout the city. You can buy a special ticket which allows unlimited bus travel for 70 minutes. All tickets must be punched in the automatic machines on the bus. Some of the newer buses, recognisable by a sign of a hand holding a coin, accept exact change. For information and maps go to the main ATAF office at 57r Piazza del Duomo (tel: 212 301); there are also bus maps in the city telephone directory.

TAXIS

Cabs are white with yellow stripes and are hired from ranks in the main piazzas and at the station. They seldom stop if you hail them in the street. Meters are provided and fares should always be displayed. The Radio Taxi system is fast and efficient—tel: 4390 or 4798.

WALKING & CYCLING

The main drawbacks to walking in the city are narrow pavements (frequently blocked by cars or motorbikes) and noisy traffic.

Bicycles can be hired from Ciao & Basta, Costa dei Magnoli, 24 (tel: 293 357 and 263 985). For those using authorised carparks, the city council offer two free bikes for the day. Information from Ente Provinciale Turismo, Via Manzoni 16 (tel: 247 8141).

Motorbikes or mopeds, useful for trips to the countryside, can be hired from Eurodrive, Via Alamanni 7/9r (tel: 298 639), Motorent, Via San Zanobi 9r (tel: 490 113) or Program, Borgo Ognissanti 96 (tel: 282 916).

Horse-drawn carriages, which can be hired outside the Duomo, are a dying form of transport, solely used by affluent tourists. If you take one, be prepared to do some hard bargaining.

BY CAR

A car within the city is a positive drawback. Traffic jams are appalling, the one-way system highly complex, the streets desperately narrow and local drivers a force to contend with. The historic centre is closed to all but holders of a special resident's permit. Exceptions have been made for tourists in the past but this concession is likely to be revoked at some time in the future. If you drive to Florence and your hotel has no car park, you are best advised to leave the car outside the centre. There is a large park at Fortezza da Basso, just northeast of the station, with a free bus service to the centre.

CAR HIRE

The main car-rental firms have offices at the airport as well as in Florence.
Avis, Borgo Ognissanti, 128r (tel: 213 629)
Eurodrive, Via della Scala, 48r (tel: 298 639)
Europcar, Borgo Ognissanti, 120r
   (tel: 294 130)

Europedrive, Via S. Zanobi, 9r (tel: 496 649 and 351 025)
Hertz, Via M. Finiguerra, 33 (tel: 282 260)
InterRent Autonoleggio, Via Il Prato, 1r (tel: 218 665)
Italy by Car, Borgo Ognissanti, 113r (tel: 293 021)
Maggiore, Via M. Finiguerra, 11 (tel: 294 578)
Program, Borgo Ognissanti, 96 (tel: 282 916)
Local companies are slightly cheaper than international firms.

GETTING OUT OF FLORENCE

A wide network of bus services operates throughout Tuscany. Fares are reasonable. The main companies are Lazzi, Piazza Stazione, 47r (tel: 294 178) and SITA, Via Santa Caterina da Siena 15r (tel: 211 487). A rapid coach service to Siena operates roughly every half an hour in season and takes 1¼ hours. Trains to Pisa depart roughly every hour from the railway station.

Several companies organise coach excursions of the historic cities and Tuscan countryside. One of the main operators is CIT, Via Cavour 56, tel: 294 306.

Having a car has obvious advantages if you're touring Tuscany. The area is well served by motorways (though tolls are expensive). Siena, Arezzo, Pisa and the coast are all within easy reach.

HITCHHIKING

This is illegal in Italy but the Agenzia Autostop, Corso dei Tintori 39, tel: 247 8626 will, for a small fee, fix up lifts (usually with long-distance lorry drivers) to all parts of Italy and Europe.

WHERE TO STAY

Despite the fact that Florence now has 370 hotels, the demand for rooms in season still far outweighs supply.

If you are going any time from June to the end of August (and at Easter) make sure you make a reservation well in advance. Accommodation ranges from de luxe hotels with pools to simple city guest houses occupying third or fourth floors of medieval *palazzi*. Whatever the category of hotel, public rooms are usually furnished with antiques and paintings. Bedrooms can be rather dark, but the main drawback of staying in the city—even if you're several stories up from street level—is the noise. Worst of all are hotels on or close to roads running alongside the river. To ensure a good night's sleep ask for a room overlooking the courtyard or choose a hotel out of the city centre. There are several charming villa hotels and *pensioni* in the surrounding hillsides, easily reached from the city.

If you arrive on spec and want a room, try the ITA (Hotel Association) offices at the railway station (open all year) or at the Fortezza da Basso (April to November only).

HOTELS

•DE LUXE

Excelsior, Piazza Ognissanti 3, tel: 264 201
The grandest hotel in Florence—a lavishly furnished 19th-century building on the banks of the Arno. Celebrities and business executives stay here. Panoramic rooftop restaurant.

Grand, Piazza Ognissanti 1, tel: 681 3861
Smaller than its sister hotel (the Excelsior, across the square) but almost as grand. It reopened in 1986 and rooms are still being added. Queen Victoria and other foreign royalty stayed here in the 19th century.

Regency, Piazza Massimo D'Azeglio 3, tel: 245 247
Small exclusive hotel on a quiet square 15 minutes' walk from the centre. Stylish bedrooms, club-like atmosphere and top-notch cuisine in garden-view restaurant.

Savoy, Piazza della Repubblica 7, tel: 283 313
Old-established hotel in centre of shopping district. Solid, old-fashioned comforts and good service.

Villa Medici, Via Il Prato 42, tel: 261 331
Sumptuously furnished hotel with large bedrooms overlooking garden and pool. Quiet setting 15 minutes' walk from centre.

Villa San Michele, Via Doccia 4, Fiesole, tel: 59451
One of the most exclusive hotels in Italy. A converted monastery (parts of which were designed by Michelangelo) on a quiet hill in Fiesole. Rooms are discreetly elegant and facilities include heated pool, piano bar and loggia for *al fresco* meals.

•**EXPENSIVE**

Croce di Malta, Via della Scala 7, tel: 218 351
Curious combination of mock-Renaissance and post-modern, but has the advantage of garden, pool and convenient location for the station.

de la Ville, Piazza Antinori 1, tel: 261 805
Plushly furnished first class hotel close to all the fashionable shops. Quiet, very comfortable rooms.

Kraft, Via Solferino 2, tel: 284 273
Civilized and efficiently run hotel in quiet location 15 minutes' walk from centre. Rooftop restaurant and swimming pool with excellent views. Very popular with Americans.

Lungarno, Borgo Sant' Jacopo 14, tel: 264 211
Delightful modern hotel on south bank of the Arno. Drawings of Cocteau and Picasso feature among the owner's impressive collection of modern art. Good views of river from front rooms.

Monna Lisa, Borgo Pinti 27, tel: 247 9751
A favourite amongst visitors to Florence. Renaissance *palazzo* with antiques, drawings and sculpture. Delightful garden. But somewhat overpriced these days.

Plaza Lucchesi, Lungarno della Zecca Vecchia 38, tel: 264 141
Comfortable, civilised and very efficiently run hotel overlooking the Arno.

•**MODERATE**

Annalena, Via Romana 34, tel: 222 402
Handsomely furnished guest house close to the Boboli Gardens.

Hermitage, Vicolo Marzio 1, Piazza del Pesce, tel: 287 216
Small, intimate and exceptionally popular hotel close to the Ponte Vecchio. Pretty rooftop terrace with views of the Arno. Some rooms very noisy.

Loggiato dei Serviti, Piazza S.S. Annunziata 3, tel: 219 165
Newly converted from a fine Renaissance building which twins Brunelleschi's Foundling Hospital (Innocenti) on the opposite side of the square. A charming, very refined hotel with tiled terracotta floors, original vaulting and old furnishings. Particularly popular with art lovers.

Pitti Palace, Via Barbadori 2, tel: 282 257
Perennial favourite with English-speaking visitors (the owner's wife is American). Pretty roof terrace and sitting rooms, convenient location just south of the Ponte Vecchio, but some very noisy bedrooms.

Residenza, Via Tornabuoni 8, tel: 284 197
Small *pensione* in upper floors of old building on the city's smartest shopping street. Homely public areas with lots of plants and pictures. Bedrooms range from rustic to modern.

Tornabuoni Beacci, Via Tornabuoni 3, tel: 268 377
De luxe guest house, very comfortable and very welcoming. Pretty rooftop terrace for breakfast and drinks. Half board terms compulsory. Particularly popular with Americans.

Villa Belvedere, Via Benedetto Castelli 3, tel: 50124
Exceptionally friendly modern villa 1/ᵢ™ miles (3 km) south of city. Sunny rooms, pretty garden and lovely views across Florence. Swimming pool and tennis court.

•INEXPENSIVE

Aprile, Via della Scala 6, tel: 216 237
One of the more appealing hotels near the station. A Medici palace with original frescoes and some painted ceilings. Huge range of bedrooms, some very simple.

Cestelli, Borgo SS Apostoli 25, tel: 214 213
Tiny, intimate guest house in narrow medieval street. Rock-bottom prices but very simple rooms and only one with private bathroom.

Liana, Via Alfieri 18, tel: 245 303
Simple hotel north of centre in former British Embassy. Quiet, pleasant but slightly faded.

Porta Rossa, Via Porta Rossa 19, tel: 287 551
Large and old fashioned, with huge spartan rooms. Favourite amongst the *literati*.

Rigatti, Lungarno Generale Diaz 2, tel: 213 022
Family-run, typically Florentine *pensione*, occupying two floors of a 15th-century *palazzo*. Lovely old furnishings and private home atmosphere. Choice of noisy rooms with a river view or quieter ones overlooking courtyard.

Splendor, Via San Gallo 30, tel: 483 427
Modest hotel close to the Accademia, set in old building with painted ceilings. Antiques and 1960s furnishings somewhat uncoordinated but good-sized rooms and very reasonable prices.

CAMPING

The closest camping site to town is the Italiani e Stranieri at 80 Viale Michelangelo, open April to October. The Camping Panoramico in Fiesole is open all year and has lovely views. For information on all sites write to Federazione Italiana del Campeggia, Casella Postale 649, 50100 Firenze.

YOUTH HOSTELS

The main youth hostel is the Ostello Europa Villa Camerata at 2 Viale Augusto Righi, out of town with quiet gardens.

VILLAS

Rarely available at short notice, but if you write to Agriturist, Via del Proconsolo 10, 50123 Firenze they will send lists of country houses, often of great historical interest and character, in the countryside around Florence.

FLATS

Self-catering accommodation, usually in flats rented out by the owners while they themselves are elsewhere on vacation, can be booked through the agency "Florence and Abroad", Via S. Zanobi 58, 50129 Firenze, Tel: (055) 490 143. Demand is very heavy in the high season and it is best to book several months in advance.

RESIDENCES

Serviced apartments, or residences, are an attractive alternative to hotels, but must be taken for a minimum of one week. Again, prior booking (several weeks in advance for the summer season) is essential. Two of the best have been converted from historic palaces and provide a taste of the life which only the more affluent Florentines know. They are the Residence Palazzo Ricasoli, Via della Montellate 2, Tel: 352151 and Residence La Fonte, Via S. Felice a Ema 29, Tel: 224 421.

FOOD DIGEST

WHAT TO EAT

•SIENA

Park Hotel, Via di Marciano 18, (tel: 0577-44803). Expensive.
Luxury hotel with pool and landscaped gardens in modernized 15th-century villa; 2 km from centre.

Certosa di Maggiano, Strada di Certosa 82 (tel: 0577-288 180). Expensive.
Small, exclusive hotel, heralded by quiet cloister of 14th-century Carthusian monastery. Country house furnishings, elegant bedrooms, pool and peaceful gardens.

Palazzo Ravizza, Piano dei Mantellini 34, (tel: 0577-280 462). Moderate.
Old-fashioned, pleasantly faded pensione. Sombre bedrooms but pretty garden and good home-cooking.

•VOLTERRA

Villa Nencini, Borgo Santo Stefano 55 (tel: 0588-86386). Inexpensive.
Small, spotless hotel in attractive 17th-century villa, just outside city walls. Simply furnished bedrooms, pretty garden and views. No restaurant.

Local dishes have their roots in rural Tuscany and tend to be simple and wholesome. The emphasis is on prime quality ingredients rather than adventurous sauces: hearty soups, Tuscan hams, pasta, meat roasted or grilled over an open fire and washed down with a bottle of good Chianti.

As in other parts of the country, local specialities are rapidly giving way to the demands of international palates but the following are a few of the typical Tuscan dishes which you still come across in some of the city's *trattorie*: crostini—chicken liver or wild boar pate on baked or fried country bread, soups such as *minestrone*, bean soup or *ribollita*, a thick soup made with bread and vegetables; *pappardelle alla lepre* tagliatelle with wild hare sauce, *bistecca alla fiorentina*—a huge T-bone steak (sold by the kilo and often shared by two or even three), *arista*—pork roasted with garlic and rosemary; tripe cooked in tomato sauce; *castagnaccio*—chestnut pie, *zuccotto*—a liqueur-soaked sponge and chocolate pudding. The traditional way to end a meal is with *biscotti di Prato* or *guadrucci*, almond biscuits which you dip into *vin santo*, a sweet dessert wine.

The typical Florentine trattoria is a *buca* or simple cellar-style restaurant with wooden tables and walls covered in paintings. Service in such places tends to be somewhat brusque but the atmosphere is lively and fun. For those with more sophisticated tastes there are a number of new smart restaurants in and around the city which combine *nouvelle cuisine* with traditional Tuscan cooking.

WHERE TO EAT

•De luxe

Enoteca Pinchiorri, Via Ghibellina, 87, tel: 242 777, closed Sun, Mon lunch and August. Reservations essential. Occupying a 15th-century palace with delightful courtyard for *al fresco* meals. Rated among the top restaurants of Europe. Excellent *nouvelle cuisine* and an impressive collection of wines.

Il Cestello, Hotel Excelsior, Piazza Ognissanti 3, tel: 294 301. Very elegant hotel restaurant with top quality Tuscan and international dishes. Popular rendezvous for business executives. Stunning views from the rooftop restaurant.

Regency, Piazza Massimo d' Azeglio 3, tel: 245 247. Top-notch food in exclusive hotel restaurant, overlooking a garden.

•Expensive

La Capannina di Sante, Piazza Ravenna, tel: 688 345, closed Sun, Mon lunch, one week August and Christmas. One of the best fish restaurants in town, patronized by the local business community. No puddings.

La Loggia, Piazzale Michelangelo 1, tel: 234 2832, closed Wed and two weeks in August. Popular tourist spot with superb panorama over the city.

•Reasonable

Cantinetta Antinori, Piazza Antinori 3, tel: 292 234. In a 15th-century *palazzo* serving typical Tuscan snacks and meals served with wines from the well-known Antinori estates. Good place for a light lunch at the bar or a fuller meal in the elegant dining room.

Bronzino, Via delle Ruote 25r, tel: 495 220, closed Sun and three weeks in August. Spacious restaurant out of the centre and named after the painter who lived and worked here in the 16th century. A favourite haunt for discerning Florentines.

Buca Mario, Piazza Ottaviani 16, tel: 214 179, closed Wed, Thur lunch and three weeks in July. Cellar restaurant with good home-made pasta and grilled meats. Very popular with tourists.

Cibrèo, Via dei Macci 118r, tel: 234 1000, closed Sun, Mon, six weeks August to September. One of the most popular restaurants in town amongst new generation Florentines. Mainly nouvelle cuisine grafted on to Tuscan cooking. No pastas. The same food, at half the price, is served in the *Vinaria* section, just around the corner.

Coco Lezzone, Via del Parioncino 26r, tel: 287 178, closed Sun and Wed evening (Sat and Sun in summer but open Wed). Crowded, chaotic white-tiled trattoria with good Tuscan cooking. Favourite haunt of locals.

Da Noi, Via Fiesolana 46r, tel: 242 917, closed Sun, Mon, Aug, reservations essential. Run by former staff of Enoteca Pinchiorri (see above). Small and intimate with good quality nouvelle cuisine and Italian dishes. No written menus but excellent English spoken.

Le Fonticine, Via Nazionale 79r, tel: 282 106, closed Sat, Sun and four weeks July/August. Friendly family-run restaurant near station specializing in Tuscan and Emilian dishes. Excellent home-made pastas.

•Inexpensive

Angiolini, Via S. Spirito 36, tel 298 976, closed Sun, Mon. Bustling, typically Florentine, in the Oltrarno district.

Belle Donne, Via delle Belle Donne 16, tel 262 609, closed Sat eve, Sun. A hole-in-the-wall near the railway station, worth visiting for simple rustic specialities.

Burde, Via Pistoiese 6, tel: 317 0206, closed evenings and two weeks in August. Authentic Tuscan trattoria with home-made soups, pastas and puddings. Tuesdays and Fridays are the best days for fish. No dinner served.

Il Caminetto, Via dello Studio 34r, tel: 296 274, closed Tue, Wed and July. Hearty simple and filling food.

Il Fagioli, Corso Tintori 47r, tel: 244 285, closed August, Sun and also Sat in summer. Simple, friendly trattoria with typical Tuscan fare.

Il Latini, Via dei Palchetti 6r, tel: 210 916, closed Mon, Tue lunch, three weeks in July and August. Typical Tuscan food at communal tables in noisy cellar restaurant.

Tarocchi, Via dei Renai 12, tel 234 3912. Lively and friendly pizzeria.

Vittoria, Via della Fonderia 52r, tel: 225 657, closed Wed, August. Basic trattoria in the San Frediano district with good simply cooked fish. No meat.

CAFES & ICE CREAM

Break, Via delle Terme 17. Simple, fun and a good choice for buffet lunch.

Doney, Piazza Strazzi 16-19. Elegant premises for afternoon tea.

Giacosa, Via Tornabuoni. 83, closed Mon. Up-market cafe where the young affluent eat home-made pastries, with the best *cappuccino* in Florence.

Giubbe Rosse, Piazza della Repubblica. Once favoured by writers and poets, and still popular, with an open air café and a dining room serving snacks or full meals.

Rivoire, Piazza Signoria 5, closed Mon. Views of the Palazzo Vecchio but prices are high.

Vivoli, Via Isola delle Stiche 7, closd Sun pm, Mon. Best ice cream in the world. Occasional queues. No seats.

EATING OUTSIDE FLORENCE

Siena: For superb setting (rather than exceptional food or reasonable prices) try either Il Campo or Mangia, both on the famous Piazza del Campo. The Al Marsili, Via del Castora 3, tel: (0577) 47154, closed Mon, an elegant restaurant in an original 15th-century building, is a better bet for food.

Pisa has two Michelin rosetted restaurants: the Sergio, Lungarno Pacinotti 1, tel: (0577) 48245, closed Sun, Mon lunch, Jan and last two weeks in July; and the smaller and slightly cheaper Al Ristoro dei Vecchi Macelli, Via Volturno 49, tel: (0577) 20424, closed Sun lunch, Wed, one week Jan and most of August. Reservations advisable. At the lower end of the market Da Bruno, Via Bianchi 12, tel: (0577) 560 818 (outside the walls) serves typical Tuscan dishes at very reasonable prices.

Arezzo: Buca di San Francesco, Piazza San Francesco 1, tel: (0575) 23271, closed Mon evening, Tue and July. Famous cellar restaurant beside the church of San Francesco. Kings, presidents and nobel prize winners have eaten here. Strong on atmosphere, not so good on cuisine. Better value food at the modern Il Torrino, Superstrada dei Due Mari, tel: (0575) 36264, eight km southeast of the town (closed Mon).

Volterra: The only restaurant of note is the Etruria, Piazza dei Prior 6/8, tel (0588) 86064, closed Thur and mid-Nov to end Dec; comfortable and congenial with good Tuscan cooking.

Lucca: Solferino, San Marcario in Piano (six km from Lucca), tel: (0583) 59118, closed Wed, Thur lunch, two weeks in August. Rated among the best restaurants of rural Tuscany and not wildly expensive.

DRINKING NOTES

The Chianti district, between Florence and Siena, is the most productive wine-producing region of Italy and every Florentine restaurant will offer a broad choice of wines from the locality. The house wine—*vino della casa*—will invariably be the cheapest but will vary markedly in quality from thin, if drinkable, young wines to full-bodied Chianti. The red table wines are usually better than the whites though these are improving with the introduction of new grape varieties that contribute fruitiness and flavour.

Most wine-lovers consider that the Chianti Classico marketed under the Gallo Nero (black cock) label is the best of the region's mass-produced wine.

At the next level up in price are the Chianti Classico estate-bottled wines, of which the most consistently good are those from Castello di Brolio and Antinori.

All these regular Chianti are drunk at any time from one to five or more years after bottling, and the best vintages of recent years are those of 1975, 1977, 1978, 1979 and 1982.

At the very top end of the market are those Chianti labelled *riserva*, which must have been aged for several years in wood to qualify for the title, and drunk five years or more after bottling.

For those who take a serious interest in wine, the *Mitchell Beazley Pocket Guide to Italian Wines* by Burton Anderson is an essential travelling companion.

THINGS TO DO

LECTURES

Florence has scores of cultural institutions and hundreds of academics from around the world come here to conduct their research. Many give illustrated lectures that range from basic introductions to the history and art of the city to the minutiae of a great painter's technique or the meaning and symbolism of his work. Lectures are a good way to meet like-minded people, learn something new and occasionally witness a tour de force performance by the world's leading authorities on their subject. Refreshments are usually served after lectures.

Perhaps the most varied programmes of talks and concerts is organised by the British Institute of Florence, Palazzo Feroni, Via Tornabuoni 2, tel 284 031. The same Institute runs courses of 4 weeks average duration in the Italian language, practical art and art history. Fees are not expensive and the Institute can arrange accommodation for students with Italian families at very reasonable cost.

The Instituto Alfieri organises lectures specifically designed for visitors every evening Monday through Friday at 9 p.m. Lectures are in English but can be given in other languages if a sufficiently large group requests it.

Details from the school at Via dell' Oriuolo 20, tel. 234 0669.

LIBRARIES

The British Institute Library, Lungarno Guicciardini 9 (tel 284 031) is open Monday to Friday, 10.00 to 12.30 and 16.00 to 19.00. The American Library, Via San Gallo 10 (tel: 296 114) Monday to Friday, 09.00 to 12.30.

Both libraries are invaluable for their large reference collections of books and periodicals about the city and its culture.

CITY TOURS

Travel agents organize day and half-day tours of the city and surrounds. CIT (Via Cavour 56, tel: 294306) is one of the main organizers. Excursions to the beautiful countryside around Florence are very popular. Some day tours take in the hillside village of Fiesole, much-frequented for its sights and stunning views. From April to October excursions are organized to the gardens of some of the great Florentine villas; and to some of the vineyards of Chianti.

CULTURE PLUS

MUSEUMS & ART GALLERIES

With 51 museums and 24 historic churches, Florence is primarily a city for art lovers. But sightseeing in the city can be as frustrating as it is rewarding. Most museums and galleries are closed in the afternoons (the Uffizi, open until 19.00 is a notable exception), famous buildings or frescoes are frequently masked by scaffolding and top sights are packed throughout the tourist season. Opening times change with alarming frequency, but hotels usually post up the latest news on official opening times and the tourist office should be able to provide you with an updated list. Remember though that ticket offices close 30 to 45 minutes before the museum itself closes. Thanks to sponsorship, some of the smaller museums are now open 21.00 to 23.00 for one or two evenings a week during summer. Look for news of these in the "Welcome to Florence" listings magazine.

KEY SIGHTS

Casa Buonarroti, Via Ghibellina 70, 09.30 to 13.30. Closed Tuesday. Small museum of works by or attributed to Michelangelo: drawings, sketches, models and two of his earliest sculptures.

Galleria dell'Accademia, Via Ricasoli, 60. Monday-Saturday 09.00 to 14.00. Sundays 09.00 to 13.00. Home of the most powerful piece of Florentine sculpture—Michelangelo's David.

Galleria degli Uffizi, Loggia degli Uffizi, 6. Monday-Saturday 09.00 to 19.00. Sunday 09.00 to 13.00. Unrivalled collection of Florentine Renaissance art. Botticelli, Leonardo da Vinci, Michelangelo, Raphael and Titian are among the many well-known artists represented. Also works by major foreign artists. There are 45 rooms in all. To avoid the worst crowds, go during lunch hour or late afternoon/evening.

Museo Archeologico, Via della Colonna, 36. Monday to Saturday 09.00 to 14.00. Sunday 09.00 to 13.00. Etruscan, Greek, Roman and Egyptian works of art.

Museo dell'Angelico (Museo di San Marco), Piazza San Marco. Monday to Saturday 09.00 to 14.00. Sunday 09.00 to 13.00. Delightful collection of works by Fra Angelico, in evocative monastery setting.

Museo del Bargello, Palazzo del Podesta, Via del Proconsolo 4. Monday to Saturday 09.00 to 14.00. Sunday 09.00 to 13.00. Famous collection of Florentine Renaissance sculpture, including works by Michelangelo and Donatello.

Museo dell'Opera del Duomo, Piazza del Duomo 9. Monday to Saturday 09.00 to 20.00 (winter 18.00). Sunday 10.00 to 13.00. Rich collection of Florentine sculptures from the Duomo, baptistry and campanile. Highlight is Michelangelo's Pietà.

Palazzo Davanzati/Museo della Casa Fiorentina Antica, Piazza Davanzati, Via Porta Rossa. Tuesday to Saturday, 09.00 to 14.00. Sunday 09.00 to 13.00. Beautifully furnished medieval town house illustrating Florentine life in the Middle Ages.

Palazzo Medici-Riccardi, Via Cavour. Monday to Tuesday, Thursday to Saturday 09.00 to 12.30 and 15.00 to 17.00. Sunday 09.00 to noon. Medici residence for nearly 100 years, built by Michelozzo. Showpiece is the exquisite little chapel, decorated with famous frescoes by Benozzo Gozzoli.

Palazzo Pitti, Piazza Pitti. Monday to Saturday 09.00 to 14.00. Sunday 09.00 to 13.00. Huge Renaissance palace housing the magnificent Medici art collection. Sumptuous galleries with works by Raphael, Titian, Rubens, Van Dyck and others. Also Royal Apartments and *Argenteria* with gold, silver and other Medici treasures.

Palazzo Vecchio, Piazza della Signoria. Monday-Friday 09.00 to 19.00. Sunday 08.00 to 13.00. Austere fortress-palace built at end of the 13th century; large rooms with late Renaissance frescoes and paintings.

MUSIC, OPERA & BALLET

The *Maggio Musicale* music festival, held from mid-May to the end of June, is a big event with top names in concert, ballet and opera performing in various venues throughout the city. Tickets are available from the Teatro Comunale, Corso Italia 16 (tel: 277 9236). Concerts, formal and informal, are held throughout the summer in cloisters, piazzas or the Boboli Gardens. The main concert hall and venue for opera and ballet is the Teatro Comunale. The opera season opens at the end of September or beginning of October. During the Estate Fiesolina, Fiesole's summer festival, concerts, opera, ballet and theatre are held in the Roman amphitheatre.

THEATRE

The main theatre is the Teatro della Pergola, Via della Pergola 18 (tel: 247 9651). Most productions are in Italian.

CINEMA

The only English-language cinema is the Astro, Piazza Simone, near Santa Croce, which shows films every night except Monday. In summer occasional English-language films are shown on outdoor screens at Fort Belvedere.

NIGHTLIFE

SHOPPING

To the casual visitor the streets of Florence seem quiet by night. But a large student population ensures that there are plenty of discos, bars and new-wave clubs once you know where to find them. Most of the clientele is young.

Florentines have been producing exquisite pieces for centuries. Although the small workshops are fast disappearing you can still find beautifully created items—from gilded furniture and gold jewellery to gorgeous leather goods.

NIGHT SPOTS

SHOPPING HOURS

Caffe, Piazza Pitti, 9—cocktail bar-cum-cafe, full of fashionable Florentines.

Caffe Strozzi, Piazza Strozzi—elegant cafe in the city centre.

Loggia Tornaquinci, Via Tornabuoni 6—smart piano bar on the top floor of a 16th-century Medici *palazzo*—popular with tourists.

River Club, Lungarno Corsini 8—elegant nightclub with winter garden.

Salt Peanuts, Piazza Santa Maria Novella, 26r—jazz club with live bands and videos.

Space Electronic, Via Palazzuolo 37—vast and ultra-modern disco with video and laser show. Lively, crowded and young.

Yab Yum, Via Sassetti, 5—large, fashionable disco.

Core hours are 09.00-13.00 and 15.30-19.00 Tuesday to Saturday. Most shops are closed Monday morning in winter, whereas in summer they open all day Monday but close all day Saturday. Also, nearly all food stores close for one additional day a week; opening hours are posted on the shop door.

WHAT TO BUY

Boutiques: Florence is a highspot for fashion, and the centre is full of top designer boutiques. The most elegant street is the Via Tornabuoni where Gucci, Ferragamo, Valentino and other big names in fashion have their outlets. Other exclusive streets are the Via Calzaiuoli and Via Roma (both of which have some stunning leather goods), Via della Vigno Nouvo and Via del Parione.

Many of the following top designers and boutiques sell clothes and accessories off the peg, but if you intend to splash out on bespoke *haute couture* it is best to make an appointment in advance.

Alex, Via della Vigna Nuova 19, tel: 214 952/218 451

Emilio Pucci, Via de Pucci 6, tel: 283 061/

283 062

Enrico Coveri, Via Tornabuoni 81r, tel: 211 263

Ferragamo, Palazzo Feroni-Spini, Via Tornabuoni 2, tel: 43951

Gianni Versace, Via Tornabuoni 13/15r, tel: 296 167

Gucci, Via Tornabuoni 73/75F, tel: 287 251/213 175/212 665

Lietta Cavalli, Via della Vigna Nuova 45r, tel: 298 572

Raspini, Via Roma 25-29, tel: 213 077

Zanobetti, Via Calimala 22r, tel: 210 646

For a wide choice of clothes for all ages try the Principe department store in Via Strozzi 21/29, part of an upmarket Tuscan chain. Cheaper shopping areas are the Via del Corso and some of the streets north of the Duomo, especially those of the Borgo San Lorenzo open-air market.

Leather is the best buy in the city. Quality ranges from beautiful creations of local artisans to shoddy goods aimed at undiscerning tourists. For top quality (and prices) start with the designer boutiques in the Via Tornabuoni or shops in streets around the Piazza della Repubblica.

Raspini at Via Roma 25-29 has superb leather shops, bags and coats as well as high quality fashions. For more down to earth prices head for the market of San Lorenzo northwest of the Duomo, where numerous street stalls sell shoes, bags, belts, wallets (as well as cheap woollen sweaters, silk ties and scarves).

Fabrics: Far from cheap, but of outstanding quality, are the textiles made by Alessandro Pucci's Antico Setificio, Via della Vigna Nuova 97, tel 282 900. The firm reproduces authentic Renaissance designs in an 18th-century mill built according to Leonardo da Vinci's design. The mill, in Via Bartolini 4, can be visited by appointment.

Bookshops: The Paperback Exchange, Via Fiesolana 31r, in the Santa Croce district, is no ordinary bookshop. For a start, it stocks just about every book ever written on Florence currently in print—and many that are no longer published. In addition, it operates a system whereby you get a credit of 25 to 40 percent of the original price of any book you trade in which can be used to buy books from their vast stock of quality secondhand English and American paperbacks. The shop is run by enthusiasts who know everything there is to know about Florence and books.

Antiques: There are two main areas for antiques—the Oltrarno, just south of the Arno, and Borgo Ognissanti, west of the centre. Look out for old frames, antique jewellery, ceramics and statues, paintings and furniture.

Jewellery: Jewellers and goldsmiths have been established on the Ponte Vecchio for nearly three centuries. Quality is still high and there's a wide choice from gold necklaces to coral cameos.

Souvenirs: Popular souvenirs are ceramics, lace, straw and other handmade goods. If you want to take home a print, try Alinari which has several branches in the city. For beautiful hand-marbled paper, the best place to go is Papiro with shops at Via Cavour 55r and Piazza del Duomo 24r.

MARKETS

San Lorenzo (see leather above) is the largest and most popular market. The Mercato Nuovo, in a 16th-century loggia, sells leather accessories, ceramics, straw goods and souvenirs. The Tuesday morning market in the Cascine park provided plenty of local colour, but dubious quality. Bargaining in all these markets is always worth a try. For food, head for the Mercato Centrale, next to San Lorenzo, a 19th-century covered market with a huge selection of cheeses, meats, fish and other food.

EXPORT PROCEDURES

The up-market shops and department stores will arrange for goods to be posted or shipped abroad.

SPORTS

Soccer enthusiasts can watch the first division local team (Fiorentina) play at the Stadio Comunale. The Cascine Park has two racecourses (one for horseracing, another for trotting), a tennis club and pool both open to the public. Of the other pools open to the public, the most appealing is the Costoli, Viale Paoli, tel: 675 744. The Ugolino Golf Club at Impruneta, eight miles (13 km) from the city, is a beautiful spot with an 18-hole course, a pool and tennis courts.

SPECIAL INFORMATION

CHILDREN

Although Florentines are indulgent towards children (those of visitors as well as their own) the city offers very little for them by way of diversion. Those who have visited Florence with children say that the Egyptian collection at the Archaeological Museum, and the working experiments of Galileo in the Museum of Science provide a degree of entertainment. There are playgrounds in the Cascine Park, and plenty of hidden corners in the Boboli Gardens where children can play ball games and hide and seek.

DISABLED

Despite difficult cobbled streets and poor wheelchair access to many sights and hotels, many disabled people visit Florence. Unaccompanied visitors will experience difficulty so it is best to travel with a companion. Sources of further information are Radar, 25 Mortimer Street. London W1M 8AB; tel 01-637 5400, and the publication Access in Florence available from Mrs V. Saunders, OUSA Office, Sherwood House, Sherwood Drive, Bletchley, Hilton Keynes HK3 6AN, tel 0908-71131.

STUDENTS

Florence no longer allows student discounts on admission fees to museums but there is no charge for entry to churches.

PARKS & GARDENS

At first sight, Florence seems to have remarkably few open spaces: most of the gardens are private and hidden behind courtyard walls. The main exceptions are the Boboli Gardens (open 9 a.m. to dusk daily, entry free) and the huge Cascine public park. Of greater interest, botanically, is the Giardino dei Semplici, founded in 1545 for the cultivation of medicinal plants, and now planted with typical Tuscan trees and flora. In the grounds, the Botanical Institute houses a small museum on the second floor (entrance from Via La Pira, open Mon, Wed, Fri 9 - noon).

Many private gardens are, however, open occasionally to the public or by appointment. The tourist office publishes a list of gardens that are open. From April to June Agriturist (Piazza San Firenze 3) organises afternoon coach excursions to the gardens of Florentine villas. These can be booked at any tour agent in Florence, and through many hotels.

FURTHER READING

Acton, Harold: *The Last Medici* (Cardinal).
Acton, Harold and Edward Chaney: *Florence, a Travellers' Companion* (Constable).
Borsook, Eve: *A Companion Guide to Florence* (Fontana).
Forster, E.M.: *A Room with a View* (Penguin).
Hale, J.R.: *Florence and the Medici* (Thames and Hudson).
Hibbert, Christopher: *The Rise and Fall of the House of Medici* (Penguin).
McCarthy, Mary: *The Stones of Florence and Venice Observed* (Penguin).
Vasari, Giorgio: *The Lives of the Artists* (Penguin).

USEFUL ADDRESSES

CONSULATES

America, Lungarno Vespucci 38,
tel: 298 276.
Austria, Via dei Servia 9, tel: 215 352.
Belgium, Via dei Conti 4, tel: 282 094.
Denmark, Via dei Servi 13, tel: 211 007
Finland, Via Strozzi 6, tel: 293 228.
France, Piazza Ognissanti 2, tel: 213 509.
Germany, Borgo SS. Apostoli 22,
tel: 294 722.
Great Britain, Lungarno Corsini 2,
tel: 284 133.
Holland, Via Cavour 81, tel: 475 249.
Norway, Via Piana 8F, tel: 228 0316.
Spain, Piazza de' Saltarelli, 1, tel: 212 173.
Sweden, Via della Scala 4, tel: 296 865.
Switzerland, Piazzale Galileo 5,
tel: 222 434.

AIRLINES

Alitalia, Lungarno Acciaioli 10-12r,
tel: 263 051.
British Airways, Via della Vigna Nova 36r,
tel: 218 655.

TRAVEL AGENTS

American Express, Via Guicciardini 49r,
tel: 278 751.
CIT, Via Cavour 56, tel: 294 306.
Universalturismo, Via degli Speziali, 7r,
tel: 217 241.
Wagons-Lits Turismo, Via del Giglio 27r,
tel: 218 851.

TOURIST INFORMATION

The main tourist office is the Azienda Autonoma di Turismo, Via Tornabuoni 15, tel: 216 544/5; open, infuriatingly, mornings only (09.00 to 13.00, closed Sun). General city information, maps and leaflets are available free of charge. A smaller office with a hotel reservation system operates from the station and is open from 08.30 to 21.00. For information on the province of Florence go to the Ente Provinciale Turismo, Via Manzoni 16, tel: 247 8141. Towns outside Florence, such as Siena and Pisa have their own tourist office.
Railway Station information office
tel: 278 785.
Pisa airport information tel: (050) 28088.

ART/PHOTO CREDITS

Giancotti, Patrizia	18/19, 35, 38, 66, 68, 69, 72, 73, 76/77, 78, 79, 81, 82, 83, 85, 92, 95, 96, 97, 99, 104, 105, 106, 108, 157L & R, 168/169, 179, 186L, 192, 202, 203, 207, 212, 227, 234, 236, 239, 240
Guatti, Albano	3, 9, 14/15, 16/17, 20/21, 22, 37, 39, 43, 74, 75, 80, 86, 87, 88, 89, 107, 112/113, 120, 121, 124, 125, 127, 128, 130, 131, 132, 135, 146, 147, 148/149, 153, 155, 156, 159, 160/161, 162, 164, 165, 166, 186R, 170/171, 173, 176, 177, 180/181, 187, 188, 189, 190/191, 194, 195, 198/199, 200/201, 206, 208, 209, 211, 213, 214/215, 218, 220, 221, 222, 223, 225, 226, 229, 231, 232/233, 235, 237, 238
Höfer, Hans	30/31, 32, 36, 40/41, 42, 48, 50/51, 58, 63, 71, 90/91, 110/111, 114/115, 116, 122, 123, 136/137, 142, 186L, 216/217
Le Garsmeur, Alain	26
National Portrait Library	61
Pamella, Alberto	101
Spectrum	98, 138, 139
Topham Picture Library	53, 109, 143

INDEX

A

Accademia di Belle Arti, 185
Acton, Sir Harold, 59, 236
Alberti, Battista, 193
Alberti family, 39
Albizzi family, 53
Alinari, 197
Allori, 144
Ammannati, 132, 238
Angelico, Fra, 45, 183, 184, 231
Annigoni, Pietro, 93, 177
Annunciation Church, 187
Archaeological Museum, 28, 68. 189
architecture, 94-7
Argenti Museum, 54, 146
Arno, river, 33, 35, 67, 68, 203
Arte di Calimala, 39

B

Badia Fiorentina, 150, 152, 231
Baldovinetti, 223
ballet, 100
Banco, Nanni di 165
Bandinelli, 132, 175
banking, 57
Baptistry, 39, 44, 121-2
Bardini Museum, 208-9
Bardini, Stefano, 208, 220
Bargello, 44, 152-4
Baroncelli Chapel, 158
Barrett Browning, Elizabeth, 61, 210, 236
Bartolini, Lorenzo, 187
Bartolomeo, Fra, 145
Bellosguardo, 235
Belvedere Fortress, 144, 147, 219
Berenson, Bernard, 62
Black Death, 38
Blok, Alexander, 117
Blue Zone, 73
Boboli Gardens, 144, 146-7
Boccaccio, Giovanni 57, 194
Borgo Ognissanti, 94
Borgo San Frediano, 212
Botticelli, Sandro 48, 49, 55, 139, 140, 197

Brancacci Chapel, 46, 212
Brogi, Giacomo, 96
Bronzino, Agnolo 49, 134, 176
Browning Institute, 61
Browning, Robert, 61, 210
Brunelleschi, Filippo
    Baptistry, 44, 122
    Bargello, 153
    Cathedral, 47, 124, 125
    Ospedale degli Innocenti, 188
    Pazzi Chapel, 159
    San Lorenzo, 175, 176
    San Spirito, 211
Brunetti, Sandra, 93-4
Bruni, Leonardo, 54, 158
Bryant, Willam Cullen, 61
Buontalenti, Bernardo 141, 146, 175, 204, 219, 238
Byron, Lord George 60

C

Calcio in Costume, 98
Calimala, 43, 121
Campanile, 123
Canova, Antonio 144
Capponi Chapel, 210
Caravaggio, Michelangelo 142
Casa Buonarroti, 159
Casa di Dante, 163
Casa Guida, 61-2, 210
Casa Torre, 95
Casino Mediceo, 185
Castellani Chapel, 158
Cathedral, 34, 43, 47, 48, 122-5
Cathedral, Fiesole, 229
Cathedral Museum, 45, 46, 125-6
Cellini, Benvenuto 131, 153
Centre for Renaissance Studies, 62
Cerchi family, 37
Chapel of the Princes, 177
Charles VIII, 55
Chimera, 29, 189
Christofori, 57, 134
Cimabue, 43, 139, 159
Cioli, Valerio, 146
Cioni, Nardodi, 195
Ciuffagni, Bernardo, 45
Concellieri family, 37
Conservatorio, 187
Conti, Primo, 93
Corsini, 59
Costa San Giorgio, 219
Costume Museum, 144, 147
Credi, Lorenzodi, 141, 142
Cronaca, 133

D

d'Agnolo, Baccio, 205
d'Angolo Bagno, 125
da Cortona, Pietro, 144
da Vinci, Leonardo, 47, 49, 106
Daddi, Bernardo, 165
Dante, 38, 57, 123, 134, 157, 163, 164
David (Donatello), 57, 154
David (Michelangelo), 49, 131-2, 185, 186
Donatello
    Bargello, 154
    Crucifixion, 159
    David, 57, 154
    Judith and Holofernes, 131, 134
    Museo dell' Opera del Duomo, 126
    Orsanmichele, 46, 153
    Palazzo Vecchio, 134
    San Lorenzo, 176
    Santa Croce, 158, 159
    St George, 153, 164
    training, 45
Donati family, 37
Duccio, 139
Duke of Florence, 56
Duomo, 34, 43, 47, 48, 122-5

E - F

English cemetery, 236
Etruria, 27
Etruscan art, 27-9, 189
Faesulanum, Museum, 228
"Firenze Nuova", 72, 74-5, 96
fashion, 85-8
Ferragamo, Salvatore, 86, 87, 95
Festa de Grillo, 98
festivals, 98
Ficino, Marsilio, 54, 55
Fiesole, 27, 227-31
Fiorentino, Rosso, 49
Firenze, Andreadi, 195
floods, 67-9, 150, 195, 208, 235
Florence, Duke of, 56
food, 103-8, 109
Forster, E.M., 117
Francesca, Piero della, 140

G

Gabinetto Vieusseux, 198
Gaddi, Agnolo, 158, 197, 222, 237
Gaddi, Taddeo, 158, 197, 223
Galileo Galilei, 57, 158, 159, 207-8, 220-1
Galleria d'Arte Moderna, 144, 146
Galleria del Costume, 144, 147

Gallery of Modern Art, 144, 146
Gamberini, 94, 95
Ghibellines, 37, 129
Ghiberti, Lorenzo, 39, 44, 46, 121, 122, 153
Ghirlandaio, Domenico, 183, 188, 195, 196, 197, 204, 205
Giambologna, Jean Boulogne, 132, 147, 153, 238
Giardino de Semplici, 185
Giardino del Cavaliere, 147
Giotto, 43, 46, 126, 139, 158
Gozzoli, 175
Gucci, 86, 87
Guelfs, 37, 129, 166
Guicciardini, 57
guilds, 34, 37, 38, 39, 43, 44, 46

H

Hawkwood, Sir John, 124
Hazlitt, William, 94
Hemicycle, 147
History of Photography Museum, 97
Hockney, David, 93
Horne Museum, 208
humanism, 54

I - L

Il Porcellino, 166
Instituto per l'Arte il Ristauro, 99
Italian language, 38, 57
James, Henry, 61, 183
La Fondinaria, 72, 74-5
La Pietra, villa, 236
Landor, Walter Savage, 60
Laurentian Library, 54, 177
Lawrence, D.H., 28, 62, 142
Lippi, Filippino, 39, 194, 212
Lippi, Fra Filippo, 45, 48, 140, 150, 212
literature, 100
Lodovica, Anna Maria see Medici, Anna Maria
Loggia del Lanzi, 131
Lorenzo, Biccidi, 219, 229
Lorenzi, Stoldo, 147
Luzi, Maria, 100

M

Machiavelli, Niccolò, 55, 57, 134, 158
Magnelli, Alberto, 93
Mann, Horace, 59
Marini, Marino, 94
markets, 105, 109, 165, 237
Martini, Quinto, 94

Masaccio, 43, 145, 146, 212
Medici, 35, 39, 53, 173-8
  Alessandro, 56
  Anna Maria, 56, 139
  Catherine, 57, 103
  Chapels, 175, 177-8
  Cosimo I, 56, 131, 132, 143, 238
  Cosimo, 39, 53, 54, 173, 176
  Giovanni di Bicci, 53
  Giovanni, 55
  Guilano, 152
  Lorenzo, 54-5, 152, 178
  Palazzo, 174
  Piero, 55
  villa, 231, 237-8
Medici-Riccardi Palace, 174
Mercato Centrale, 105, 109
Mercato di Sant' Ambrogio, 237
Mercato Nuovo, 109, 165-6
Michelangelo
  Bargello, 152
  Casa Buonarroti, 159
  David, 49, 125, 186
  Laurentian Library, 177
  Pietà, 126
  Medici Chapels, 178
  Medici-Riccardi Palace, 174
  Museo dell' Opera del Duomo, 125, 126
  Palazzo Vecchio, 133
  Uffizi, 141
Michelazzi, 94
Michelozzo, 132, 174, 183, 185, 222, 231
Michelucci, 94, 95
Modern Art Gallery, 144, 146
Modern Art Museum, Prato, 93
Monaco, 140
Moorehead, Alan, 62
Museo dell' Opera del Duomo, 45, 46, 125-6
Museo di Firenze com' era, 155
Museum Bardini, 228-9
Museum Faesulanum, 228
Museum of Anthropology and Ethnology, 154
Museum of Porcelain, 144, 147
music, 99-100

N - O

National Library, 68
Neptune Fountain, 132, 147
new town, 73, 74-5
Niccolini, 159
Nightingale, Florence, 61
Ognissanti, church, 196
opera, 99-100
Opera del Duomo, 125-6
Orcagna, Andrea, 165
Orsanmichele, 46, 153, 164, 165
Ospedale degli Innocenti, 48, 188
Ospedale Santa Maria, 155

P

Palatine Gallery, 143, 144
Palazzeschi, Aldo, 100
Palazzo Bardini, 208-9
Palazzo Bartolini-Salimbeni, 205
Palazzo Corsini, 203
Palazzo Davanzati, 166-7
Palazzo degli Affari, 95
Palazzo del Populo, 129
Palazzo dell' Arte della Lana, 165
Palazzo di Parte Guelfa, 166
Palazzo Ducale, 131
Palazzo Gondi, 150
Palazzo Masetti, 203
Palazzo Medici, 174
Palazzo Nonfinito, 154
Palazzo Pandolfini, 185
Palazzo Rucellai, 97, 197
Palazzo Torrigiani, 210
Palazzo Vecchio, 34, 56, 67, 131, 132-4, 206-7, 209
Parco Museo di Seano, 94
Pazzi Chapel, 48, 159
Peoples' Palace, 129
Peri, Jacopo, 57
perspective, 46, 47, 57, 212
Perugino, 49, 236
Petrarch, 57
photography, 96
Piazza del Duomo, 121
Piazza della Repubblica, 34, 163
Piazza della Signoria, 34, 67, 129
Piazza San Marco, 183
Piazza Santa Croce, 156
Piazza Santa Maria Sovraporta, 166
Piazza Santissima Annunziata, 187
Piccolomini, Aeneas Sylvius, 54
Pietà (Michelangelo), 126
Pisano, Andrea, 121, 126
Pisano, Giovanni, 43
Pisano, Nicolo, 43
Pitti, Luca, 143
Pitti Palace, 93, 131, 142-4
Poggi, Giuseppe, 94, 155, 224
Poggio a Caiano, villa, 237
Pollaiuolo, 49
Pollaiuolo, Antonio and Piero, 223
Ponte alla Carraia, 203
Ponte Santa Trinita, 95, 203
Pontormo, Jacopo, 49, 238
Pope Boniface, 38
Pope Clement VIII, 56
Pope Eugenius IV, 39, 125
Pope Innocent VIII, 55
Pope Leo X, 56
Pope Pius II, 54
population, 73
Porcelain Museum, 144, 147
Porte San Giorgio, 219
Pratolini, Vasco, 100
Praz, Mario, 59
Pucci, Emilio, 85, 86, 98
Pulci, Luigi, 103, 106

Q - R

Quercia, Jacopo della, 44
quatrocento, 37, 140
Raccolta d'Arte Contemporanea, 93
railway station, 94
Raphael, 43, 144, 185, 203
Rembrandt, 142
Renaissance, 45, 47, 122
River Arno, 33, 35, 67, 68, 203
Robbia, Andrea della, 188
Robbia, Luca della, 123, 126, 222, 223
Robbia, School della, 75
Rogers, Samuel, 60
Rosai, Ottone, 93
Rossellino, 152, 158, 223
Rossi, Vincenzo de', 133, 147
Rubens, 145
Rucellai Giovanni, 193, 197
Rucellai Palace, 97, 197
Ruskin, John, 60, 139, 142

S

Sacchi, Claudio, 94
Salone dei Cinquecento, 133
Salutati, Collucio, 39
Sangallo, Giulianoda, 198, 238
San Domenico, 231
San Lorenzo, 48, 175-8
San Marco, 45, 54
San Miniato, 222
San Pancrazio Museum, 94
San Spirito, 211-2
Sant' Alessandro, 229
Sant' Ambrogio, 237
Santa Croce, 48, 157-9
Santa Felicita, 209
Santa Margherita, 163
Santa Maria del Carmine, 46, 212
Santa Maria Maddalena dei Pazzi, 236
Santa Maria Maggiore, 57
Santa Maria Novella, 47, 193
Santa Trinita, 204-5
Santi Apostoli, 205-6
Santissima Annunziata, 157
Santo Spirito, 48
Santo Spirito Leather School, 99
Santo Stefano al Ponte, 206
Sarto, Andrea del, 49, 144, 187, 237, 238
Savonarola, 55, 129, 131, 184
Science Museum, 207
Scoppio del Carro, 98, 121
Shelley, Percy Bysshe 60
Smollett, Tobias, 59
Soderini, Piero, 55
Spandolini, Pier-Luigi, 95
Spanish Chapel, 195

St Minias, 222, 223
Starnina, Gherardo, 140
"Stendhal Syndrome", 23
Strozzi family, 39, 195
Strozzi Palace, 198
Susini, Francesco, 147

T

Tarquinia, 28
Tchaikovsky, 220
Tempo Israelitico, 236-7
theatre, 99
Thomas, Dylan, 62
Titian, 141, 144
Tito, Santi di, 134
Toledo, Eleanora di, 143, 195
Tornabuoni family, 195
Torre del Gallo, 220
Torre della Castagna, 164
Torrini, Franco, 97
trade guilds, 34, 37, 38, 39, 43, 44, 46
trecento, 139
Twain, Mark, 141, 203

U

Uberti family, 129
Uccello, Paolo, 47, 124, 140
Uffizi, 45, 48, 56, 139-42
Università Internazionale dell'Arte, 99
Utens, Giusto, 155

V

Vasari, Giorgio, 43
   Palazzo Vecchio, 132, 133, 134
   Santa Croce, 157
   Uffizi, 48, 139
Verrocchio, 154
Vespucchi family, 196
Via del Calzaioli, 164
Via dell'Ardiglioni, 212
Via della Vigna Nuova, 88
Via Maggio, 210
Via Tornabuoni, 88, 197-8
Viale, 34
villas
   della Petrela, 238
   di Castello, 238
   Gherardesca, 60
   i Tati, 62

    La Pietra, 236
    Medici, 231, 237-8
    Palmieri, 60
    Poggio a Caiano, 237
    Stibbert, 235
Vinsanto, 108
Viottolone, 147

W & Z

wine, 104, 106, 108, 109
Woolf, Virginia, 61
Zoological Museum, 210